You're a
Better Parent
Than You Think!

Raymond
N. Guarendi

You're a Better Parent Than You Think!

A Guide to Common-Sense Parenting

A FIRESIDE BOOK
Published by Simon & Schuster
New York London Toronto Sydney Tokyo Singapore

FIRESIDE
Simon & Schuster Building
Rockefeller Center
1230 Avenue of the Americas
New York, New York 10020

Published in 1986 by Prentice Hall Press

Originally published by Prentice-Hall, Inc.
First Fireside Edition 1992

FIRESIDE and colophon are registered trademarks
of Simon & Schuster Inc.

Manufactured in the United States of America

10

Library of Congress Cataloging-in-Publication Data

Guarendi, Raymond.
You're a better parent than you think!

Includes index.
1. Parenting—Psychological aspects.   2. Discipline
of children.   3. Authority—Psychological aspects.
I. Title.
HQ755.8.G83   1985   649'.1   814-16022
ISBN 0-671-76595-7

Contents

Preface

This book is dedicated to your mental health. It is not a "how-to-parent" book. I don't intend to tell you how to raise your child by my methods. The purpose of this book is to build your confidence and peace of mind as a parent. It is to put authority into your hands, where it belongs.

Much has been written about how to raise a well-adjusted child: how to build the child's self-esteem, confidence, sense of responsibility; how to buffer the child from destructive anxiety and guilt—in essence, how to help the child emerge from childhood in the best possible shape. But not nearly so much has been written to help parents emerge from parenthood in the best possible shape. Parenting has its own unique fears, worries, and frustrations. Parents, too, need their confidence bolstered and their self-image enhanced; especially these days.

A line popular on T-shirts says: "Insanity is hereditary. You get it from your kids." There is some truth to this. Being a parent can be hazardous to your emotional health. And while you strive to foster your child's emotional well-being, you may be neglecting your own and sacrificing your needs and rights to an unhealthy degree. Effective parenting means considering *your* mental health as well as your child's. You must accept yourself as a fallible human who can make mistakes—many of them. You need to be able to discipline without feeling guilty or anxious that you're causing your child psychological harm. And you need to get out from under the influence of paralyzing child-rearing myths and practices. In short, you must feel confident in yourself and in your own decisions. Unfortunately, nowadays too many parents don't.

By the end of this book I believe your mental health as a parent will be better in the following several ways:

1. You will gain trust in your own instincts and good sense. You will view yourself unquestioningly as the prime decision-maker for your child's welfare.
2. You will be a more relaxed, easygoing parent. You will realize that your youngster is more "normal," even better adjusted, than you probably give him or her credit for.
3. You will have no doubt, and neither will your children, as to who's in charge in your home. You will more comfortably, calmly, and easily discipline.
4. You will be less prone to blame yourself for all your child's frailties and troubles.

One parent who attended one of my workshops summed up well the feelings I hope you'll gain from this book: "I feel better about both me and my kids. When the dust clears, I think I will have done all right after all. I guess I'm a better parent than I thought."

Acknowledgments

To Kathie Chaffee, for clinical, editorial, and humorous inserts. To Jan Stadulis, for adding polish while subtracting words. To Carol Hoppel, for tireless typing and retyping and unflappable patience. And most of all, to Randi, for everything.

To Mom and Pop,
who trusted themselves

1
The Child-Raisers: The Media, the Experts, and Everyone Else

John's parents constantly worried about handling him in the "wrong" way. "Should we make him stay in bed when he cries even if he says he's scared?" They thought that if they made mistakes now, John would suffer later in life. They feared planting the seeds of psychological disturbance. "What if he really is afraid? What effect could that have on a four-year-old? Couldn't he develop a phobia?" Their relentless second-guessing prevented their making firm decisions and sticking with them. "One time we actually had to block the bedroom doorway to keep him in his room. It worked, but he became so upset, we never tried it again."[1]*

Keith's parents drove themselves ragged searching for the reasons behind his unmanageable behavior. "Getting him to do schoolwork is an endless struggle. Do you think he has a learning disability? We read an article that said these kinds of problems come from a poor self-image." They felt inadequate as parents

---

*Throughout this book I will use case histories from my own experience to illustrate a point. A footnote after any example means that you can find out how the case was, or wasn't, resolved in Chapter 11, "How the Story Ended." Often enough, you don't get the whole story from your own kids; I didn't want to add to your frustration by withholding information about the kids in my examples.

because Keith seemed to be slipping out of their control. "Our doctor told us he may be hyperactive. That could be why he's so hard to discipline. We're going to change his diet and see if that makes any difference. If that doesn't help, maybe he needs medication."[2]

Gina's mother doubted her parenting because her family and friends always criticized her as out of step with everybody else. "I try to make Gina listen to me when people are around, but everyone says I'm being too strict, that she's just going through a stage. They tell me I'm old-fashioned and that Gina is going to rebel when she's older." The opinions of strangers likewise bothered her. "People look at me like I'm some kind of ogre when I discipline her in public. I'm to the point where I just want to avoid a scene at all costs, and Gina knows it." More and more she questioned her style of discipline. "Does spanking your children really make them aggressive? Is it true you should never use the word 'no' with your toddler?"

If you've had these or similar doubts about your parenting, you have plenty of company. I talk with many parents who are plagued by the uncertainty that they might not be raising their children the "right" way. Even some of the most capable, conscientious mothers and fathers are feeling insecure and underestimating themselves. The pattern is becoming distressingly familiar: parents constantly worrying without reason, habitually second-guessing their decisions, easily swayed by others' opinions. If I were to pick one word for such parenting, it would be *tentative*. It is lacking in resolve and a firm trust in good commonsense judgment.

Why are so many parents losing their trust in their own abilities? The answer to this question has many parts, some of which will come up naturally as this book progresses. In this first chapter we will focus on what for many parents is the prime cause of their shrinking self-confidence: other people. Nowadays nearly everyone is telling parents how to be parents. We are in the midst of a rush into child-rearing awareness—a rush that is having an unexpected backlash on parents. It is breeding worry, guilt, indecision, and a host of other uncomfortable emotions that can undermine self-assured parenting. Who are the people affecting your resolve as a parent? Basically, they fall into three groups: the media, the experts, and other parents just like you.

Parenting by Media
or *"Kids, don't let your parents watch too much TV."*

You can't browse through a rack of popular magazines, skim the paper, or catch a handful of TV talk shows without coming across somebody giving you the do's and don't's of child-rearing. Early-morning voices forecasting a 30 percent chance of showers have been replaced by invitations to "spend an hour with noted child authority Dr. Justin Case, who'll tell you how to handle sibling rivalry." Magazines supply quizzes to test your skills as a parent or to check out your child's level of adjustment. Bookstores pack several rows of shelves with parenting manuals, and radio call-in programs host child experts to grab more listeners. One well-known psychologist even offers call-in telephone service. Who knows, maybe someday somebody will open an office with a drive-in window for parents whose children have six different problems or less! (MasterCard and Visa accepted.)

Advice about how you should raise your kids is everywhere. You are told what words to say to make Morris eat his spinach, when to spank him and how hard, and why never to be inconsistent. You are shown the "tested" new ways to raise him, and warned about using the untested old ways. In short, you are exposed to more standards and guidelines for being a good parent than any group of parents before you. It's no wonder you sometimes feel unsure of how you're measuring up. There's so much to measure up to.

One quick and easy way to measure your parenting competence these days is the child-rearing quiz or survey. It has become routine practice for magazine covers to try to grab your attention with headlines like these: "Is Your Child Hyperactive?"; "Test Your Skill As a Parent"; "Experts Tell You How to Keep Your Child Happy"; or my favorite, "Ten Research-Proven Steps to Raising a Well-Adjusted Child." Now, what self-respecting parent wouldn't be driven to seek the knowledge underlying such titles?

Let's look more closely at this child-rearing fad and how it might mislead a vulnerable parent. A mother is upset because her ten-year-old son Delroy has recently pilfered a small toy from a department store. To Mom's knowledge, Delroy has never before been light-fingered, so his behavior comes as a total surprise. Because stealing ranks high on her list of most-feared behavior,

3

Mom is wondering where she went wrong and if this act is a sign of deep-seated conflict or problems to come. Looking over a stand of magazines, a headline catches her eye: "Is Your Child a Thief?" Anxiously flipping to the article, Mom finds a series of twenty questions. Do you notice money missing around the house? Does your child want to wander through stores without you? Does your child frequently come home from school with things s/he claims others children have given to him/her? At the end of this quiz is a scoring system: "If you answered 'yes' to less than five questions, you have little to be concerned about. Research has shown ... scoring between five and ten 'yes's,' this is a sign of potential trouble .... Ten to fifteen could indicate the need for professional counseling .... Over fifteen—serious problems already exist ...." Following this last warning is a list of "signs" that a group of adults convicted of theft exhibited when they were children. The logic used is misleading, however, because even though most antisocial adults do in fact show certain problems in childhood, this in no way means that any youngster who presents these problems will go on to become a thief. But Mom doesn't realize that. After tallying twelve 'yes's,' she starts to wonder if Delroy does indeed need professional help. Her own judgment of how to handle the stealing has effectively been distorted by a "test" that could best be considered a piece of entertainment.

Despite their broad appeal, these do-it-yourself child assessment kits are highly deceptive. They foster the false expectation that "you, too, can explore the hidden meaning behind your child's behavior"—even if there's really not much to explore. Typically, these packages contain heavy-sounding statements, like "Research has found that left-handed children are more likely to show learning difficulties," or "Studies show that middle children have identity problems." What if your middle son, Joey, also happens to be left-handed? Must you now be vigilant for learning and identity problems? Not at all. These tests offer only generalizations, they have little value for understanding any individual child. But because they appear to be based on scientific research, they can look very legitimate. Beware. You can be fooled into imagining problems that don't exist or overreacting to those that do.

Certainly most child-rearing advice is not so neatly packaged. However, no matter what form it takes, the media are relentlessly pushing you to the experts for answers. As they do, you can become less and less willing to trust yourself. Your judgments are not expert ones, therefore you may wonder if they're good enough. You don't understand everything your child does, so you might feel you have to look for the explanation somewhere. It doesn't matter that kids can be unpredictable and impossible to fathom. Your impression is that good parents should be able to somehow uncover the reasons for and then resolve every problem their kids have. And, of course, the people who know the *real* reasons are the experts! Too much reliance on the experts, however, only breeds a sense of uncertainty. You lose the ability to make confident decisions on your own. You become more susceptible to poor advice.

A simple parallel to a machine can be drawn: If you overload a machine, you bring on problems. The machine runs less smoothly, parts break down, and overall efficiency is lost. I'm reminded of an episode from the old television series *Star Trek* in which the ship's captain outwits a supercomputer by feeding it contradictory data. The computer tries to process all the data simultaneously and only succeeds in burning out its circuits.

Fortunately, I don't know many parents who are burned out from too much information, but I do know quite a few who are operating less efficiently. They are suffering from *information overload*. In trying to do everything by the book, or should I say by all the books, they've taken in too much too quickly. They aren't sure anymore how to handle even some of the most routine situations. If something goes awry or their youngster behaves a little out of the ordinary, they panic. Are they to blame? Will she be OK? For these parents, child-rearing has become an uptight, guilt-ridden affair. Their obsession with doing the perfect job is the very thing that reduces the quality of their parenting.

Now, I'm not suggesting that you rely totally on yourself and avoid all outside advice. That would be the other extreme. Much helpful information is conveyed through popular channels. Take advantage of it and you will overcome a good bit of the uncertainty inherent in being a parent. I am suggesting, however, that you need to learn how to digest this steady diet of material; otherwise, it could overwhelm you.

The key to reducing information overload, therefore, is to view any kind of child-rearing advice for what it is—an idea that *might* help. No one way is *the* way to a well-adjusted child, and you certainly don't have to apply all you read and hear. Selectively attend to what you can use. And always remember that most of child-rearing still involves good-sense judgments by parents. It always will. The sooner you become comfortable with that reality, the more calmly and self-assuredly you will parent.

Who(m) do you trust?

Not only are you bombarded with advice from all angles, but much of the time the advice is contradictory. Dr. X says method X is a good way to raise kids and recommends it wholeheartedly. Dr. Y says method X is a bad way to raise kids and warns it will lead to stunted emotional growth. Who is right? Whom do you listen to?

Actually, "Who is right?" is an irrelevant question. "What works well?" is the question to ask. It provides one solid means of determining whom to listen to. Some experts advise parents to sit their child in a chair to emphasize a lesson. Others believe spanking is justified at times. Still other experts feel that if parents consistently notice their child's good behavior, they will seldom have to punish the bad. There's nothing "wrong" with different approaches to the same problem—if they work. Anyone who tells parents they should be acting differently when they are getting decent results is doing them an injustice. Your style is not automatically wrong just because an expert says so. Look hard enough and you can always find someone or something directly opposed to your technique. If your approach is working, don't tamper with success. As the old saying goes: "If it ain't broke, don't fix it." If your approach is not working, get rid of it, even though an expert says it's the right thing to do.

One mother told me of her struggles to keep her two-year-old from mauling her house plants. Even though Mom moved as many plants as possible out of reach, Amanda still managed to grab hold of those fascinating hanging leaves, breaking stems and on occasion toppling a plant or two. Mom had read an article that said the best solution to this problem would immediately be to whisk Amanda away from the plants every time she came close. This would stem trouble before it took root. That's not quite what happened. Instead, Mom quickly found herself engaged in a contest of wills, carting Amanda out of plant range several times per hour, while Amanda enjoyed the game. In fairness to the article, maybe this strategy would have flowered with another two-year-old less headstrong than Amanda. But to deter Amanda, clearly something else was needed. The idea that sounded so good on paper wasn't working too well in real life.[3]

Child-rearing specialists too often imply that their ideas are suited for all children under almost all circumstances. This attitude misleads parents because it underestimates the tremendous differences among kids and parents. What's good for me may not be good for you. What's right for my child may not be right for your child. In assessing an expert's advice, ask yourself some simple questions: Can I do this? Will I be comfortable with it? Will it work for my child? These questions will move you away from seeking "rightness" and toward seeking "usefulness."

The Words of Prophets
or *"I'm OK, you're OK, but your kid's neurotic."*

A couple attending a workshop on sexual education for young children were considering adopting a little boy about two-and-a-half years old. The boy's infant years had been marked by neglect and chaos. From birth until he was removed from his home, his mother had treated him as though he were a girl, dressing him in feminine clothes and calling him "Carla." The couple was hesitating to adopt this youngster because a doctor had told them that he would definitely carry "emotional scars" for life and would always be unsure of his sexual identity. Imagine that—doomed to a life of instability by age two and a half! Indeed, it's possible that this little fellow could experience problems as a result of his early confusion, but a warm, stable home life from age three on would do much to counter any such problems.[4]

A father described for me the troubles he was having with his seven-year-old daughter Diane. As we talked, I formed the impression that Diane's was basically a garden-variety behavior problem. That is, she had learned at a young age how to get around Dad and was growing more defiant and manipulative as she grew older. I guess you could say that as she matured, she was becoming more immature. I recommended to her father that we

7

spend several sessions discussing more effective discipline practices. When I assured him that because of Diane's young age he could probably bring about change within a few months, he looked surprised. He said a former therapist had warned him that "these types of problems take years of therapy to resolve." He had been led to believe that what was essentially common misbehavior would need lengthy individual treatment to "cure," when in reality things would improve when he stopped giving in to his daughter.[5]

The following example represents the epitome of professional "godliness." A distraught mother told me that on the basis of one evaluation, a clinician had pronounced her six-year-old son "psychologically bizarre." He based his conclusion on the boy's habit of rocking back and forth whenever he became frustrated. Granted, rocking is not your typical six-year-old's response to frustration, but it doesn't necessarily mean that serious disturbance exists either. The clinician further warned that if the rocking didn't stop soon, more severe maladjustment would follow and could eventually lead to a personality with a potential for mass murder. (And he seemed like such a cute kid to me.)[6]

The above situations all have one common denominator. They illustrate reckless statements and predictions made in the name of understanding children's behavior. Most professionals certainly do not make such statements. They recognize their limits and the limits of their profession. But every profession has those who speak irresponsibly and are believed simply because they are authorities. Child psychology is no exception to this rule. Many parents believe that child specialists can mysteriously see and understand what others cannot. They can delve into a youngster's psyche, ferreting out the hidden motivations and potential ramifications of any piece of behavior. Hence, no matter how farfetched an expert's statement, parents are often reluctant to question it. I related the story of the six-year-old rocker and potential mass murderer to an intelligent friend who, I thought, would quickly see how ridiculous the clinician's prediction was. Instead of shaking her head in disbelief, she replied, a bit unsure of herself, "Can he really say something like that?"

Experts have no third eye or ear that allows them to probe deeply into a child's mind. They do have specialized training and experience working with parents and kids, but, like all humans, experts make mistakes. They can form false impressions, they can make inaccurate assessments, and they can give poor advice. Because parents give weight to their opinions, experts have to be particularly careful about what they say. They can do much damage with interpretations and predictions that are accepted as gospel truth.

A common term in psychology is *self-fulfilling prophecy.* Essentially, this means that if you expect something to come about, it may eventually do so just because you looked for it. Fortune-tellers try to create self-fulfilling prophecies to make their predictions look accurate. Experts must take care not to create self-fulfilling prophecies.

The following incident illustrates well how something can come to pass primarily because an authority said it would. Eleven-year-old Susan had exhibited learning problems since her early elementary school years. She had not been blessed with good reading skills, but through effort and a strong desire to achieve, she was maintaining respectable marks. Susan's teacher, however, wondered if Susan had an "underlying" reading disability, so she referred her to the school psychologist for an evaluation. The psychologist's opinion was that Susan was definitely learning-disabled and that if she were not immediately placed in a special class she would suffer irreparable damage. The placement committee disagreed with the psychologist and recommended that Susan remain in her regular class, where she was doing well. Within weeks after the evaluation Susan's grades had plummeted to D's and F's. The teacher had believed the psychologist's doomsday warning; Susan had begun to react as expected.

Avoiding professional gods

Again, I want to stress that most professionals act professionally. They are highly qualified to help and they realize their limits. But should a professional overstep his or her bounds, you probably do not have the training or experience to know for sure. Therefore, keeping the following points in mind may help you avoid becoming a victim of professional "godliness."

First: There's an old joke about a mother who took her son to see a psychiatrist. After the evaluation, the psychiatrist said, "Your boy is maladjusted." The mother asked, "Can I get a second opinion?" The psychiatrist replied, "Sure, he's ugly, too." If a professional offers an outlandish-sounding observation about your child and is reluctant to explain that observation, seek a second opinion—from a different professional. A statement that sounds absurd and contrary to common sense might be just that.

Second: Experts use the word "probably" a lot when they talk about kids. If they really know what's going on, they say "very probably." This is not so much a sign of their uncertainty as of their awareness that many factors are involved in any behavior. Beware of anyone, then, who absolutely predicts how your child will turn out, especially far into the future. The farther any behavior is from the present, the more difficult it is to predict. Too many variables can affect the outcome. For example, I can usually anticipate fairly well how an eight-year-old will react to his parents' new rule that he has to bring home uncompleted schoolwork. But my accuracy drops fast if I try to predict his success in college because of their rule.

Some examples of professional "godliness" would be: "Your six-year-old is headed for a life of crime." "If your son doesn't outgrow his hyperactivity, he'll never make it through high school." "She is insecure because you refused to let her sleep in your bedroom when she was younger." "Problems like this are never resolved. They stay with a child throughout his life." These statements could in fact be true, but no one can see into the future, or the past for that matter, with such infallibility.

Third: Personality tests are a common source of inaccurate, and often harmful, evaluations of children. Abuse of tests occurs because many people—experts and parents alike—still view tests as some kind of magic, as mysterious tools that allow the tester to probe where no one else can. In reality, tests have no such power. Indeed, most psychological research suggests that tests don't tell you nearly as much as does observing a child and talking with her parent(s). Quite simply, personality tests don't give anyone a permit to make statements that cannot be questioned or explained. If someone uses them that way, then I again advise that you consider consulting another professional.

Relatives, Friends, and Other Experts
or *"If he were my kid..."*

You don't need a license to be a parent; there's no rule book to follow. So, anyone can have an opinion about how kids, in particular yours, should be raised. Relatives, especially, grant themselves a familial right to comment on your parenting. Grandma thinks you're too hard on Oscar. Grandpa says you let him get away with murder. Aunt Clara reassures you that Oscar's dad also sassed anyone over four feet tall when he was little, and he outgrew it. But your sister-in-law warns you that her son was just like Oscar and he didn't outgrow it; he only got worse. And so on, down the family tree.

Prior to the last few generations, anyone pushing advice on parents was pushing just that—advice. It was an opinion. If parents didn't agree with it, they usually said something akin to: "You raise your kids your way. I'll raise mine my way." Nowadays, though, opinions aren't always just opinions. Frequently they carry added weight. They are backed by the experts: a new theory, an article, a quote. And other parents won't hesitate to use these backups, not only to make their own opinions more credible, but to make you doubt yours. Your mother can quote the doctor on yesterday's talk show. Your sister-in-law can buttress her viewpoint with the parenting course she had. Your best friends can compare Oscar to their nephew who the school psychologist said is emotionally fragile. And even when others don't cite an expert who agrees with them, you can still upset yourself by wondering if they know something you don't.

Hazel was a conscientious mother who had some nice ideas about how to raise her kids. She also had a precocious three-year-old son, Tony, whose purpose in life was to test those nice ideas daily. To do this, he made use of a versatile talent: He could vomit at will. If he didn't like a meal, he wouldn't keep it down. If he became angry, the next thing out of his mouth after his screams would be his lunch. Typically, Tony would throw up between one and three times a day, sometimes more, probably just to stay in practice. Well, you can imagine the variety of remedies people pushed upon Hazel to properly manage this unusual problem. Most of them implied that she was overly demanding and too hard on her kids. That was why she was having troubles with Tony; he was rebelling. By the time I saw Hazel, she didn't know which way to turn. She was not only unable to hold down Tony's vomiting, but she was also feeling inept overall as a mother. The continuous regurgitation of opinions from family and friends, along with Tony's skill at creating upheaval, had finally taken their toll. As I spoke with Hazel, my opinion was that she wasn't as rigid or demanding as some wanted her to believe. She genuinely attempted to teach her children the value of discipline and self-control, and because of this she was accused of not letting her kids "be kids." Actually, Hazel was very good at letting her kids be kids; she just didn't let her kids be brats. Most of our counseling centered on getting Hazel to trust her own good judgments and not to worry so much about what grades others gave her as a mother.[7]

Hazel typifies many parents who become upset when other people tell them that they discipline too much, they are too strict, they expect too much. These are the standard criticisms leveled at parents who practice consistent discipline, who feel that the parent should have clear authority in the home. And by authority, I mean a willingness to warmly but firmly set boundaries on a child's behavior when necessary and to hold her responsible for her actions. I don't mean an authority that is rigid or dictatorial in nature. In fact, such parents are not hard-hearted dictators or stifling disciplinarians; quite the contrary, they are conscientious parents who expect responsibility and self-control from their kids. And because they do, they are easy targets of permissive ideas and myths. Like Hazel, they are genuinely trying to parent well. But they question their own methods, not because they don't work, but because other people disagree with them. They rely on their judgment in other areas of their lives, but not where their kids are concerned.

People who find fault with your parenting very often fail to realize that they are looking at legitimate differences between your style and theirs. They are too quick to view everything in terms of someone being right and someone being wrong. They don't recognize your right to instill those behaviors and values you feel are important to your child's ultimate adjustment as an adult.

My parents wanted to teach me to spend money wisely, so they gave me a monthly allowance barely above poverty level. I had no choice; I was forced into frugality. Some disagreed with my parent's skimpy stipend, but my folks didn't agree with those who gave extravagant wages for taking out the garbage. Because my parents emphasized fiscal responsibility, I learned to be a bit more penny-wise than the average person. As far as I know, I'm not maladjusted because of it. I just developed values different from those of some of my friends.

If your daughter displays her temper in the grocery store, and you choose to quietly walk away from her, that is your prerogative. Others might disapprove of your style, and that is their prerogative. But you do not have to adjust your parenting just because you have an audience. If you leave your infant with a sitter every Saturday night, the relatives might think you're an unfit parent. They're not considering that some parents need more time away from the kids than do others. If you don't agree with Uncle Nick that you should "just ignore" Butch's nagging to watch big-time wrestling on TV, that is your decision. Maybe Uncle Nick has an exceedingly high level of tolerance for badgering. He can become blissfully oblivious to it, and in time Butch winds down. You believe, however, that your rights are being infringed upon by this mosquitolike droning, and you've told Butch that any more will lead to his removal from the room. The issue is not who is right, you or Uncle Nick. Either approach can work, and the choice basically depends upon who is parent.

In searching for the ideal parent, we have constricted our views of what are proper ways for parents to think, react, and feel. Others will regularly try to convince you that you are somehow not being a good parent just because you have ideas that are unlike theirs. You will be better able to resist these manipulations if you recognize that ultimately your parenting has to be founded upon your choices. Of course, I'm not implying that you ignore everybody, as many people will have valid, helpful advice. But don't try to alter everything that is you because of messages that you aren't the model parent. Someone who tries to make you think there is a deficit in your child-rearing may simply have a narrow-minded view of things.

The majority doesn't rule.

Not only are your peers and elders quick to point out when and how you're falling short, but even your kids join the chorus. "Most of my friends don't have to use their allowance on school supplies." "Carson's mother lets him stay up until eleven." "Faith's parents don't mind if we stay at their house by ourselves as long as we call and let them know how we are." As you've probably noticed, kids always make sure they point out who has it easier. They never liken themselves to Siegfried, whose father makes him finish all his homework before he goes outside, or to Madge, who helps her mother all day Saturday with housework. Kids draw comparisons that are supposed to make you feel guilty, unfair, or mean. They want you to change your mind, and if you show signs of wavering, they'll expand their range of comparisons, citing every "nice" parent they can think of, maybe even making up a few. Their goal is to convince you that you just aren't the in-touch parent that Carson's mother or father is.

Seasoned parents have comebacks to these tactics: "Well, you're not Carson." "I don't run my life the way Faith's parents run theirs." "That may be OK for Sherman, but that's not OK for you." Or the classic "If Marlin jumps in the lake, are you going to jump in, too?" Beneath these confident-sounding retorts, though, many parents do wonder if indeed Marlin's parents have better ideas than they do, if indeed Marlin's parents are better qualified to raise children. Competent parents often question themselves because others do things differently. "Dating at fourteen seems to be the routine practice nowadays. Maybe I am a little behind the times." Or "Most of Wyatt's friends have BB guns. I guess he's old enough to have one. But it's against my better judgment." This *consensus parenting,* or looking to the majority to guide one's actions as a parent, is on the rise. The driving force behind such parenting is the assumption that the answer lies somewhere out there in how everybody else raises their kids. Maybe other parents know more. They can't all be wrong, can they?

A basic rule of child-rearing, and disciplining in particular, is that the majority doesn't always provide a good example. More parents are asking less help from their kids around the house. Do you want less help from your kids? Many youngsters are allowed to decide pretty much for themselves the effort they'll put into their schoolwork. Is this the freedom you want your nine-year-old to have? Most households don't place a time limit on phone calls. Does that mean you shouldn't enforce one if you think it's necessary? If Marlin's parents jump in the lake, are you going to jump in, too?

When you believe in what you're doing but feel unsure of yourself because others seem to be raising their kids differently, keep in mind three unalterable realities: You are unique; your children are unique; your situation is unique.

Let's say you've decided to initiate a one-hour reading period on school nights for Page. You want to give her more exposure to the benefits of reading, while at the same time hoping she'll develop some self-discipline in this area. Page doesn't like your idea and nightly complains that her classmates aren't "forced to read." And in fact, from what you know, most parents don't have a requirement like yours. At times, Page puts up such a fuss that you're beginning to wonder if it wouldn't be better to imitate the majority of households and not have a set reading time. Maybe you are wrong in "pushing her too much."

REALITY #1: YOU ARE UNIQUE.   For your own reasons, you feel more strongly than most parents about the value of reading, both as a hobby and as a discipline. Since you want to teach Page to share your appreciation for reading, you pay more attention to fostering this skill than does the average parent. And that is your right.

REALITY #2: YOUR CHILD IS UNIQUE.   Page needs structured time to do anything that involves reading. She is not a poor reader, but if left to read only when she feels like it, Page seldom, if ever, looks in the general direction of a book. Homework assignments are put off, carelessly whisked through, or "forgotten." Instead of a nightly game of twenty-one questions about homework, you have found that an evening reading session saves arguments. Or, Page might be different from her peers in that she's more intelligent than most, but she's also a slider. She doesn't push herself to do any more than she has to in order to get by. A predictable reading hour forces her to make use of her intellect and also shows her that initially distasteful activities can sometimes turn out to be enjoyable once she starts them.

REALITY #3: YOUR SITUATION IS UNIQUE.   You have a particularly stressful job. After dinner, you and your spouse both prefer an hour or so to unwind, read, pursue hobbies. It is your time for quiet, and it's a logical time for Page to learn how to enjoy a good book. Other families might not need or prefer this way to relax, but this time is important to you. And Page is learning to respect it.

Consider these three realities when you're looking all around you to confirm the soundness of your parenting. And remind yourself that other people don't live with your children; you do. The majority isn't responsible for your children; you are. You know them far better than anyone else does. You are the one who has to decide what is best for them and for you.

One More Time...

Too much advice can be paralyzing, especially when it is contradictory advice. Overreliance on the experts can make you mistrust your own judgment. The opinions of family and friends can create uncomfortable uncertainty. Listening to everybody will only confuse you. In the final analysis, you have to decide which advice is helpful to you and which isn't.

Homework

At the end of each chapter I will suggest several brief exercises to help you better incorporate into your parenting the concepts discussed in that chapter. By the way, the assignments are due a week from Friday.

1. Take a simple count of the number of articles, talk shows, books, school programs, and other things you come across in any two-week period telling you how to be a good parent. You'll give yourself an idea of how much child-rearing material you are really exposed to. I have a feeling you will find that you've underestimated it.

2. Note which of these sources are most likely to present information in "here is the answer" style, as opposed to "here are some ideas." It will greatly ease your parental mind if you learn to translate automatically any "here is the answer" message into "here are some ideas."

3. Begin a discussion with relatives or friends about a personally trying child-rearing issue (such as toilet training, school achievement, or discipline). State that you would like suggestions for better ways to deal with your child in this area.

Watch how quickly the participants begin citing experts, personal experience, and other sources to give you "the answer" or "the way" to solve your problem, rather than focusing on your particular needs and situation.

4. Over a one-month period, keep track of the amount of unsolicited advice you receive from well-intentioned relatives and friends. Notice that the closer the relative or friend, the more likely the advice is to be dogmatic, absolute, and critical. Begin to interpret these intrusions for what they are: well-meaning, if undiplomatically presented, efforts to control the decisions you make with your child. There's no problem in choosing to listen as long as you remember you're in the best position to make the final decisions.

5. Ask your youngster, "Which of your friends do you think has the strictest parents?" Then ask, "Why do you think that?" and "Why do you never compare me to these parents?" I think you'll find your child's answers enlightening. I think you'll also let him or her know that you're on to this particular manipulation.

2
A Collective Mythology of Parenthood

Too much advice from others can make it difficult for you to parent decisively. But there is an even bigger roadblock to self-assured parenting. I'm referring to several beliefs widespread among parents today. These beliefs all center around what it means to be a good parent, and most likely they are playing a big part in how you are raising your children. There's just one catch. The beliefs have *no basis in reality!* They are myths that probably underlie much of your parental guilt, worry, and frustration.

In virtually all aspects of our lives, we humans hold beliefs that aren't true. And in so doing we cause ourselves much unnecessary grief. If you can recognize the parenting myths in which you believe, and give them no power over you, you will rid yourself of many of the unpleasant feelings you thought were a natural part of parenthood. You will also be able to parent with more composure and confidence.

Parenting Myth I:

There is a psychologically right way to handle every situation.

or *One spanking after each tantrum and two at bedtime.*

"How should I deal with a child who picks on his younger brother?" "What's the best way to get Carol to listen to me?" "What am I supposed to do to stop my son from tattling?"

Notice how these questions begin: How *should* ... What's *the best* ... What am I *supposed* to do? They all ask: What is the *right way* to do such and such? Parents more and more are phrasing child-rearing questions in this way. They are seeking prescriptions for behavior, just as they do for physical illness. Undoubtedly, getting a foolproof prescription (effective up to twelve hours) to cure tattling, or any other perplexing childhood behavior, would greatly simplify your parenting, but alas, it's not realistic. Child-rearing Question #62—How do you stop a child from tattling?—has no pat answer. How you stop your child's tattling depends on you, your child, and the nature of the tattling. Like any behavior, tattling involves too many factors for one answer to fit all circumstances.

Who is fostering the myth that there is a correct way to handle every situation? Nearly everybody—the media, the experts, and most of all, parents themselves. The media perpetuates this myth through their style of presenting child-rearing advice. Usually, you are enticed with something like this: "Tune in tomorrow when Dr. Arch Eaver will show you *how* to make your child an achiever and discuss his latest book, *The Way to Build a Child's Self-Confidence.*" Anything so worded says: "Here is the answer." It creates the false impression that there are surefire paths to any results you desire. On the other hand, it's much less common to come across this: "Tune in tomorrow when Dr. Eaver will offer his suggestions for improving your child's school achievement and self-confidence." The message here is: "Try these ideas." Again this is not a message you'll receive often, because as raising children gets tougher, ideas just can't compete with answers.

Experts also feed into the *right way* myth if they imply that their way is the only way to shape a mentally healthy child, and that any parent who follows other practices is falling short of ideal parenting and is risking the child's welfare. Fortunately, most experts don't speak with such godlike assurance. Instead, they recommend or advise. They recognize that good kids can be raised in different ways, and they tell parents so.

But even when experts offer only advice, many times parents still make an illogical leap: They view opinion as fact.

Someone with credentials said it; therefore, it must be the psychologically right way to do it. Once you believe this, you're primed to doubt your own ideas. In effect, you give yourself a standard by which to judge your parenting—an expert's word. I was eating breakfast at a restaurant once, and a mother and her son were seated in a booth behind me. The youngster ordered something he thought looked tasty, but when it arrived, he decided it didn't look as tasty on his plate as it did in the menu. He started whining and angrily pushed his food back toward the waitress. His mother immediately insisted he apologize and eat what he ordered or not eat at all. After a pouting "I'm sorry," the little fellow played with his food a few minutes, tasted a small bite, and much to his surprise, liked it. Before I left the restaurant, I walked over to the mother and identified myself as a psychologist. Suddenly her expression read: "Oh no, what did I do wrong?" When I complimented her on how she handled her son, she seemed surprised. Apparently she thought I was going to chastise her for not practicing sound restaurant parenting, and she looked relieved to get confirmation that she'd done just fine.

If you don't recognize it as a myth, the *right way* notion can also stifle your creativity as a parent. You can become reluctant to trust your own resourceful solutions to problems for fear they're "incorrect." You might reason that the more unusual or novel your idea, the more chance you have of doing something wrong.

A father once related to me that his five-year-old son had been kissing boys at school. The youngster's teacher was getting nervous because she hadn't yet found a way to stop the kissing, and she feared possible sexual problems. When Dad found out about his son's affection for his classmates, he had an idea. His son's hero was the Hulk, so Dad told him that the Hulk wouldn't kiss people if they didn't want to be kissed. Apparently, the little guy wanted to emulate his hero, because he soon started keeping his lips to himself. The strategy was successful, but dad still wrestled with doubts. What if he missed something that was troubling his son socially? Maybe he should have had a long father-son talk. Was the Hulk a good model? Dad certainly could have tried other approaches. Some would have worked; some would have failed. His creative solution was one that worked. Why look any further?[8]

Another parent shared with a workshop group how she once and for all silenced her eleven-year-old son's weekly threats to run

20

away from home. One morning, after her son had become angry over cold toast, or something similarly unbearable, he vowed to leave town after school and never return. Mom didn't argue. She just quietly handed him his lunch wrapped in a road map. From that day on, the threats ceased. I thought Mom's style had merit, but a few parents asked: "Didn't you worry about looking like you didn't care if he ran away?" This veteran mother responded that her son didn't seem too badly scarred by her lack of concern. That evening, he returned home from school and handed her the Ohio Highways lunch bag. Mom had driven home her point.[9]

Most problems can be handled any number of ways, and often the more creative ways work best, even though you wouldn't find them in a book of "how to's." You and your child are unique, and books can only offer general suggestions. How cleverly you use those suggestions, or come up with your own, is up to you.

To sum up, the notion that there are approaches you *should* use, advice you *must* follow, and words you *have* to say in order to raise a well-adjusted child is a debilitating myth. The reality is that your methods can be effective or ineffective, helpful or useless. Instead of judging your actions as right or wrong, apply the key question put forth in the last chapter: Is this working or isn't it? This is a much more meaningful test of your methods, and it will make you less likely to downgrade yourself as a parent.

Parenting Myth II:

**If you handle a situation well,
your child's behavior will immediately improve.**

or *"We've tried everything. Nothing works."*

How often I hear these words. They are the lament of defeated parents. As parents describe how they've spanked, reasoned with, ignored, and denied their child every privilege except breathing, I often find that along the way they tried things that would have worked quite well—if they had used them regularly enough or stuck with them long enough. They mistakenly assumed that had they found the proper approach, life would surely have become more tolerable by now. If only they could figure out the *perfect* line of reasoning, deny just the *right* privilege, or reinforce the *exact* behavior, Ripley wouldn't tell lies anymore, Gloria would keep her room clean enough to find the bed, and Dusty would like baths.

This kind of reasoning undermines an ingredient crucial to effective parenting—persistence—because it convinces you to give up too quickly. Pinball parenting, or bouncing from idea to idea looking for the one that will put you instantly in control, only makes you feel less in control. You start to grope for answers, feeling at a total loss as to where to turn next. Then a self-defeating cycle begins. As a problem behavior gets worse, you become frustrated and impatient. You're prone to drop an idea because it isn't working fast enough. But every time you give up, the problem only becomes more stubbornly entrenched. Then you get even more frustrated, more impatient, and less willing to stick with anything ... and on and on. This cycle can quickly bruise your image of yourself as a smart parent. Surely a smarter parent would have matters under control sooner.

Although it would be nice to take command of a situation with a few well-phrased or perfectly timed strategies, you just can't count on it. I humbly learned this lesson some years ago at the hands of a five-year-old. After I had finished playing a softball game, this youngster walked up behind me and began taking practice swings at the back of my legs with a baseball bat. Now, I've always been allergic to wood colliding with my body at twenty-five miles per hour, so I bent down and said, "Hey, that's not cool. Enough of that." My teammates immediately saw their chance: "Big-time, big-city psychologist. 'That's not cool. Enough of that.' A true pro with kids." My reputation was at stake, so I racked my brains for the flawless response to a baseball-bat-wielding five-year-old. Exuding professionalism, I bent back down and tried again: "You know, I won't let you hit me with that bat. I'll just walk away because I don't like being hit. But I'll tell you what, if you put the bat down, I've got a ball and we can play catch." I felt sure that I had covered a range of appropriate responses, and I expected to be in charge any second. But I guess the little guy hadn't read the same books I had, because after my mini-speech he just looked at me unruffled and said, "Stuff it, Jerkface," and walked away.

Needless to say, my confrontation with the unknown ball-player did little to enhance my professional reputation. But it did impactfully impress upon me this: Don't make the mistake of grading your technique after one, or even several, tries. You can deal with a situation beautifully, and it may still blow up in your face. One-shot tries, or brief intense spurts of trying an idea, are usually not enough to bring on desired results. Finding good ideas is only the first step, very often the easiest. Staying with your ideas is the part that can push you to the limits of your parenthood. Happily, most kids respond fairly quickly to a good approach consistently used. Some kids, however, are experts at outlasting their parents. They have learned that, no matter what happens, if they put up enough fuss, their parents will eventually relent and try something else, or maybe try nothing else, giving up altogether. If this is your youngster's style, you'd better be prepared to be part parent and part bulldog, for you will need to stick with any approach for a long time.

Parents also can get tricked into foresaking an idea too soon if they overlook the fact that the purpose of an act of discipline need not always be to produce results the first time it is used. Its purpose might be to reap results the second time the misbehavior occurs, or maybe not even until the misbehavior and the discipline are paired many times. An example will clarify this. A colleague of mine who tutors preschool children in their homes was having more than her fair share of trouble with one little boy—call him Norman. Whenever Norman lost interest in the activity of the moment, he would ignore, throw, or destroy whatever was in front of him. During a recent tutoring session, Norman had flung a set of blocks from the table to the floor. This was definitely not part of the lesson plan, so the teacher told Norman to pick up the blocks. He refused—not surprisingly, since I doubt that Norman would have chucked the blocks just to go bend down and retrieve them. Because the teacher felt that trying to convince Norman to retrieve the blocks would result in a prolonged and futile struggle, she allowed him to leave the blocks strewn and move on to the next scheduled activity—lunch preparation. This activity Norman loved and had been quite anxious to start. I suggested that the teacher might have instead told Norman one time that all blocks must be gathered and the lesson completed before lunch fun would begin. She replied that Norman's reaction to that would probably be to pout, throw a second fit, and swallow the loss of lunch rather than clean up his mess. What could she do then? My answer: Nothing, not with Norman anyway. Fix lunch with Norman's mom, enjoy it, and then quietly leave. Granted, for that visit, in one sense the discipline wouldn't have "worked"; that is, it wouldn't have instantly motivated Norman to correct his behavior. On the other hand, it would have sent Norman a clear message for the next time a block-splattering incident occurred: No more fun until the mess is cleaned. In the future, Norman will know what will happen when he loses control and will be a bit less stubborn. And if he still remains immovable, a second or third repeat might be necessary. Eventually Norman will understand his choices. And that is often what discipline is supposed to do.

There are four realities that will help you overcome the belief that if your child's behavior doesn't improve as quickly as you think it should, you aren't parenting well. These realities are basic principles of learning, and they exert a powerful influence on your child's behavior. Focusing on them will help you remain resolute and optimistic while you wait for your approach to have a positive effect.

The longer any behavior has been a problem, the longer it usually takes to turn it around. An eight-year-old who has been talking back since he was six can be taught respect a lot more quickly than a fourteen-year-old who's been verbally abusing you since he was six. That fourteen-year-old has a solidly ingrained habit under his belt, and he is not about to give it up quietly. I recall consulting with a teacher about a youngster who had given headaches to every one of his teachers since the first grade. Five teachers and thirty-two bottles of aspirin later, he was eleven. I offered the teacher suggestions for managing the little migraine-maker; she gamely tried them for three weeks and then discarded them because they "didn't work." Five years of disruptive, negative behavior can't be brought under control in three weeks, no matter how good the ideas.

The older the child, the harder you will probably have to work to change a problem behavior. Trying to stop a two-year-long habit of backtalk from your fourteen-year-old will take more effort than trying to curb the same two-year-long habit in your eight-year-old. Older kids see things more their way, and they are less willing to be influenced by you. They also can learn more clever, subtle, or sophisticated ways to resist your best efforts.

An approach is only as good as its follow-through. Nearly every child-rearing book ever written has emphasized consistency and following through with what you say, and rightly so. These are linchpins of effective parenting, and they can make or break even the most well-thought-out strategy. Suppose you have a rule that Filbert cannot watch TV until he dries the supper dishes. Most of the time you stand by your rule, but about every third night you allow Filbert to finagle TV while the dishes sit. Tiring of the hassle, you throw in your towel and dry the dishes yourself. Overall, then, your rule is only about 66 percent effective; however, it would be much closer to 100 percent effective if you enforced it daily. By letting Filbert periodically dodge the dishes, you're keeping his resistance strong. In effect, you are paying off like a slot machine. A slot machine only rewards every once in a while, but players relentlessly crank away, putting up with mostly unpleasant results until they finally hit pay dirt. The tenacity of kids rivals that of the most inveterate gamblers. If your children discover they can play you until you eventually cash in, even if it's only one time in five, they will challenge virtually every approach you try.

What may be the most important fact of discipline is this: the effectiveness of any discipline depends not only upon the quality of the approach itself, but very much upon your style in implementing it. Even a mediocre approach used confidently and consistently is more beneficial than the most brilliant approach used tentatively and sporadically.

Kids often act worse for a while just because you are finally handling them well. In fact, if you test a new strategy and your youngster's behavior worsens, this is a positive sign you're on the right track. Confusing? Let me illustrate. Patience likes to nag. She pounds away at you until you break. One good way to silence her nagging would be to tune it out, to tell Patience that you are now going to ignore any more appeals. The first few times that you do become oblivious, however, she will probably carry on louder and longer. Finding that the usual level of badgering isn't high enough anymore to wrench your attention, Patience amplifies it, trying to make you respond in your old ways. Don't be disheartened; Patience's flare-up is only temporary. Once she realizes she is not going to wear you down through her persistence, she will slowly abandon her efforts. In the end, your strategy will work. To illustrate this phenomenon more broadly: I frequently talk with parents who have set weak and indecisive limits on their youngster's behavior. After our initial parent assertiveness session, they march out of the office determined to show their child who is parent. When they return, they're more discouraged than before and convinced their child is beyond even the power of the shrink: "He got worse." That's not surprising. Mom and Dad are starting to put firm limits on Butch, and he doesn't like it. So he's becoming more uncontrollable, trying to get around those limits. Even though his folks are finally taking charge, those first few days, weeks, or even months may find Butch harder to manage. And he won't stop escalating his unmanageability until he realizes his folks are not going to be bullied back to the old order.

Once again, behavior change is a process. It takes time, patience, and above all, effort. Much of your feeling of futility in dealing with difficult behavior probably doesn't come from your lack of good ideas. It comes from your lack of stick-to-itiveness in using those ideas. There are many things in life that can be fixed quickly. Behavior is not one of them.

Parenting Myth III:

**If you handle a situation poorly,
your child will suffer now and in the future.**

or *It's not all right to be wrong.*

"If I force my daughter to do her homework, couldn't that just make her hate school even more?" "What if I punish Danny for something he didn't do?" "How can I be sure what I'm doing now won't hurt my kids emotionally later in life?"

Questions like these reflect what may be the most pervasive fear among parents today: the fear of harming their child psychologically, of accidentally creating some emotional hang-up that will plague a youngster for life. One mother told me she worried about disciplining her son too much because she didn't want him to grow up with bad feelings toward women. Another parent shared with me his inability to make his three-year-old daughter

Trisha stay in bed. One night in desperation he blocked the bedroom doorway with a baby gate. After a prolonged fit of crying and gate-rattling, Trisha finally gave up and fell asleep. That was the first and last time, though, that her father ever used the gate. He felt there was too much risk of psychological damage if he had to go "that far" in disciplining his daughter.

It's no surprise that parents are as anxious as they are. They've been warned about and made to feel responsible for just about every problem and quirk their children develop. Everything from a bellyache to dropping out of high school has been blamed on parents. Nearly every child-rearing, and in particular disciplining, technique has been accused by somebody of not being good parental practice. Consequently, parents have become uncomfortably cautious. They endlessly weigh their actions because they don't want some negative repercussion returning to haunt them someday. And they waver in their decisions, at times making no decision at all for fear of making the wrong move. Ironically, it is their own indecision that most often brings on trouble.

Certainly your parenting is extremely influential in shaping what your child will be like as an adult. If you consistently parent poorly, your child will probably develop problems that carry over into adulthood. The key words here, though, are *consistently* and *probably*. You have to handle your child poorly not once or twice but *repeatedly* before you lay the foundation for *potential* future troubles. Just as it takes time and perseverance to teach healthy habits, it takes time and perseverance to teach unhealthy ones. A rebellious, out-of-control teenager does not appear overnight or because Mom and Dad miscalculated at crucial developmental periods several years back. Totally unmanageable adolescents usually result from many years of inadequate, neglectful, or ineffective parenting.

Naturally, you don't want your kids to have an unhealthy emotional reaction to something you've done as a parent. And if you're like most parents, you worry about two kinds of reactions—those you see and those you don't. Those you see—pouting, temper tantrums, hostility, crying—generally occur when your child doesn't like what you're doing. As a responsible parent, you will see these reactions often, especially when you discipline. The great majority of the time, they are no cause for concern, even though they can get pretty ugly. Kids have a remarkable talent for appearing as though their inner world could collapse any second because of you. Younger children give uninhibited displays of facial contortions, grotesque postures, and inhuman grunts, growls, and wails. Older kids can present a more calculated loss of control, looking as if the hostility within them is beyond sanity. They'll spew things you never thought would be in their heads, much less come out of their mouths. I'm reminded of a youngster who used this tactic whenever he was disciplined for bullying his sister. He would fly into a rage and detail all the terrible ways he'd get revenge on his sibling when he had the chance. Hence, he kept his parents worried that their attempts to stem his aggression were only filling him with more aggression.

It is these intense, dreadful-looking outbursts that can shock you and convince you to abandon your discipline. You don't want such outward craziness to cause any inward craziness. Don't be alarmed; it won't. What you're seeing are severe temper tantrums. Your youngster is discovering that you or the world is not going to behave as she would like. And you won't traumatize her by making her realize this fact of life, no matter how often or how dramatically she shows her displeasure. I have never known a single child emotionally scarred by not getting her way during a relentless temper outburst, but I have seen many who have problems because they got their way too much.

Carl was one such child, and one of the most extreme cases of the *it's not all right to be wrong* myth I ever saw. Carl had realized early in life that his mom was terrified of overly frustrating him, so, to manipulate her, he had mastered the fine art of "look what you're doing to me; I'm losing my mind" crying. And sure enough, every time the tears began, Mom's panic began because she was convinced she would cripple Carl emotionally if she allowed him to sob too long. Over a period of years, Carl had learned he could get whatever he wanted by marathon wailing. On one occasion, and this has to be some kind of record, he cried for nine hours straight to ensure Mom wouldn't leave the house. A partial list of the concessions Mom had allowed Carl to wring from her included the following: she couldn't go to the store without Carl; she couldn't talk on the phone while Carl was home; Carl decided his own bedtime; and when Carl and Mom had the chance to move into a larger apartment, Carl cried the opportunity away. In every sense except doing chores, Carl ran the household. When I attempted to convince Mom that she would have to take a firm stand and outlast Carl's crying, she helplessly said she couldn't do that. She told me I obviously didn't understand how sensitive a child Carl was.[10]

Carl's reaction to his mother's every wish was immediate and unpleasant—he sobbed interminably. This proved unhealthy for Carl, but only because his mother gave in to him constantly. Unlike Carl's mother, you needn't fear the negative reactions you see from your children. In fact, sometimes these reactions can give you valuable information about your methods.

Let's say you're tired of verbally wrestling with Bruno about his homework. You've decided to allow him to complete whatever amount of schoolwork he desires, hoping the impending bad grades will motivate him to buckle down. Two months later, Bruno hates school even more, and his grades have dropped by at least one letter in every subject. Your strategy isn't working; it is only making matters worse. But at least you know that and can learn from your mistake. As with a temper tantrum, you can see what is happening and then do something about it.

It is when you can't see what is happening, however, that you may feel most anxious. Or, put another way, are you creating some hidden emotional conflict within your youngster, and will this conflict show up later in life as some form of maladjustment? Twenty years from now, will he be sitting in an encounter group, painfully recalling the time you went berserk and threw out several of his most treasured toys because he was not caring for them properly, pinpointing the experience as the turning point in his life, as the event that showed him life is cruel? What a sure way to drive yourself batty! Since you can't know what subtle, silent ill effects your actions might be having on your youngster's psyche, you can't do anything about them. You just have to wait helplessly until they surface; then you can futilely scour the past, trying to pinpoint where you went wrong. In the meantime, you must torture yourself with worry that you could be damaging your child's emotional well-being without realizing it. After all, only an expert can *really* know if unseen problems exist and when and where they will erupt.

As a psychologist, if I had to put together a set of notions to make parents anxious, I don't know if I could do better than what they do to themselves. And the real tragedy is that so much of parents' anxiety is caused by misconceptions. First of all, we experts cannot predict adult maladjustments on the basis of a few childhood experiences. Some old psychological theories said we could, but experience has taught us differently. Second, even if we could do such predicting, most serious problems don't come about this way. I can't stress this enough. Children who grow up making a total shambles of their lives almost always have experienced long-term patterns of poor or ineffective parenting. Their pasts are riddled with neglect, abuse, or lack of guidance. And even then it's amazing how some of these children not only survive their chaotic or pitiful upbringings, but actually go on to lead reasonably stable lives. Of course, children from solid homes can also hit rocky periods while growing up, but more often than not these children eventually put their lives back in order. They don't stay on a path to lifelong maladjustment.

We adults underestimate how emotionally durable kids are. They are not fragile little beings who shatter under stress. They won't be psychologically ruined by your parental mistakes, even if you do blunder badly. When you get upset that you might have mishandled any particular situation, remind yourself: That situation is only one of the thousands you'll share with your child over many years. If you're a loving, responsible, limit-setting parent, you already have the basics. The odds are much in your favor that your kids will mature into responsible adults, even if they do pass through some rough stretches along the way.

If you care how you parent, if you want to improve, overall you're probably doing fine. But there will be many times when you won't parent as well as you think you should. You do not have the consistency of a machine, nor do you need it to raise good kids. You will have bad days. You will misjudge, overreact, underlisten. You are going to lose your cool and fling personal insults. Sometimes you'll be unfair and blame Jimmy when Rover actually did it. In short, you're unavoidably human, and humans make mistakes in even the simplest things they do. You'd better expect to err frequently in doing something as complicated and prolonged as raising kids. In all likelihood, your kids will survive your humanness and go on to be human parents themselves who will make mistakes with their kids.

The fear of doing your children emotional harm won't ruin just your parental peace of mind; it may also ruin your ability to act firmly and decisively with your kids. You can slip into a wishy-washy style of second-guessing yourself, ruminating over your every move, eventually becoming paralyzed by your own indecision. Here is a hypothetical sequence of events. You decide that Carlisle will have to pay for the window he carelessly broke while shooting at the cat with his BB gun. As you think more about your decision, you start to feel guilty, or worse yet, wrong. Maybe you acted too hastily or were too harsh. Carlisle is taking forever to earn the money, and he's growing surly under the weight of his self-prolonged punishment. He's also more rotten to the cat each day. Fearing the ill effects of dragging out Carlisle's penance, you take the two dollars he's earned thus far and forget the rest. Or, to use another house-pet example, for the third time this week, Kitty didn't feed the dog. So you restrict her to the house for the evening. She begins to plead and sounds truly contrite, promising never to starve Rover again. Now you're torn. You want to follow through on what you've said, but you don't want to be callous toward Kitty's genuine remorse. Wavering back and forth, you finally decide to let the whole incident drop, as Kitty trots off to play outside. Once you send your kids the message that your decisions lack resolve, they will quickly learn how to take advantage of your uncertainty. You are teaching them to do the very thing that is encouraging your indecisiveness—that is, become emotionally distressed when they don't get their way.

I'm certainly not implying that you should never reconsider your decisions and change them if need be. Sometimes, in the heat of the moment, you'll impose a punishment that far surpasses the crime, assuming a crime was even committed. For example, you may later find out it was Rover, not Carlisle, who chewed the door frame. Or, you may simmer down after a fit of rage in which you grounded Kitty for one month because she was fifteen minutes late for supper. However, in general, taking a clear, firm stand greatly reduces conflict between you and your children. Indecisiveness invites challenge and testing. If you don't succumb to the irrational worry that you will accidentally harm your youngsters emotionally while you're trying to be a good parent, you will act with more authority and credibility. Your kids will better know what to expect, they will better be able to live with your rules, and they won't have the constant temptation to push you to change your mind. And at those times when you realize you could have handled things better, be patient. Your kids will give you many future opportunities to polish up your approach.

Parenting Myth IV:

Psychologically sophisticated approaches are best.

or *There's always a way to make things difficult.*

This myth goes like this: If an approach looks psychologically sophisticated, it must delve deeper into a child's psyche and get to the root of a problem better than other approaches. It is guaranteed to bring to the surface and resolve all the complex motivations underlying a child's behavior. Parents who believe this myth are not likely to apply the acid test by asking, "Does it work?" They believe that their child's overall emotional health is benefiting from the approach, and that the positive results will be seen someday.

You can stand at the back door for an hour, telling your son how you empathize with all his anger and distress because he has to quit playing and come into the house, but if he stays outside, acknowledging you only enough to argue, your approach isn't getting through. It may seem the psychological thing to do, it may sound good, but it's not working. And if it's not working now, it's not likely to have positive results sometime in the future.

Probably the most popular version of the *sophisticated is best* myth is the Reverse Psychology Tactic. The R.P. Tactic is based on the belief that subtly manipulating your child into behaving a certain way shows more parental savvy than simply asking his cooperation or telling him what you expect. The logic is that competent parents should always be able to reason, convince, or "psych" their child into behaving well. Not only is this logic fallacious, but it will regularly draw you into exasperating duels of wits with your child that you may not always win.

Suppose your three-year-old daughter Lovina is refusing to kiss Grandpa goodbye, and you've been trying to persuade her otherwise for the past ten very embarrassing minutes. You've told her that Grandpa's feelings will be hurt, that he'll cry, and that he won't want her to come over again, all to no avail. That does it. Lovina's forced you to reach for your ace in the hole. Holding

Lovina close to Grandpa's cheek and, counting on her natural tendency to behave counter to your wishes, you firmly demand that she not kiss Grandpa because he doesn't want to be kissed anymore. On the one hand, if Lovina figures out your tactic, she may become even more obstinate. On the other, if she doesn't catch on to what you're doing, she may well kiss Grandpa, but only at the cost of disobeying you to do so. And how long will you be able to "outsmart" her like this?

One of the simplest yet most elegantly effective ways to deal with your youngster's problem behavior is to tell her clearly what you expect and what you plan to do if she behaves otherwise. No games, no behavioral trickery, just straightforward communication of your expectations and consequences. This is such an indispensable means of keeping you an easygoing parent that it will be elaborated on more fully in Chapter 6. For now, I want to emphasize that getting yourself caught up in trying to manipulate your youngster psychologically into doing what you'd like can rapidly give you a case of mental battle fatigue.

In our love for sophistication, we have devalued common sense. Routinely, I ask parents what they think would be a good way to manage the situation they're telling me about. Quite often they come up with sound ideas that they feel are too simple to work. Common sense, they feel, is sufficient for common problems, but for really hard-core problems, something more psychologically advanced is called for.

A school official once called me because a student had been urinating on the school's front bushes. Because the official suspected this behavior might be a sign of "emotional problems," he hadn't even tried the standard school discipline with the boy. Instead, he asked me: "How should you solve a problem like this?" I offered what I thought was a logical suggestion, something that should be tried before anything else: "Tell him not to urinate on the front bushes anymore, and then tell him what you're going to do if he does." The administrator was obviously disappointed with my common-sense advice. I could sense him thinking: "This guy went to college for nine years, and this is the best he can do." He believed there just had to be a more profound answer to this unusual problem. Maybe there was, but why search for it if a simple one will work? Why make things more complicated than they are?"[11]

There is an informal rule of science called the Law of Parsimony. This rule states that one should find the simplest, most economical way to explain something or to change it. In other words, use as few steps as possible to achieve a goal. The Law of Parsimony applies well to raising kids. Simple, level-headed approaches are the first, and generally the best, route to take. For instance, you find out that your child has taken a toy from the neighbor's yard without permission. You immediately require that he personally return the toy, apologize, and, if necessary, pay for any damage, loss, or inconvenience. This is certainly not a revolutionary new technique. It's an intuitive response that parents have used as long as there have been toys and neighbors' yards. And it still applies. You don't need to use tailor-made phrases or deep interpretations. A sensible explanation of why it's wrong to steal, backed up with some consequences, will provide a good lesson about stealing in most cases.

Parents are sometimes reluctant to rely on common sense because children today live in a complex world that breeds complex problems. Don't complex problems need complex solutions? Not necessarily. Most of the problems your kids present you with can still be solved with straightforward approaches. You just have to be prepared to stick with those approaches longer, using them more consistently and more often.

Responsible parenting has always involved instincts and good sense. That will never change. You will needlessly complicate your parenting if you believe that because something is common sense, it's not good enough. Decide upon some well-defined, solid principles and you'll have the foundation to build upon for good parenting.

Parenting Myth V:

You must know the reasons behind a behavior to change it.

or *You must know why before you try.*

Some of the toughest questions parents ask me have the word "why" in them. "Why does Cindy hate school?" "Why is Buddy so immature?" "Why can't Chris control his temper?" I have to admit that to many of these I'm forced to answer, "I don't know." But that doesn't mean something can't be done.

The *you must know why* myth may be the oldest of the parenting myths. It has its roots in the earliest days of psychology, when theories about kids focused almost totally on why they behaved as they did, saying that the answer lay buried somewhere in past unresolved conflicts and hurts. As other viewpoints became popular, less emphasis was put on the past. Nevertheless, many of these viewpoints also said that in order to change behavior, one must first identify its causes. This old and erroneous idea still governs parenting today.

Because of the *you must know why* myth, you may think that really good parents should be psychologically slick enough and insightful enough to elicit their children's true inner feelings (as opposed to false outer feelings, I suppose), resolve the dilemmas caused by those feelings, and thus enable all conflicts to evaporate. After all, isn't that what Robert Young was so good at on *Father Knows Best?* Ah, real parenthood should unfold so nicely.

Knowing *why* sometimes helps. It sometimes doesn't. But either way, it's not necessary. Look at your own behavior in this respect. If you procrastinate, do you understand all the reasons why? Does this mean you can't work at changing yourself? When you have a headache, do you always know where it came from? Nonetheless, you do things to get rid of it, don't you? In fact, most of the time you are forced to change yourself without ever completely understanding how you got that way. The same observation is true of children. You can't always understand them, but you may still have to change their behavior.

If you're like many parents, though, you feel uneasy when you can't figure out your kids. You're afraid of acting prematurely or being unfair. "What if we punish Jimmy, and we miss something that is upsetting him?" Even if something is upsetting Jimmy, and you're not aware of it, he is still responsible for his actions. Maybe the kids at school made fun of his designer lunch box. That gives him no excuse to come home and push around his sister. "But," you ask, "won't a behavior keep coming back if its causes still exist?" Again, not necessarily. In fact, part of maturing and adapting to this world is learning new behavior in the same old bad situations. You want Jimmy to learn how to ignore name-calling instead of getting upset by it, or to realize that he can get good grades even if his teacher doesn't like him. You need to teach Jimmy that he can change his behavior even though his environment or the people in it may not change.

If you are preoccupied with *why,* you may also waste energy looking for complicated explanations that don't exist. One of my colleagues was seeing a family for counseling. During a session, the father repeatedly badgered his teenaged daughter to tell him why she smoked. Each time, she doggedly answered, in true teenaged fashion, "I don't know." Finally, the therapist stepped in, "Will you please tell your father why you smoke?" The girl then confessed, "Because I want to. I know you don't like it, but I don't care." That was too obvious for Dad. "Quit trying to avoid the issue. Why do you *really* smoke?" He was convinced they couldn't get anywhere until they got to the psychological bottom of things.

You will endlessly frustrate yourself trying to comprehend everything your child does. Children can be baffling creatures whose motivations are oftentimes impossible to discern. I often hear, "You're a psychologist. You should know why kids do that." On the contrary, it's because I am a psychologist that I've learned to be content with not always knowing why. I keep my sanity better that way.

Along a much broader line, foster or adoptive parents must face a far more frustrating reality. Save for a few general facts, they know little about their new son or daughter's past. Overall, they have to accept the child as he or she is. Bad habits, attitudes, emotional troubles all have to be handled from the present forward. There is no luxury of knowing why.

Of course, much of the time you are in fact able to figure out the reasons for your child's behavior, or at least what you think the reasons are. Even so, you are often unable to do anything about them. Nevertheless, you can still solve the problems they cause.

If the reasons are in the past, they are beyond your reach. You can't go back and undo them. Suppose your fourteen-year-old daughter Cindy hates school. Her attitude has been building for years. Why? By now, the reasons are so many and so complex that you could never identify them all. And even to try would probably be a waste of time. Your main concern is getting Cindy to school *now.*

If the reasons are in the present, they may still be beyond your reach. "Cindy is so hard to manage after she comes back from a weekend with (*fill in the appropriate relative*). It takes me a week to get control again." But if Cindy has to visit that relative, and that person won't cooperate with you in disciplining her, then you are forced to handle Cindy when she's with you, in the here and now. You can't eradicate all the present causes of her unmanageability.

I can pull a similar illustration from my own family. My younger brother Mike began to dislike school intensely during the middle of one school year. His attitude manifested itself in crying spells, slipping grades, and assorted illnesses. My mother couldn't understand what was happening, because Mike had always enjoyed school. Looking into the change, she learned that Mike's teacher, for personal reasons, was having a difficult year in the classroom. And my brother, who was a sensitive little guy, was reacting. There was little my mother could do about the classroom situation, so she supported Mike but still insisted that he attend school, "sick" or not. She also held him responsible for his grades. Eventually, Mike pulled out of his slump, even though the "cause" was still there.

The reasons for a child's behavior regularly come purely from his own peculiar motivations. In other words, the *why* lies inside the child's head. Just as we adults perceive the world in our own unique and sometimes distorted ways, so too do kids. They misperceive what they see and experience, and then act upon their misperceptions. The result is behavior that seems to have no logical explanation or basis. And what frustrates us adults even further is that kids often can't or won't explain what is going on. To use another school example, I remember a second-grade girl who started a pattern like my brother's. After about a year and a half of liking school, without warning she began to feign illnesses. Her dad spoke with her, with her teacher, and with school personnel and could find no reason for her puzzling behavior. Obviously, something was upsetting this little girl, but she wouldn't open up about it. Dad felt helpless, but he didn't let the behavior become a habit. He still sent his daughter off to school, and a few weeks later the illnesses disappeared. Where did they come from? Dad never found out. They were one of those many "out of the blue" things that kids do that catch parents completely off guard. Nevertheless, you must deal with them, and they usually resolve themselves.

Always asking *why* can be an exercise in futility. That's because you can't always know why, and even when you can, you may not be able to do anything about it. To save yourself much misdirected energy, replace your *why's* with *what's* and *how's*. Instead of asking "Why is this happening?," ask "What can I do about it?" or "How am I allowing this problem to continue?" These questions will guide you toward causes over which you do have control. You may not be able to change the past, the environment, or what's in your child's head, but you can change you. And you are often the strongest influence on your youngster's actions. Learning to respond in ways that will reduce tensions and increase your self-control will be the focus of later chapters.

One More Time ...

You will gain composure and self-assurance as a parent if you replace several common myths with the following realities: (1) Labeling your parenting as "right" or "wrong" only deceives you into grading yourself. Your actions can be far more accurately judged by how well they work. (2) There are seldom instant cures to problem behaviors. Most likely, improving your child's behavior will take time and effort, no matter how good your methods. (3) If you care how well you parent and are willing to learn from your mistakes, you will not emotionally damage your child through errors in judgment committed in good faith. In fact, you are probably asking for more trouble by being afraid to make mistakes, and thus not decisively establishing your parental authority. (4) Even in this age of scientific sophistication, effective child-rearing still involves hefty doses of common sense. You don't need to be up on all the latest psychological techniques to raise a well-adjusted child. (5) If you wait to understand all the reasons for your children's behavior before you act, your kids will grow up robbed of much of your guidance. Accept your children for what they are—baffling and unpredictable at times—and work to change their behavior even though you can't always understand it.

Homework

1. If you have more than one child, recall a particular behavior or developmental task, such as toilet training or weaning, that you tackled with each. If you have only one child, find another parent who faced the same issue with a youngster of a similar age. Were the children approached in exactly the same way? Did they respond in exactly the same way? Probably not, because what was "psychologically right" for child A may not have been "psychologically right" for child B. In other words, what works with one may not work so well with another.

2. Pick an especially troublesome behavior—one of your child's favorites. Decide what consequences to place upon it and convey these to your child. Then set a date at least six weeks hence to review your progress. During the first week of your approach, count how many times the behavior occurs. Make a similar count during the last week. Compare the two. Most likely, the problem will have subsided, but maybe so slightly you wouldn't have noticed if you hadn't tallied the score. You'll have evidence your approach is beginning to work because you stayed with it.

3. Think back to a time when one of your parents overreacted to a situation in the family. Make sure your memory is of something neither of your parents did regularly—that is, of an isolated incident of overreaction. Has it scarred you emotionally? Did it impair your adjustment from that moment forward? How often have you and your siblings laughed about it as adults?

4. Recall an occasion in which you totally lost control in dealing with your child and in one fell swoop committed nearly every child-rearing sin known to man. Who stayed upset longer, you or your child? Who had the harder time letting the incident die?

5. Think of people you know who make a practice of never telling you directly what they would like you to do for them. How do you feel when they do this? Confused and off-balance? If they would simply convey their wishes, you would probably feel less suspicious, less resentful of being manipulated, and more likely to give them what they want. Kids operate in the same way. They

generally respond more positively to simple, clear-cut messages and approaches than to obscure ones.

6. Identify an undesirable personal habit that you've broken. Make a list of all the reasons you can remember for the original development of the habit. How many of these reasons had any relationship to the methods you finally used to break the habit? For example, if you started smoking in order to look grown-up and fit in with the crowd, did you eventually quit smoking by convincing yourself you didn't have to look grown-up or "fit in" anymore? Not only do *why's* often elude capture, but they have the distinct habit of changing over time.

3

Personality:
Remembered Myths
and Forgotten Realities

The last chapter exposed several parenting myths that make the tough work of being a parent even tougher. This chaper will uncover a few more myths of a different ilk—the personality myths. Like the parenting myths, these myths can add anxiety and confusion to your parenthood, thereby hindering your efforts to act decisively. By giving you a false picture of how your kids develop, think, and behave, the personality myths can influence you to parent in ways that will do nothing but create problems for you and your youngsters, now and later.

This chapter will also reinforce two very obvious, but very ignored, realities about personality. Most likely, you are well aware of these realities, but just as likely, you forget them from time to time. And forgetting a reality can cause you as much grief as believing a myth. Let's look first at the most widely believed myth about personality.

The Personality–Finality Myth
or "It all started in my childhood."

I often pose this question to parent groups: How many of you believe that a child's personality is pretty much developed by age six? Typically, over half of the parents raise their hands. I then ask if any of the believers have children between the ages of five and six. Several usually do. "Well, then," I warn them, "you'd better get going. You have less than a year to teach all the traits, habits, attitudes, and beliefs you want your child to have as an adult."

Quite understandably, nobody takes this tongue-in-cheek warning seriously (except maybe those with horrendous five-year-olds). Few parents believe their work is complete before their children even begin first grade. Such a belief is contrary to all observation and common sense. On the other hand, many parents do believe that the years prior to first grade are the most crucial in shaping the kind of adult their child eventually becomes. Indeed, this notion has been on the child-rearing scene for some time. It gained popularity several generations ago, when Freud said that the adult personality, and especially adult maladjustment, could be traced back to early childhood. According to Freud, if one could look back to just the right moments in childhood, one would find the roots of almost all adult emotional turmoil. Since Freud, others have reshaped this idea, adding and subtracting their own individual biases, but the basic notion still remains intact: Personality is molded in the first several years of life.

This observation has some truth to it. Some early behaviors are the forerunners of later characteristics. First experiences can be impactful. They have a head start on whatever follows, and they occur at a time when a child is most impressionable. However, to say that personality is *molded* in the first several years of life is psychological nonsense. Only a small fraction of what children become originates in their preschool years. The rest of the personality is formed through complex psychological and biological processes that continue until the end of life. As an example, look at your own personality. The attitudes and opinions you hold today were unknown to you as a young child. At age six, did you have any inkling what political party you would now be registered with? Had you settled on what characteristics you would value in a spouse? Back then, your reasoning powers were simple; your morals were only starting to form. When you were in kindergarten, could you state an opinion on capital punishment and support it with logical arguments? Not unless you were *very* bright or read a lot. Some of what you are at present may have started in your early childhood, but it is just as accurate to say that much of what you are at present has no relationship whatsoever with your early childhood experiences. You are much too complex a being to have had your adult character shaped at a time when you were just beginning to understand your world.

The experts have scared parents by putting so much weight on the "formative" years. These years aren't all-powerful in and of themselves. Their ultimate impact is determined by the rest of childhood, and by adulthood, for that matter. Early characteristics can either gain strength or disappear as a child faces new experiences. Likewise, early problems may or may not lead to later maladjustment, depending upon what the rest of the child's life is like. I have known many youngsters who were given little parenting or guidance as young children. They were unloved, unsocialized, and undisciplined. Everything about their young lives pointed to trouble ahead. Then these kids were finally given a chance. They were removed from their nonhomes and placed with caring foster or adoptive parents. The transformation was gradual but remarkable. Many ugly habits acquired in early years were left behind. The children's personalities more and more reflected their new lives rather than their old.

These kids thrived because, like all humans, they possessed a precious ability—the ability to change and adapt. And this ability does not start to die out at the ripe old age of six. As long as we are alive, we can change. We may not want to or know how, but the capacity is there. That part of us we call personality can always be altered; it is never a finished product.

Prime time for the "it's not all right to be wrong" myth

The *personality-finality* myth can make you especially anxious because of its timing. It hits right when you're most vulnerable to it—during your own early parenthood. Raising your firstborn is an uncertain affair. You're on new and unfamiliar ground, so you may parent as if you're walking on eggs, at least at the beginning. Further aggravating your uncertainty is hearing over and over that mistakes made during these early years can reverberate throughout childhood and even adulthood. And there's the rub. The years in which you're feeling most unsure of yourself are also supposed to be the years most crucial to your child's future adjustment. What a prime time for the "it's not all right to be wrong" parenting myth, which was exposed in the previous chapter. Not only must you watch for any immediate ill effects of your parenting, but now you also have to wonder about all the possible long-range effects, too. What if your first experience with toilet training didn't pass as smoothly as you had hoped? Did you breed a future sixteen-year-old chain-gang member as a result?

I knew one mother who began this kind of worrying even before her first child was born. Her pregnancy had been unplanned, and she felt confused and unready for the role of motherhood. Nevertheless, she accepted the responsibility of a child, and although feeling her way with much trial and error (as do we all), through the years she was a fine parent. Her son, who was nearing adolescence when I met him, reflected her conscientiousness; he was maturing into an admirable young man. But Mom nonetheless battled doubts. She still struggled with lingering fears that her premotherhood confusion had somehow caused unseen emotional damage in her son, even though there was no evidence whatsoever of such damage. In essence, because of a myth she lived for years with the uncomfortable uncertainty that her son might not be as well-adjusted as he seemed to be.

Recognizing two realities will help you be a more relaxed parent during your youngster's early years. And, as is true throughout all of parenthood, staying relaxed means recognizing realities.

First, you cannot make harmful mistakes during these years anywhere near as easily as you might think or have been led to believe. In fact, the most recent research suggests that a child's early emotional experiences are very poor predictors of how she will turn out later in life. There are far too many intervening experiences; there are also too many physiological changes taking place. Therefore, if you genuinely attempt to raise your child well, your chances of causing emotional damage through errors or inexperience are miniscule.

Second, if you do make some poor parenting moves, you'll see the results then and there. The problem will not disappear into your child's head, fester a while, and then show itself six years later. This notion comes from old and inaccurate psychological theory. Resolve the problem at the moment, and it will truly be gone, not just temporarily out of sight. If it does return, as much problem behavior will, that doesn't mean some covered-over trauma was lying just below the surface waiting to erupt. It means the conditions were right for your child to exhibit old familiar habits again.

One parent's insights about the *personality-finality* myth will serve well to close this section: "Parents are always told that the crucial years are from birth to six. Why couldn't the crucial years be from six to twelve, after we've had time to gain some confidence and experience? I didn't start to relax until after I had three kids and my oldest was heading into high school. Then I finally looked back and decided I must not have done too badly after all as a rookie parent. In the meantime, I worried a lot unnecessarily."

Is it too late?

Parents often worry that it's too late to do anything about the way a child is. "Maybe we didn't catch the problem early enough." "Perhaps he's been this way too long." "What if the damage was done years ago? Can we do anything about it now?" In some cases, these concerns are understandable, especially when voiced by parents whose fifteen-year-old has been house ruler since he was in kindergarten. Indeed, they may not be able to overcome the effects of years of letting Junior be parent; their worries are grounded in reality. But many such worries come from parents with seven-, eight-, and nine-year-olds. Some parents even wonder if it's too late when their kids are five or six years young.

What breeds these premature fears? Once again, the *personality-finality* myth is usually the culprit. If you believe that your child's personality is molded early, then it naturally follows that his personality becomes resistant to change early. Thus your time to lay down a sound personality base is relatively brief.

I once saw a talk show whose guest was a child specialist speaking about the development of self-concept. During a question-and-answer period, a mother asked for suggestions about how to build her son's self-esteem. The specialist began his answer by saying it was important for her to realize that a child's self-concept is generally formed by the age of six. After hearing that, Mom didn't appear to listen anymore. The expert's warning was clear: If your youngster is past six, there's little you can do. Too often, parents are handed this brand of outmoded theory. You are led to believe that you have a mere few years in which to make any significant impact on your youngster's development. You might even hear something that implies, "Don't make mistakes early because you may never be able to undo the damage." Such a warning is among the best at creating needless anxiety for parents. It not only puts a time limit upon behavioral change; it also convinces you that your child's habits are much more solidified than they actually are.

Let's say that your four-year-old daughter Harmony is a real handful, sometimes two. She revels in creative name-calling, she persistently refuses to do as she is asked, and temper tantrums are her forte. Initial psychological diagnosis: Transient Brathood. During the past few years, though, you've more or less tolerated Harmony's rebelliousness because you believed she was too young to really know any better. She would outgrow these bad habits. But slowly and painfully, you started to realize you were wrong. Harmony isn't outgrowing her habits. On the contrary, they are becoming more numerous and harder to ignore. Is it getting too late to change Harmony's "basic" personality? Is she doomed to float from Transient Brathood (ages three to six) through Intermediate Impossible (ages six through twelve) into Acting-Out Adolescence (ages twelve to eighteen)? Even if you change her on the outside, will she still be contrary underneath? Fortunately, the answer to all of these is "no!" Harmony's personality is just starting to develop; she is still extremely malleable. It is far too early to think that no matter what you do, Harmony will always have in her that piece of nastiness she learned as a young child. If you change her on the outside, she will eventually change on the inside.

The *personality-finality* myth is a remnant of an outdated and simplistic psychological theory, but it has been slow to die out. A child's character is not molded during a few critical years early in life. Your child is the sum total of his genes and all that he has experienced up to this very moment, no matter how old he is. The early years are no doubt important because they start some patterns, but they are only one part of a very complex whole.

The Jekyll-Hyde Myth
or *"It's as though he has a split personality."*

"He can act one way in one situation, and then totally the opposite in another. It's as though he has a split personality." According to clinical reports, only a few hundred documented cases of split, or multiple, personality exist in the world. Yet, if I were to accept parents' assessments of this rare disorder, I alone would see at least a few hundred cases a year. What parents are seeing is not a rare disorder but a common feature of behavior. Kids can behave quite differently from one situation to the next, sometimes so much so that you can't conceive of how such extremes could come from the same child. Tornado Tommy becomes Tranquil Tommy when his dad's around. Eve's teacher tells you at parent conferences she wishes she had a whole classful of Eves, and your mouth drops. She can't be referring to that uncontrollable creature that flouts your every wish at home. Ah, but she must be. There's no other Eve in her class. Different situations have different expectations, and Eve, like all kids, learns very quickly what those expectations are.

I work with special classes for children with severe behavior problems. Youngsters are considered for these classes because they have a history of resisting classroom rules. They leave their seats every two minutes, complete a small fraction of their work, and habitually challenge the teacher's authority. Their relations with both peers and adults alike are full of conflict. Adults who describe these youngsters use uncomplimentary terms like hyperactive, aggressive, uncontrollable, and mean. Once placed in the special classroom, though, many of these kids don't fully live up to their labels. In fact, a few totally belie their past reputations. What causes the miraculous transformation from Mr. Hydes to Dr. Jekylls? For the most part, the operating rules of the new classroom. Expectations are clear-cut and consistently enforced. The kids know what behaviors will lead to what consequences, and they respond well to the fairness and predictability of the class. Previous teachers are sometimes amazed at the overnight changes in their former incorrigibles. They expected these youngsters to remain incorrigible, at least for a while.

Why are we so surprised when kids act differently from what we expect? In part, the answer relates to the traditional view of "personality." Most people consider personality to be made up solely of traits. A trait is a label we use to describe someone: honest, good-hearted, lazy, carefree. Traits are just one aspect of personality, however. They are only general categories that we use to describe habits, and habits can be strengthened or weakened depending upon the situation in which they occur. For example, your argumentative daughter may never argue with her boyfriend. Or, good-hearted Joe can act very selfishly with Grandma. Kids simply do not behave according to their traits in all situations. And if you expect them to, you will not only be disappointed, but you also may find yourself bewildered by seemingly erratic behavior.

When you characterize Joe as good-hearted, you are really saying that Joe acts good-heartedly most of the time. So, when he doesn't, you're surprised. You might even wonder if something's wrong with Joe because he's acting "out of character." In all likelihood, nothing is wrong with Joe. He's just responding to his surroundings. Maybe Grandma gives Joe everything he wants, so with Grandma, Joe takes instead of gives. And that's understandable. Grandma consistently teaches Joe how not to act good-heartedly.

Because kids' behavior depends so much upon where they are and who is present, it's not unusual for them to show certain "traits" to one parent and not the other. For instance, one parent might see more defiance, or carelessness, or even a higher activity level, than the other. Although there could be many reasons for this, often the difference occurs because one parent is more secure and consistent in setting limits. That parent teaches the children that he or she expects to be treated well. And the kids are very aware, even at an early age, of which parent that is. If you are the abused parent in your family, it is most likely not because your kids have some ingrained drive that motivates them to give only you trouble. It's probably because you are teaching them that you will tolerate being mistreated, at least some of the time.

But even if you've taught your children to treat you well generally, they still know when and where they are most able to succeed at not treating you well—in the cereal aisle at the grocery store; the back seat of the car (just out of arm's length, naturally); at church, during the sermon no less—and their behavior can change accordingly. Normally eager-to-oblige Mercy might resort to behavioral blackmail in the store if she picks up cues from you that it'll be profitable. Or your usually lovable Broderick may not be so lovable at Grandma's house when he sees how Grandma repeatedly comes between what you said you'll do and what you actually do. Kids don't take long to figure out when your normal operating rules are temporarily suspended, and this can encourage them to behave quite unlike what you've grown to expect.

Indeed, kids are much more skillful at sizing up situations and adults than most of us give them credit for. They can discern subtle changes in the rules that we grown-ups miss totally. Brian, age nine, and Marc, age seven, were two spunky, precocious brothers who took turns giving their mother fits. If one behaved well for a while, the other would become more unmanageable and pick up the slack. They worked like a wrestling tag team, each taking over when the other got tired, thus ensuring no lull in the action. Mother was single, working, attending college, and raising three boys under age ten. In her spare time, she breathed. Needless to say, Mom was feeling a bit overwhelmed. However, after several counseling sessions, she was slowly establishing peace on the home front. The boys still continued their tag-team ways, though, when they were with her and her boyfriend, Paul. And Mom couldn't understand why. Aha! Any psychologist should realize they were jealous of this new man who was taking a share of their mom's affections, so they were trying to make life miserable for him. A plausible explanation, but with just one catch. The boys liked Paul and were generally well-behaved when they were alone with him. Well, then, Mom and Paul must clash on child-rearing methods in front of the boys, right? Sort of. Even though they didn't always agree about discipline, Mom and Paul never disagreed—openly, that is—in the boys' presence. Instead, they shot glances at each other, shifted uneasily in their chairs, left the room, or gave off other wordless messages meant only for adults. But these messages were being intercepted by young eyes and were being interpreted, quite correctly, as a lack of a united front. After Mom and Paul learned to save their nonverbal arguments for later, the boys gradually decreased their part-time unmanageability.

So, is there a split personality lurking within your child because he acts one way in one situation and totally opposite in another? Only in the sense that every child's behavior is highly dependent upon what is expected or allowed in a given situation. And when two situations, or adults, have very different operating rules, a child will quite naturally behave by the rules of wherever he is. The belief that Jekyll-Hyde behavior is abnormal is a myth. The reality is that to varying degrees every child is a Jekyll-Hyde. Once you determine what it is about you, or a particular situation, that breeds unexpected or unwanted behavior, you can stop worrying about your child's "split personality" and start taking action to bring the behavior more into line with what you'd like. There will be more about ways to take such action in later chapters.

The Ugly Phase Myth
or *"It'll pass ... I hope."*

Childhood is filled with stages. Children pass through stages in speech, intellect, muscular coordination, and many other areas. As they do, they replace immature skills with newer, more sophisticated ones. This ongoing process of growing out of old patterns into new ones is the way much of a child's development occurs. It isn't surprising, then, that parents also talk about behavior, especially nasty behavior, as a stage. Comments like these come regularly from parents and nonparents alike: "Oh, he'll outgrow it," or "It's just a phase she's going through; it'll pass." Most kids do outgrow childish language or immature reasoning skills naturally, but most don't outgrow nasty behavior naturally. They have to be taught to outgrow it. If not, "stage" behaviors can become a style and soon escalate into other forms of undisciplined and irresponsible behavior. In other words, without effective parental intervention, the "terrible two's" can become the "tantrum-prone three's" can become the "fiery fours" can become ...

Susan didn't want to attend first grade. Every school morning she cried and refused to step onto the bus. So Mom dutifully drove her to school, and like a Geiger counter, Susan became more perturbed as she neared her destination. By the time she entered the school doors, she was screeching at peak volume, desperately clinging to her mother and begging to go home. At the principal's urging, Mother usually left and Susan was escorted to class, where her weeping slowly tapered off as the morning passed. On some days, however, when Susan's crying was particularly intense, Mom would relent and let Susan spend the day at home. This pattern went on for about a year and a half before I saw Susan and her mother. When I asked Mom her impression of Susan's behavior, she said she thought it was a stage Susan was going through. She was hoping that as Susan got older, she would learn to like school. Two points about Mom's reasoning struck me. One, a year and a half is a long stage. And two, did Mom intend to stand idly by waiting for Susan to change her attitude toward school? I also asked Mom if the crying was confined only to school mornings. She said at first it was. Then Susan began to wail at bedtime. She soon moved to turning on the tears in stores when she wasn't bought what she wanted. Eventually, Susan sobbed just about anytime she was denied her wishes. You can see what was happening. Instead of dying out, the crying was gaining strength and filtering into other areas of Susan's life. The "stage" was spreading! In time, Susan would probably outgrow the act of crying itself, only to replace it with other forms of resistance, such as defiance, "sickness," or hostility.[12]

Kids are natural psychologists. If they stumble upon a tactic that works, they stay with it. Susan's crying proved valuable in one situation, so she tried it elsewhere, and it worked there, too. She wasn't about to give up a good thing by outgrowing it. As long as you allow undesirable behavior to continue, it's not likely to fade as your child matures or gets old enough to reason with. If you wait for that day, bad habits may become so entrenched mere reasoning won't budge them.

No question—kids do pass through periods where one particular form of misbehavior predominates. Toddlers often hit a stage where the word "no" comprises 50 percent of their vocabulary. Preschoolers can rage through tantrum periods. Young

51

adolescents may get very lippy as they strive for independence. You can expect many such "phases" from your kids, but you don't have to tolerate them. If you don't yield to temper tantrums, they will be outgrown. If you do yield, however, temper tantrums at age three can become verbal abuse at age five. Continuing to submit can pave the way for surly belligerence at age nine. Yield still more and you may face total unmanageability at age fifteen. The form of a rebellious behavior may change as a child grows, but its purpose doesn't.

Fortunately, children sometimes do seem to outgrow nasty behavior stages "spontaneously," and you can't pinpoint anything you did to aid the process. Obviously, there are reasons for the changes. Either you are unknowingly responding differently to your youngster, or factors other than you are entering in. Nevertheless, it is unwise to hope that unidentified causes will eventually pull your youngster out of an ugly phase. For one thing, as I've stressed, unless you take action, the odds are stacked against you that the stage will pass. But more importantly, passively waiting for a phase to be outgrown is not good for your parental mental health. It reduces you to the role of helpless bystander and puts your child in control, a role he's not nearly old enough to handle.

THE FORGOTTEN REALITIES

Operating under the influence of misguided beliefs about your child's personality will definitely raise your level of parental anxiety and lower your level of parental authority. But failing to operate under certain realities can create just as much trouble for you. Even though the following realities about personality are among the most basic truths about kids, they are still among those most often ignored by parents.

Personality Reality I:
All Children Are Not Created Equal.

The most obvious reality about children is that no two are alike, physically or emotionally. Every child has a personality as unique as her fingerprints. Even siblings often bear little resemblance to one another. While Venus is docile, shy, and spacy, her brother Milo is talkative, adventuresome, and stubborn. Jack cries easily, turning everyday frustrations into catastrophes. But his sister Jill has an envious ability to take life's tumbles in stride. What causes these vast differences in makeup, even within the same family? Certainly, parenting is a major factor. But there is another factor that parents frequently overlook—*temperament,* or a child's *nature.*

Consider a litter of puppies. Before those puppies are taught anything, each behaves differently. One puppy nips at any hand that reaches to pet her. Another cowers next to his mother at the sight of strangers. A third scrambles eagerly out of the box to explore his surroundings. Children are not puppies (for starters, puppies are easier to housebreak, less rebellious as they get older, and generally more grateful dependents). Like puppies, though, children have unique inborn temperaments. Every child's body is predisposed, or preprogrammed, to act and react in its own individual way. And it is these inborn predispositions that influence how a child responds to her world. As a parent, you need to realize how powerful these temperamental characteristics can be. They can make your parenthood a relative breeze or a daily storm.

At the breezy end of the child-rearing continuum are those children who almost seem to raise themselves. You may not think you will ever have such a child, but contrary to popular belief, they do exist. These children readily accept guidance and discipline, and if they do challenge you, it's short-lived. They learn quickly what you expect and how to avoid conflicts. It isn't that these kids necessarily lack spirit or independence; they just don't seem to relish pitting their will against yours. At the other end of the continuum are those children who push you beyond your limit. They are active, bold, and seem bent on opposing you at every turn. They have a creative flair for finding trouble in even the most everyday circumstances. Most parents believe they have at least one of these youngsters residing in their home; actually on some days most parents feel their whole brood fit this category. My mother still tells horror stories about one such cyclone who dwelled in her home—me. Besides constantly running at full throttle, I was also contrary and "bullheaded." If my parents said that it was cold outside, I'd say I didn't need a jacket. My mother could discipline me fifty-seven times in a row for the same transgression, but as soon as she turned her back, I'd try it a fifty-eighth time. If left unsupervised for too long, I'd find something to take apart or destroy. When my nine-day-old sister came home from the hospital, I sneaked into her room and greeted her with a shoe in the face. She was an intruder into the domain I wanted to misrule. Fortunately for me, my parents were determined not to let me take over. If they had to discipline me fifty-eight times before I learned my lesson, they did so. They knew they had to make me curb my natural instincts somewhat, or both they and I would pay more heavily as time passed. They persisted as long as necessary to teach me some self-control.

It is by no means easy to persist, though, with a strong-willed child. Such a child can bring out feelings of inadequacy in the most capable parents. So many approaches that you try don't seem even to dent this one's armor of obstinacy. And despite your best efforts to teach him otherwise, this child repeats the same self-defeating behavior with baffling regularity. Consequently, you might conclude your parenting is at fault; somehow you must be doing something wrong. But that is so often not true. You may be parenting well; your methods may be good ones. They may simply need more time to produce results. They aren't going to work as rapidly as they would with a more docile child.

Or you may be underestimating the degree of consistency you need to reach this child. Maybe with his easier-going sibling you can get by with following through on your statements only 67 percent of the time. But with this little spitfire you must average at least 92 percent consistency even to get him to hear your voice, and 99.9 percent follow-through to persuade him to alter his ornery actions.

Then, too, you may worry that you're making more "mistakes" raising this child than you are with your others. You probably are. A strong-willed youngster will test your stamina and your patience far more than will most children. You'd better expect to make more mistakes and overreact more often. Child-raising is like any other skill. The more difficult it is, the longer it takes to master, and the more errors you make along the way.

And while you're trying to master your temperamental tempest, watch out for the *nothing works* parenting myth, which was exposed in the last chapter. Parents of strong-willed children are especially vulnerable to this myth. Because an approach isn't working as quickly as you think it should or prayed it would, you might drop it prematurely and move onto something else. Continue this exhausting pursuit for very long and soon you'll feel like your whole bag of tricks is empty. And your Buckley is only five years old. In trying any discipline with a hard-to-raise child, remember that stick-to-itiveness is vital. It is as important, if not more important, than the discipline itself.

Temperament can also explain why one of your children seems to be having an unusually tough time growing up. It may be that Jessica's nature makes her more likely than her siblings to create hardship for herself. As a parent, you have to deal with those hardships, even though you may not be causing them.

I consulted with a mother and father about their nine-year-old son Jerry. Compared to his brother and sister, who were both close to him in age, Jerry was having more than his share of growing pains. He was a bright boy, but he consistently hid his intelligence by acting impulsively and immaturely, especially when frustrated. Although adept at sports, Jerry was highly competitive and flared up at an opponent's slightest infraction of the rules. He also seemed to be in the middle of much of the family's arguments and friction, often becoming angry quickly and leaving the scene tearfully. While the other family members talked out their disagreements after calming down, Jerry would keep his thoughts to himself, emotionally withdrawing from the family. Overall, Jerry's parents described him as being negative and unhappy much of the time.

Jerry's parents were intelligent, well-educated people who were conscientiously trying to meet the differing needs of their children. They couldn't understand what they might be doing, consciously or unconsciously, to provoke Jerry's behavior. They wondered where their parenting was faulty. Half believing the *personality-finality* myth, they kept combing the past for mistakes they'd made with Jerry that they hadn't made with the other two. My impression was that Jerry's parents weren't to blame. Generally, they didn't evoke or feed his behavior. Rather, Jerry was temperamentally quite a contrast to his two more mature and even-tempered siblings, reacting to situations much more unpredictably than they did. Jerry's parents would indeed have to work harder to understand and change Jerry's approach to life, but they weren't fostering it. Jerry was uniquely Jerry, and he had much to learn about how to quit creating his own distress.[13]

Like Jerry's parents, you may be too ready to blame yourself for your youngster's troubles. You may be underestimating the power of other factors, particularly temperament. Not all problems are the result of poor parenting. The quality of any parenting interacts with a child's makeup and learning experiences away from home to form the whole picture. Did you ever wonder why some kids can grow up with almost no guidance and still turn out fairly well-adjusted while others who have the benefit of concerned parents seem to have endless troubles? Again, part of the answer has to do with individual temperaments. Certain innate predispositions render some kids more likely than others to make life a daily struggle. Returning to the puppy analogy, some puppies will instinctively nip at your finger unless they are repeatedly taught otherwise, while other puppies need much less instruction to look for bones elsewhere.

Even though no two children are alike, no two temperaments created equal, all children share a common right. No matter what their temperament, all children deserve to be taught how to live in this world. Some just take a lot longer to teach than others. If you have a particularly challenging child to raise, don't lose faith in the impact of your parenting or allow yourself to become discouraged. Hold two truths to be self-evident: One, that this youngster would be difficult for *anyone* to raise; and two, that to get through to him you will need persistence and effort far beyond what is required of most parents. Establishing your authority may take time, and holding on to it may seem a constant struggle, but the outcome will be worth it. In the end, you will have followed the much easier path.

Personality Reality II:
The Earlier, the Easier

There is a bit of child-rearing folklore that says: From birth to six, you teach kids; from six to twelve, you guide them; and from twelve to eighteen, you pray for them. This little piece of wisdom contains a big truth: As children get older, your influence over them declines. Therefore, the ease with which you can teach healthy behaviors or eliminate unhealthy ones also declines. If you allow unmanageable behavior to grow as your child grows, you may someday confront an ugly reality: Your power to change your child's character for the better has slipped away over the years, along with your authority. To avoid one day finding yourself in this powerless position, follow a basic axiom about asserting your influence and authority as a parent: The earlier the easier.

FROM BIRTH TO SIX, YOU TEACH KIDS. You have the distinct advantage of being your child's first teacher about the world. What you impart early falls upon an unquestioningly open and receptive mind. If you teach your child to respect you and your expectations, life will be that much more pleasant for both you and her later. You will have a foundation to build upon naturally as she matures and your relationship changes. And when problems develop, as they inevitably will, don't panic. Just about anything learned in these first years can be unlearned. Even if your preschooler is parent of the house, you can probably regain your parent status with some simple, straightforward ideas used consistently. Lest you're asking, "Quick, what ideas?", I'll have some suggestions in Chapters 6 and 7.

If it's so easy to establish authority during these early years, why is it that so many parents don't? Perhaps the most common reason centers around the hopes and expectations of first-time parenthood. A challenging, somewhat scary phase of your life is beginning. You're aiming to make it as near perfect as possible. Your relationship with your young one is going to be mutually pleasurable, your times together happy ones. No destructive conflicts or ill feelings will mar your tender first years together, not if you can help it. Alas, these may be your desires, but don't expect your little one always to go along. When he doesn't, and he gets sad or mad or just plain bad because you've denied him his wishes or had to cap his inborn exuberance, you hurt. You really meant to avoid these rough spots. The temptation to yield to exorbitant demands, temper outbursts, or misbehavior to keep peace or to make the "parent-child interface" reciprocally satisfying can be almost overwhelming. Can't you discipline him when he's older, when he better understands what you're doing? Right now in his young mind all he believes is that you're just being mean and that you really must not love him.

Yes, it does hurt you more than it hurts him when you have to discipline him and watch his anger and disappointment well up. But an inescapable reality of parenthood is that these rough spots are inevitable, no matter how much we experts tell you how to make child-rearing a time of total fulfillment for both you and your child. To varying degrees, depending upon the child's nature and the effectiveness of the parent's disciplinary style, all parent-child relationships will have unpleasant and painful moments as the parent establishes himself or herself as parent. You can choose to face these moments when your child is young and when, believe it or not, it's most easy. Or you can try to skirt them, to put them off until your youngster is older, only to find yourself most likely face-to-face with frequent and uglier clashes. Sadly, many parents choose the latter course without realizing it. Their struggles to keep life pleasant at any price during these first years succeed only in allowing their kids to develop more in-grained and durable bad habits that will eventually have to be handled anyway. As one mother fretted: "I know I should take charge when he's young, but it's so hard. He seems so innocent and emotionally fragile." No doubt disciplining can be hard in the early years, but if you delay it, it becomes even harder later. There is one reassuring note, however. No matter how upset your youngster makes herself, no matter what she temporarily thinks of you, she will recover quickly. She won't stay sullen as long as an older child might when she is disciplined. As my mother would comment during my pouts: "He bruises easy but he heals quick."

Before moving ahead, I want to briefly clarify that in this section I have been referring primarily to disciplining toddlers and older preschoolers—children who are old enough to show a basic awareness of their behavior and its results. As I have been speaking of discipline, it is neither necessary nor advisable with infants.

FROM SIX TO TWELVE, YOU GUIDE THEM. You certainly don't stop teaching, but now your youngster is making more decisions on his own. The eager-to-please, dependent little child is fading, and inklings of the future adult are emerging. Your child is learning to think and reason in adult ways. His motivations are more complex, and sometimes completely incomprehensible. (Refer to the *you must know why before you try* parenting myth of Chapter 2.) Not only are you unable to figure your child out as easily as you used to, but you can't control him quite so easily, either. Indeed, from six to twelve so many characteristics start to take on adult shape that I believe these years are as influential, if not more so, than the early years. At age five or six, children are very flexible. Their potential for change is tremendous. But as they near adolescence, some fairly well-established characteristics are present. If you want to alter a few of your twelve-year-old's habits, your chances for success remain good, but be ready for resistance. Most likely, he won't accept your good intentions as readily as he would have a few years ago.

During these transitional years, you also need to watch for a widespread misbelief that can draw you into hours of uninterrupted exasperation. That is the misbelief that somehow, some way, you should always be able to reason with your youngster. After all, he's becoming more adultlike, and don't adults talk things out? Don't you reason with adults to get your point across? Sometimes. Did you ever try to change the mind of an adult who completely disagrees with your viewpoint? Likewise, you can reason with kids, sometimes. Not all the time. To be sure, reasoning is the first approach to try. There is danger, however, in reasoning too much. To put it simply, reasoning doesn't always work. With kids, even adultlike kids, there comes a time when reasoning must end, when you as parent must say, in effect, "These are my reasons. Like them or not, this is the way it will be." Overreasoning, or trying to make your children understand and accept all your parental actions and decisions, is a paralyzing ritual. We will discuss it, and ways to counter it, in much greater detail in Chapter 8, "Five Tested Ways to Drive Yourself Batty." For the moment, let me introduce it to you as possibly the single greatest eroder of parental authority during these middle years.

FROM TWELVE TO EIGHTEEN, YOU PRAY FOR THEM. This doesn't mean you give up on them, although you're not unusual if you entertain that temptation frequently. This temptation reaches its peak during the teen years. But as bleak as things can sometimes look, your youngster isn't beyond hope. You still can teach and guide, but you might find yourself praying a little more, too, especially if you've allowed unmanageable behavior to build upon itself for years. At this late age, turning around long-standing problems can be an arduous, erratic process, sometimes one without the happy ending you anticipated.

I work with many parents who have lost control over their adolescents. The complaints are all too similar: "He doesn't listen; nobody knows anything but him." "She won't follow any rules; she wants to do as she pleases." "He's almost impossible to live with; he wants no part of the family." Of course, to some degree these complaints describe how most teenagers behave at times. But in the cases I'm referring to, home has become an unbearable place. And most of the time it is apparent that the kids didn't suddenly get rebellious as they hit adolescence. On the contrary, they had been pushing their parents around for years, and quite successfully. If Mom and Dad finally stand their ground, they still can't be sure of making the ground peaceful. They are struggling against two potent factors: long-standing habits and dwindling control. These parents are trying to undo years of lax parenting that have resulted in their children developing the deeply ingrained habit of doing as they pleased. Mom and Dad are attempting to turn around long-standing habits at a time when their influence as parents is at rock bottom. Indeed, they may finally start to assert some of their long-dormant authority, but sometimes they start too late, having lost too much respect to be effective teachers. Now their youngster will have to learn from another teacher—life. And regrettably, sometimes life has to teach pretty harshly before a teenager realizes his parents had something worthwhile to say.

To varying degrees, almost all parents are tuned out by their adolescents during those first tentative strivings for independence. This period of parental impotence is unavoidably rocky terrain for parents, and for adolescents, for that matter. But those parents who are ignored longest and most completely are those who from day one have never consistently taught their children to listen to and respect them.

If you've permitted your parental authority to be usurped for the past fifteen years by a chronically rebellious youngster and you've finally resolved to take charge of your home, ready yourself for some very stormy moments. It's almost certain your teenager will neither understand nor agree with your new-found assertiveness. Why should she? For a decade and a half she's grown increasingly accustomed to dictating home life; now you're trying to end her reign. And regardless how reasonable, how fair, how compromising your rules and limits, your adolescent isn't going to see them your way. She will accuse you of being a dictator (what irony!), of not loving her, of favoritism toward her siblings, of telling her how to live her life. She will in all likelihood become even more unmanageable, disrespectful, and determined to flout your rules. Threats to run away may become a by-product of every disagreement. You have little option but to stand firm during this turbulence. For if you don't, you will only perpetuate more of the same turmoil. Additionally, you will have to work hard at not being dragged into the "overreasoning" trap. Expect not to be understood. If you're braced for the accusations, the guilt tactics, and the general nastiness unleashed upon you by a surly adolescent, you will find your resolve gaining strength and even becoming a bit more acceptable to your youngster. You will be less likely to feel that it is you who are at fault and that maybe you are the unfeeling ogre your youngster says you are. But most importantly, you won't be so tempted to give back immediately that which you've at last taken, and which was rightfully yours all the time—your authority.

Keep *the earlier, the easier* personality reality in mind. It is often forgotten by parents—often at heavy expense. Although behavioral change is always possible, it becomes more difficult as a child gets older. Establish your rightful parental authority early, therefore, and you will head off many no-win confrontations between you and your child later. You will also save her from much painful learning at the hands of teachers less gentle than yourself.

One More Time ...

Replacing three personality myths with three personality realities will reduce much confusion and anxiety: (1) Personality is not laid down by the age of six. Personality development is an ongoing process that occurs throughout life. As a parent, you have more than just a few years to mold your child's character. (2) Children do not have split personalities. What seems to be Jekyll-

Hyde behavior is most often a child's learned response to different situations and different adults. Change the rules and expectations, and a child's behavior can change dramatically. (3) Although much of a child's development occurs in stages, it is erroneous to believe that when undesirable behavior occurs it is a stage and you are prudent to let it "run its course." Unless taught otherwise, your child may indeed pass through his stage, but only headed toward more advanced and more intransigent forms of problem behavior.

Always reminding yourself of two other prominent realities will also avert confusion and anxiety. (1) Every child is temperamentally unique; thus, every child is like no other to raise. You may have to put far more parental concentration into raising one child than another. (2) Turning around a child's undesirable behavior becomes more difficult as she grows older. Therefore, establish your authority early and you will have the control necessary to teach your youngster how to live in this world.

These first three chapters have attempted to help you feel that as a parent, you are psychologically OK. The next chapter will help you to feel that as a kid, your child is psychologically OK.

Homework

1. Write out five beliefs you firmly held when you graduated from high school, but which you no longer adhere to. Surprised at how your views have changed over this relatively short period? This is one short but compelling demonstration that personality is ever-evolving.

2. Think of two people with whom you behave quite differently. Now think of two situations in which you behave differently. Do you have a split personality? Of course not. And neither does your child. He, like you, simply changes his behavior as the time, the place, and the people change.

3. Identify a misbehavior or ugly "trait" your youngster shows only to you and not to your spouse or some other adult. Imagine how this other, more fortunate adult might react if your little darling showed this characteristic to him or her. Now compare it with your reaction. This mental workout can give you valuable clues about what you can do differently to exorcise this particular demon from your child's personality.

4. This next exercise is for those of you with more than one child. Rate each of your children on the following characteristics as they displayed them at age two.

1	2	3	4	5
Shy				Outgoing
1	2	3	4	5
Sedate				Active
1	2	3	4	5
Easygoing			Emotionally reactive	
1	2	3	4	5
Compliant				Stubborn
1	2	3	4	5
Relaxed				Tense

Notice the individuality even at this very young age? A brief reminder of the power of temperament.

5. Recall a grade-school teacher you admired and respected. Determine specifically what that teacher did to establish authority and when in the school year the teacher established it. Conversely, think of a teacher who chronically struggled to control his or her class. How long did it take this teacher to regain authority after he or she allowed it to slip away? Did the teacher ever regain it? A parallel can be drawn between a well-respected teacher and a well-respected parent: Both follow similar guidelines in asserting their rightful and necessary authority.

4

Is My Child Normal?

The more I talk with parents, the more I notice a parallel between parents and first-year medical students. Lest you think the only thing they have in common is years of challenging work ahead of them, let me elaborate. Common among beginning medical students is a "disease" called, not surprisingly, *medical student's disease*. Its main "symptoms" are a preoccupation with one's own physical aches and pains and the fear that they are a sign of some disease or disorder recently studied. The irrationality of this disease is obvious. Although physical complaints could be symptoms of some serious affliction, they seldom are. Most aches and pains indicate either a minor problem or no problem at all, just daily, transient discomforts. For instance, headaches could conceivably point to the presence of a brain tumor, but in actuality they rarely do. Novice medical students, however, because they are deluged with information about all that their symptoms could possibly mean, tend to worry proportionately. In a sense, they become casualties of their own incomplete knowledge. They know just enough to worry too much.

In much greater numbers, a similar disease afflicts parents. Let's call it *enlightened parent's disease*. Its primary symptom is the tendency for parents to see psychological maladjustment in their offspring where none exists. And this disease is becoming epidemic as more parents hear about more psychological disorders, the symptoms of which to some degree could fit almost all children. Consequently, while trying to stay alert for the slightest inkling of disturbance in their kids, parents are looking too hard. They are overinterpreting, giving even normal quirks undeserved significance. Like the fledgling medical students, parents are suffering from their own overawareness: They know just enough to worry them too much.

Certainly, a healthy sensitivity to the problems of childhood is something to strive for. But our sensitivity is reaching beyond healthy. It is bordering on an obsession—an obsession with finding maladjustment. Labels like *hyperactivity, learning disability,* and *middle-child syndrome* are being hung on more and more kids, by experts and parents alike. And as these labels proliferate to envelop just about every piece of unconventional childhood behavior, our view of what is normal is shrinking. We are accepting a smaller range of aggressiveness or shyness or activity as normal. We are marking more behaviors as atypical and therefore as signs of something being wrong with a child. If this trend continues, my hunch is that in a decade or so we will be able to pin at least one "childhood disorder" label on every child in our society.

Even the labels themselves convey our preoccupation with extremes. Kids aren't active anymore; they're *hyperactive.* They don't have learning problems; they have learning *disabilities.* They don't have bad experiences; they suffer emotional *scars* or *trauma.* With such terms permeating our daily language, it's not surprising that parents are getting nervous and reaching for reassurance that their kids are indeed psychologically OK. Seldom do I simply hear something like: "My child likes to play by herself." More commonly, I hear: "My child likes to play by herself. Is that normal?"

Part of the reason so many parents are falling victim to enlightened parent's disease is because of the word *normal* itself. The term resists clear definition. If 50 experts were asked to define *normal,* most likely 50 differing definitions would result. This is not so much due to disagreement among professionals as it is due to the vagueness of the word normal. Capturing the essence of *normal* is like trying to capture the essence of words like *love, life, personality, happiness.* All are elusive, and their meanings depend upon many factors, not the best of which is who is doing the defining. Whether, for example, a given behavior is normal depends upon the behavior itself, where it occurs, with whom, how often, to what degree. One thing can be said about *normal,* though. It is normal to not always be sure of what normal is.

One of my colleagues told me she was concerned about her thirteen-year-old son Eric. In school, Eric was maintaining an A–B average. He excelled in a number of organized sports and was popular with his peers. At home, he was usually easy to get along with, helpful around the house, and courteous to visitors. "Definitely sounds like a troubled youngster to me," I said. "What's the concern?" Well, Mom asked, didn't Eric seem too well-adjusted for his age? Was it normal to be so content in early adolescence? Shouldn't he at least be refusing to clean his room?

If you're wondering how normal your child is, this chapter will try to answer some of your questions and ease some of your apprehensions. Stretching your view of what is normal will not only bring a sense of relief, it will also bring more parental poise. You will be less prone to overreact to behavior that looks atypical but in reality is to be expected.

The Many Faces of Abnormality

Perhaps the best place to begin relieving the symptoms of enlightened parent's disease is with those terms that are used to label children abnormal. There are many such terms; some are specific (for example, *hyperactive, school-phobic*), others more general (for example, *emotionally disturbed, behavior-disordered*). Later in this chapter we will focus on some specific labels and misconceptions associated with them. For now, let's look at general labels of abnormality.

EMOTIONALLY DISTURBED. This is probably the best-known marker of abnormality. It is pinned on any youngster who, in someone's eyes, is acting in an excessively unusual way. The major problem with this description is that it is extremely misleading. Except in a few rare disorders, a child's emotions don't become disturbed. Emotions can well up at unexpected times, in unexpected ways, or with too much or too little intensity, but this doesn't mean something is inherently wrong with a child's emotional makeup. Suppose that eight-year-old Melody averages nine violent temper outbursts per day. Because this rate is well above the norm for eight-year-olds, Melody risks being judged emotionally disturbed by anyone who believes that something must be internally out of order for any child to lose control so consistently. Granted, nine tantrums a day is a bit exceptional, but maybe Melody's parents submit to her outbursts and reward them. In this context, Melody's actions become more understandable. Pronouncing her emotionally disturbed does nothing to reduce her explosiveness. It only frightens her parents and distorts the real issue. Melody's emotions are not disturbed; it is her behavior that needs altering.

BEHAVIOR-DISORDERED. Any child who misbehaves regularly is a candidate for this diagnosis. Where is the line separating a behavior problem from a behavior disorder? There is no line. There is a large gray area in which someone makes a judgment as to what constitutes a problem and what constitutes a disorder. Again using little Melody as an example, let's make a few additions to her problem list. Besides temper tantrums, Melody sasses her parents about three times an hour, fights with two of the neighbor's kids every day, bullies her little brother half the time he's within arm's length, and in any given week breaks about two-thirds of the school's rules. Now, this is enough rowdiness for any three kids, let alone one. So, if Melody's parents seek professional assistance in managing her, they might be told she has a behavior disorder. But in the true sense of the word, Melody has no disorder. She simply displays much hard-to-manage behavior. The difference between a behavior problem and a behavior disorder is not qualitative; it is a matter of degree. A behavior disorder is just a lot of problem behavior.

PSYCHOLOGICALLY TROUBLED. Although not quite as alarming as its cousin *emotionally disturbed,* this phrase too is deceptive. It suggests that the psyche is malfunctioning, that something is not quite straight inside a child's head, and that therefore she is acting abnormally. Actually, children most often act abnormally because they've learned to do so or because they know no other way to act, and not because they suffer from some psychological defect. *Psychologically troubled* is a catchall category for any child who, once again in somebody's opinion, is a little too withdrawn, cries too much, has one too many fears, is overly sensitive, or shows any other behaviors that seem too much or too little for a youngster that age. Put another way, the term covers a wide gamut of behaviors that cause more problems for a youngster than for those around her.

Let's make much-maligned Melody our problem child a third time. First, though, we'll have to alter her personality. We'll replace her explosiveness and misconduct with shyness and timidity. Melody is now a quiet girl. At school she hugs the background, plays alone at recess, and needs to be coaxed to join any group activity. Melody is no management problem, but her behavior is obviously unlike that of her more gregarious classmates. An adult viewing her might even conclude something is psychologically awry with Melody. Why else would she be so withdrawn? Well, maybe Melody is shy by temperament. Or maybe she hasn't yet learned how to interact comfortably with others, so she plays it safe and avoids them. Or maybe Melody sees how uneasy her mother is in unfamiliar situations, and she's mirroring a style she's picked up at home. No doubt Melody could benefit by becoming more sociable, but to infer that some psychological short circuit or cross-wiring is the basis of her shyness is not only inaccurate, it's harmful. Melody's head doesn't need to be worked on. It works as well as yours and mine. Melody needs to find better ways to view and interact with the world; then her "psychological problems" will most likely disappear.

These are but a few of the more widespread labels of abnormality. There are others—*emotionally troubled, psychologically maladjusted, behaviorally disturbed*—all variants on the same theme. But whatever the particular wording, such labels all pose several dangers:

1. They are overused. Too casually and too often, they are invoked to describe what is mainly inexplicable or problem behavior.

2. They are scary-sounding. They falsely imply that it is the child who is abnormal, rather than his behavior, and that correct-

ing the abnormality will be a protracted affair because the child's character has to be reshaped.

3. They are vague. They are broad descriptions that serve little purpose other than to say: "This child is acting unlike most kids." Using them is similar to answering "Because she is sick" when asked "Why does this person have pneumonia?"

4. They lead to circles of reasoning that in the end reveal nothing. Suppose Melody has been pronounced emotionally disturbed. Once attached, the label can serve a dual purpose. It not only describes Melody's behavior, it also becomes a means to explain it. Why do we call Melody emotionally disturbed? Because she throws temper fits. Why does she throw temper fits? Easy: because she's emotionally disturbed! The behavior justifies the label; then the label is used to explain the behavior. All that is accomplished is to make us think we understand more about a problem than we really do.

5. They paralyze parents. Once such a marker is stamped on a child by a well-meaning psychologist, schoolteacher, or family doctor, the child's parents often lean toward overcaution in their parenting. After all, if a child's behavior fits into some "syndrome," this implies she's different, perhaps not responsible for her actions. And if she's not responsible, how should Mom and Dad react to her? The irony is that while children who manifest behaviors that fall under these labels often need their parents to be extra confident and firm, by the very act of labeling we undercut parents' ability to be confident and firm.

If these terms are unnecessary, even detrimental, what can replace them? Why not direct descriptions of how a child is acting? If Bernard is terribly afraid of dogs, then Bernard is terribly afraid of dogs. It's not necessary to take another step and call Bernard cynophobic (a funny word for "fear of dogs"). What for? Labeling him cynophobic offers no help in understanding Bernard's fear. If Melody becomes wildly irrational when her immediate wants are somehow blocked, then we can say that Melody becomes wildly irrational when she doesn't get her way. Is she emotionally disturbed? The question is meaningless. If it were put to a vote by one hundred renowned psychologists, probably half would vote "yes" and half would vote "no." Whatever the final tally, the task remains the same: to teach Melody some self-control instead of categorizing her behavior.

If someone should pin one of these tags on your youngster, before you become too alarmed or chastise yourself for failing somewhere as a parent, think over what these terms actually mean and their uselessness. This will ease your guilt and help redirect your energies toward solving the problems you're facing, rather than worrying about how disturbed your child is.

Out of Sight but Not Out of Mind
or *"Is it normal to look normal and not be normal?"*

Recall the mother in the previous chapter who worried that her son, although looking adjusted on the outside, might not be so on the inside? Her anxiety was that some suppressed psychological conflicts were evolving in her son's head, beyond reach of her parenting, and that she could never really be sure he was growing up as he seemed to be. He looked OK on the surface, but who knows what was happening underneath?

Many parents share this brand of uncertainty, although not usually as intensely as did this mother. Typically, the doubt is a vaguely bothersome feeling that flares every so often when a youngster behaves incomprehensibly or out of character. Understandably, you too might have these concerns. You want your youngster's healthy exterior to reflect a stable interior. However, to worry without evidence that your otherwise normal-acting Kathi might possess a not-so-normal psyche is a no-win dilemma. By its very nature, the *out of sight but not out of mind* worry defies resolution. Because it is based on the fear of troubles unseen, of troubles that may not exist, this worry is untestable. Without some concrete signs, you can't know in fact whether or not problems are there.

On the surface, then, it looks like there will always be that piece of doubt about how your child is truly developing "down deep." Fortunately, in this instance the surface is misleading. Down deep, you do have ways to settle your doubts.

Begin by observing your youngster's behaviors and attitudes. Do they generally seem OK? Then most likely they are. Does your child look fairly typical to you? Then most probably he is. It is rare that children who look normal on the surface are abnormal underneath. For the most part, with kids, appearances are not deceiving.

If you deal well with what you see, you will be laying the foundation of what you don't see; in other words, the external lessons you teach form your child's "internal personality." Qualities like responsibility, self-control, and altruism are all learned from the outside in. They are first introduced through a child's experiences, and only over years do they slowly become part of her character. Therefore, teach your child well on the outside and she will learn well on the inside.

But, for you diehard worriers, assume for a moment that your child is in fact developing some in-the-head conflicts that you, and maybe even she, are unaware of. Eventually, in one way or another, these conflicts are likely to show themselves, allowing you to handle them openly. Trying to guess where they are before you even know where to look invites more upheaval than it saves. You begin to chase shadows or make too much of minor peculiarities. In the end, you confuse yourself and your youngster, who much of the time may not even know what you're getting at.

It is a sensitive parent who notices the tiny, telltale signs that indicate that a child wants help but somehow has not yet asked for it. It is also a sensitive parent who knows not to imagine or search for problems without evidence; and who, when a search is undertaken, knows to stop looking when the looking turns up nothing. There are few better ways to limit your ability to parent than to second-guess your every move by wondering how your child's interpretation of it will affect her internal makeup years from now.

Psychological vs. Behavioral Problems
or *"It's better he's bad than disturbed."*

The mother of seven-year-old Donny described what she considered his most severe problem: He cried at the smallest disappointment. If his bus was late, he cried. If a playmate cheated in a game, he cried. If told to eat his split peas, he cried. As Mom detailed the specifics of the crying—its frequency (five to ten times a day), its duration (up to ten minutes after the traumatic incident), and its nature (part whine, part cry, with a sniffle or two in between)—it became apparent that she feared the crying reflected some underlying emotional imbalance. When I asked about any other problems, Mom much more casually mentioned that Donny also talked back, defied her authority, and was daily difficult to control. She added, however, that these habits didn't disturb her so much since they were just behavior problems. In so assessing things, she focused most of her concern and energies upon the crying, while neglecting the need to curb Donny's defiance.[14]

This parent's perception of what kinds of problems are most worrisome is a common one. It is based on the following assumptions: Problems that look "psychological" or "emotional" in nature—fears, excessive crying, worries, nightmares—are the "deeper" problems. They evolve through complex mental processes, so they will take more time and effort to change. On the other hand, problems considered misbehavior—aggression, defiance, unruliness—are more observable, thus more normal and easier to correct. They aren't anchored as solidly in a child's makeup as psychological troubles. Although at first glance this reasoning appears sound, I can offer both my own experience and the studies of others to show that it is faulty.

Most of the children I see as a psychologist for several Head Start classrooms fall into two groups. By far the larger group is composed of those kids who are unruly in the classroom. They don't like rules; they persistently clash, verbally and physically, with both peers and adults; and they are easily upset when things in the environment don't act as they would like. These kids are the "acter-outers," the challengers of social limits. Their problems are behavioral in nature. The second group includes kids who, while behaving differently from most of their classmates, offer few management problems. These children might be excessively passive, reluctant to join classroom activities, anxious around unfamiliar adults or in new situations. They are often quick to cry and slow to talk. Fears of all kinds can also be present. Overall, these children show difficulties that are typically viewed as psychological. Compared to the behavior problems, however, it is the psychological problems which more often improve as the year progresses. Fears are outgrown, initial shyness slowly yields to a growing familiarity with the class, and communication opens up as early anxieties melt away. The management problems are not only less likely to resolve themselves on their own, they are also more resistant to any adult's efforts to modify them.

My observations of these Head Start children are made only over the span of one school year. But researchers have come to similar conclusions using a much longer time frame. They followed a group of kids from childhood to adulthood to see what sorts of problems would be most likely to persist and what sorts would be most likely to fade with age. They found that the "psychological" problems were more often resolved as a child matured, while the behavior problems, especially the severe ones, more frequently led to social troubles in adulthood if not corrected in youth.

What does this mean for your parenting? It certainly does not mean you can disregard the problems that look more psychological. They too need your attention. But it does mean that such problems may not be as alarmingly abnormal nor as predictive of where your child is headed as you might think. Exaggerating their significance can also interfere with the need to act on those problems that are "just behavior."

THE VOGUE LABELS

Having answered some general "Is my child normal?" questions, let's now turn to the most prevalent, and most misunderstood, "disorders" of childhood. Though few in number, these disorders take in the majority of kids diagnosed as atypical, either behaviorally or emotionally. They also account for a good many false notions about what is and isn't normal. In one way or another, you're probably familiar with each of these names. They are *hyperactivity, school phobia,* and *middle-child syndrome*—the vogue labels.

Hyperactivity: An Epidemic
or *"Don't get hyper; he's just active."*

If one were to list the most overused and misunderstood childhood diagnoses of the past few decades, hyperactivity would far and away rank as number one. So much has been written about hyperactivity—its symptoms, causes, cures, and long-range effects—that a discussion of the subject could fill many books much larger than this one. My aim is not to review hyperactivity as a condition, but to clear up a few widespread misconceptions and point out the main problems caused by the label itself.

Actually, hyperactivity is not the official name of the diagnosis that envelops more kids, particularly boys, than any other. Over its relatively short lifetime, what is now popularly known as hyperactivity has had more than forty names, including learning disability, impulse disorder, hyperkinesis, and minimal brain dysfunction. Currently, the official title is *attention deficit disorder with hyperactivity*. But, like a rose, by any other name this disorder is the same—a source of misinformation and worry for parents.

To begin with, what is hyperactivity? Contrary to common belief, hyperactivity is not just a lot of motion. Rather, it refers to a cluster of characteristics that appear to be loosely related to one another. Most prominent are a high activity level, impulsiveness, a short attention span, and a lack of stick-to-itiveness. Kids with these characteristics are described as constantly on the go, driven by motors, flitting like flies from place to place—all phrases that suggest a fast-moving, easily distracted youngster. In essence, these are the basics of hyperactivity, although at one time or another almost every immature or undesirable behavior has been placed beneath the hyperactive umbrella. One article alone listed ninety-nine signs of this condition, many of which, as you can imagine, would apply to almost any moving child. To elaborate on such open-ended lists would only further cloud an already fuzzy picture and lead you to be unnecessarily alert for meaningless "symptoms."

What causes hyperactivity? Here the picture becomes even more confusing. To put it simply, we don't know exactly what causes hyperactivity, although everything from brain damage to lipstick has been accused. Some experts think that some kind of subtle miswiring in a child's brain is one cause. Where is the faulty wiring? Nobody knows for sure. Other experts contend that diet is a factor, especially sugars and artificial additives. There is some evidence for this, although not nearly as much as the media feed us. Many physical disorders can also lead to hyperactive

74

behavior, but these embrace only a tiny fraction of those kids diagnosed as "hyper." And finally, there is a mounting tally of highly suspect villains, which include soft X rays (no such thing exists!) and allergies to substances in magic markers, permanent-press clothes, soap, and perfume.

All told, hyperactive behavior has many alleged causes, some legitimate, others best ignored. But even all the legitimate causes still probably account for only a minority of so-called hyperactive kids. The rest can be more accurately described as either temperamentally active, developmentally immature, underdisciplined, or some combination of the three. No vague disorder is necessary to explain their behavior.

During my first year as a consultant to special classes for kids with behavior problems, I spent much of my time with the boys who made up the elementary class. Although disparate in age and in kinds and severity of problems, the boys all shared a common distinction. At one time or another in their young lives, all had been diagnosed as hyperactive. Interestingly enough, while they were in the special class, which was taught by a strict but fair teacher, the boys were anything but hyperactive. In fact, they were better behaved than most of the kids in regular classrooms. Why this seeming contradiction? Why were these "motor-driven" boys able to exert this degree of self-control? Most likely because they never were hyperactive in the true sense of the word. That is, nothing was out of kilter in their systems. These were basically active and undisciplined kids; a few weren't even that active, just very undisciplined. In a setting where they knew they had to temper their impulses, their "hyperactivity" slowed dramatically.

These boys provide a lucid example of possibly the most insidious aspect of the hyperactivity diagnosis—the ease with which it can be called upon to explain all manner of hard-to-manage behavior. Being so openended, the term "hyperactive" can fit many children, and distinguishing between the true hyperactive child and the temperamentally active child with a penchant for testing limits is not always possible. Kids who mimic perpetual-motion machines and who want to do as they wish the moment they wish are prime targets for the hyperactive label simply because their behavior is so exasperating to adults. But a fast-paced, impulsive youngster—even one extremely so—is not necessarily hyperactive. And labeling him in this way unjustly conveys the impression that something in him warrants changing, rather than the idea that changes may be needed in what or how he is being taught. By nature or learning history, some kids move at a velocity well above that of other kids their age, but difference does not mean malfunction.

Of Diet and Discipline
or "Fast foods = fast kids?"

Besides causing you unnecessary consternation about your youngster's development, the hyperactive label also sets in motion other misconceptions. Two of the most common have to do with overestimating the impact of diet and underestimating your child's ability to act responsibly because he is handicapped by an affliction. Let's take a bite out of the diet controversy first.

With increasing publicity and fanfare, diet is being recognized as a factor that can affect a child's behavior. Sugars, artificial colors, preservatives, all have been linked by one researcher or another to problem behavior. Grandma's admonition that we are what we eat is finally getting scientific support, in some cases anyway. But somewhere between the research and actual parenting practice, we are getting recklessly ahead of ourselves. The *control the diet, control the behavior* rationale is being carried to extremes, especially with active children. How tempting it is to believe that Herb's rowdy behavior is due mainly to what he eats, and that with only the proper dietary adjustments he will become a new child. Then you could insightfully explain to your neighbor that the reason little Herbie ran through her garden is because he downed one too many bottles of pop that afternoon. Indeed, it would be extra nice to be able to stem Herbie's mischief by feeding him two apples, five teaspoons of wheat germ, and one slice of melba toast (plain, of course) a day. Unfortunately, except with certain food allergies, diet hasn't been shown to have this kind of control. While it is safe to view diet as *one* possible part of a child's troubles, it is unsafe to put too much weight on diet. Here are two examples why.

Billy was an active, periodically explosive eleven-year-old cared for primarily by his grandmother. Grandma admitted that she spoiled Billy, but she still maintained that sugar was the chief culprit of his rebelliousness. So, as much as possible, she eliminated the white stuff from Billy's diet. According to Grandma, this did seem to subdue Billy a bit, although with any child it is hard to tell whether improvement is due to a change in diet or to a change in the parents' view of the child because they know he's on a "special diet." But even a slowed-down Billy was no more mindful of Grandma's rights and authority. He still treated Grandma as he always had—with disrespect and relentless demands. To change this, Grandma didn't need to cut down on Billy's sugar; she needed to practice more consistent and firm grandparenting. And that would be much harder than changing Billy's diet, in the short run anyway.

A more extreme case of the *control the diet, control the behavior* rationale was nine-year-old Frank. Frank's mother was convinced that most of Frank's nasty behavior came from diet-caused allergies and hyperactivity. And even though there were few signs of any physical allergies, Mom believed Frank had "behavior allergies," so she put him on practically a roots-and-berries existence. I felt sorry for the little guy. Whenever his class went to a restaurant for a treat of their choice, Frank would drag along his unsalted crackers and thermos of grapefruit juice. I think I'd have problems too if I ate that sort of stuff day in and day out. The interesting thing about Frank's diet, though, was that it didn't seem to work when his Mom was around. Anytime Mom visited the class, Frank almost immediately became more whiny and disruptive. As soon as Mom left, Frank settled down. Now, unless Frank was managing to gulp down a taboo food secretly right before Mom's visit, it seems most likely that his flare-ups were coming mainly from how he and his mom related to each other. Mom's preoccupation with Frank's diet was only blinding her to the real factor maintaining Frank's behavior—her own reaction to it.[15]

Frank and Billy, along with their folks, were casualties of an overreliance on the power of diet. Certainly your child's eating patterns can have some influence on his behavior and certainly not all diets are alike—some have merit, some are pure fad—but be careful not to search too long and too hard for dietary answers at the expense of overlooking your own power as a parent. No diet, no matter how good or how controlled, is a substitute for responsible parenting.

At this time in our understanding of the relationship between activity level and diet, about the most accurate statement that can be made is this: There is a percentage of active kids who become less active when certain foods are taken out of their diet; however, this percentage is small. Further, manipulating a child's diet won't alter undesirable characteristics that are learned, like irresponsibility, disrespect for others, and selfishness. These qualities develop over long periods of time, and a child has to be taught, not dieted, his way out of them.

"Don't blame me, I'm hyperactive."

The hyperactive label brings another hazard: It can pull you into an escalating cycle of tolerance for nasty behavior, as it did to the following parent.

A fiery seven-year-old once threatened to dismantle my office piece by piece until I put an abrupt stop to his wrecking plans. When I interviewed his frazzled mom, she told me she hadn't really put steadfast limits upon her son ever since a professional had said he was hyperactive and shouldn't be held responsible for his behavior. But rest assured, the professional also said, in time her son's whirlwind tempo would slow. Mom said she was trying to be patient, but things just seemed to be deteriorating. I had three initial questions. If the boy isn't responsible for his behavior, who is? Would Mom survive until her son grew older? What kinds of bad habits would he accumulate in the meantime?

The impression given this parent is one that all too often accompanies the "hyperactive" handle. That is the idea that any "hyper" youngster shouldn't be held accountable for his actions because he suffers from a disorder and therefore can't really control himself. Such reasoning only begs further trouble. Granting a youngster license to act without restraint or consideration for others merely opens the door for more uncontrollable behavior. It prevents learning of self-control and allows irresponsibility to build upon a high activity level. A child is not likely to learn from limitless tolerance; both he and his parents will be victims of it.

There is absolutely no reason why any "hyperactive" youngster should not have to answer for his actions. In the first place, as I've argued, most kids called hyperactive are probably not so in the clinical sense of the term. They have as much potential for self-control as the next child, even though it might take them longer to develop it. Second, even if a youngster is genuinely hyperactive, he still must be taught restraint. Otherwise, his inborn wiriness can feed upon itself until it is uncontrollable. More so than most kids, a hyperactive youngster needs supervision and close guidance. He needs to experience repeatedly some guidelines to operate by. To state it simply, if a child is not to be held responsible for his behavior, how then will he learn to act responsibly?

If this whole hyperactivity issue leaves you with more questions unanswered than answered, don't feel too lost. It does the same for those of us who work with it daily. Repeating a few key points, however, should help tie together this confusing package. While there is a minute percentage of kids who could be considered truly hyperactive in the sense that some neurological or physical problem underlies their behavior, the vast majority of so-called hyperactive kids have no such identifiable problem. They are simply temperamentally, maturationally, and/or behaviorally different from other kids. And labeling these youngsters does nothing but create new problems: (1) It leads both a child and his parents to feel that his actions are guided by some obscure malfunction in his makeup rather than by his choices and their parenting. (2) By making the problem seem internally caused, this label pushes parents to seek cures such as medication, diet, therapy—all of which may benefit a few select kids, but none of which takes the place of responsible parenting. (3) Calling a youngster hyperactive can nurture the unsound belief that he should not be considered answerable for his behavior—a belief the exact opposite of the one needed to teach an active child self-control.

Parent Fear #102: School Phobia
or *"He's absent due to illness; he's sick of school."*

School phobia—literally a fear of school—like hyperactivity is a term that has been stretched far beyond its legitimate boundaries. Originally, school phobia wasn't even considered the fear of school itself, but rather the fear of separation from one's parents.

Supposedly, a school-phobic child suffered assorted fantasies and anxieties about what could befall her or her parents while she was apart from them, and therefore resisted leaving their side. As this definition proved too narrow, school phobia was broadened to include those kids who were afraid of the school situation itself. However, it didn't stop growing there. It has continued to swell to its current status—a phrase too quickly thrown upon any child who shows any resistance or uneasiness at the idea of attending school.

Of all the kids I see who resist going to school, only about one in ten could legitimately be considered school-phobic. There is that small handful of kids who are severely anxious about something in the school environment, and their fear virtually paralyzes them. But the great bulk of so-called school phobics have no such debilitating anxiety. They either flatly don't want to go to school or they are uncomfortable with something related to it. They might hate getting up in the morning, dislike a teacher, be terrorized by a bully, feel intimidated by a new school—the reasons are limitless. But these do not a school phobic make. Because school is the work of childhood, at one time or another almost every child will have hang-ups about it. Very few, though, actually become so distraught they couldn't get near the school even if they wanted to, although some can look pretty phobic. Tom was one such boy.

During my early days as a psychologist, a school principal asked my help in getting Tom, one of his seventh graders, back to school. Through the clarity of hindsight, I see now that Tom basically just disliked school. It had too many requirements and it interfered with more preferred pursuits, like sleeping in and watching game shows. But at the time, because Tom reacted so violently to any efforts to return him to school, he had everybody convinced, myself included, that he was truly terrified of that huge building and all its kids. To nudge Tom past his fears, I arranged with his mother to let me pick him up in the morning and escort him to school. My idea was an elementary one: to expose Tom to the school piecemeal—first the building, then the hall, then staying for one period a day, and so on, until he could comfortably attend a whole day of classes. All this was to take place over a week or so with my encouragement and support. Well, it was easy enough to motivate Tom into my car, although even this surprised his mom, because he was usually "sick" every morning. But after my first successful step, things began to bog down. No matter how gingerly I guided Tom through each phase of our plan, whenever he thought he might have to remain at school, even for a few minutes, he went berserk, wailing, pleading to go home, promising he'd stay tomorrow. But tomorrow never came. I thought I was seeing my first bona fide case of school phobia. Finally, after I had emptied my whole bag of approaches, the juvenile probation officer stepped in and, under threat of court action, forced Tom back to school. Within a few days Tom was attending regularly and showing few traces of his former terror. I guess all his "phobia" needed to evaporate was a little forceful prodding backed by some unpleasant consequences.

Tom's opposition to school was extreme, but most kids who resist school do show some signs of discomfort or anxiety. Most common is the early morning "I don't feel good" complaint, which usually arises when a child misinterprets or uses morning's natural sluggishness as a dubious illness to try to escape school. This is a good dodge. It's convenient, hard to check, and sufficiently vague to allow for midafternoon TV viewing and late-afternoon total recovery. Other anxieties center around taking tests, a disliked teacher, gym class, and talking before a group. These are typical troubles and seldom signal any broader fears or maladjustment. Help your youngster in whatever way you see fit to tackle whatever it is, real or imagined, that is bothering her. But hold one principle nonnegotiable—she has to tackle it *at school*.

Since faking illness or bodily pains is probably kids' most time-tested method of skirting school, you can count on facing at least a few times during your parenthood when you're not sure whether your youngster is really ill. How might you reduce your uncertainty? Obviously, you can check out the complaint with a doctor. But repeated doctor visits are time-consuming and expensive. Besides, many kids still claim some untraceable or exotic discomfort even after being given a clean bill of health. Therefore, you may need a few diagnostic tests of your own. I have two to suggest. First, if Betsy is sick, then she needs bed rest, at the absolute minimum during school hours, but better during part or all of the evening, especially if her illness has become suspiciously recurrent. If she is in fact sick, she won't be totally upset by the boring prospect. If she is only vying to stay home, after a day or two in bed (without TV, comic books, or Barbie dolls), even school will start to look tolerable. Second, if you can't be home all day to supervise and you suspect Betsy is opting for daytime freedom at the cost of being bedfast in the evening when you're home, send her to school with the suggestion that when she feels ill she can ask to lie down in the nurse's office until she recovers. Few kids will take the nurse's office over class for very long.

As parent, you know your youngster's moods and her ploys. You might misread her "symptoms" now and then, but don't let a fear of this keep you from acting resolutely on the school issue.

So, is your youngster now, or will he ever be, a school phobic? Highly unlikely. Will he ever show resistance or anxiety over something connected with school? Highly likely. Almost all kids do. There are many effective responses to these problems, but allowing a child to remain home is not one of them. Granting a youngster indefinite school leave while waiting for his "school phobia" to disappear will only strengthen it. Successful resolution to any school problem, be it resistance or phobia, almost always involves getting the child back to school before he wants to go.

Media Disorder #13: Middle-Child Syndrome
or *"What do you expect? He's our middle one."*

Middle-child syndrome is a relative youngster to the child-rearing scene. It enjoys neither the attention nor the reputation given to hyperactivity or school phobia. In part, that's because it doesn't embrace nearly as many kids. By definition, it can't. As the name states, *middle-child syndrome* is limited to middle children. (Although I did know one firstborn who supposedly suffered from this syndrome, possibly because she had two imaginary siblings—one older than she, one younger.) Those of you with one or two kids needn't be too concerned yet about MCS—you know a disorder has arrived when you can call it by its initials—because you don't have a middle child. Nevertheless, in case you someday have more children, thereby creating this precarious role for one of them, you might want to read on.

What are the signs of this syndrome? A syndrome is defined as a cluster of symptoms that occur together. The main ones are these: (1) Feelings of isolation, of not belonging. Enjoying neither the parental attention and expectations given to the eldest, nor the relaxed parental standards experienced by the youngest, the middle child is supposedly lost in the shuffle, caught in between, with no unique position of his own. (2) Identity problems. The middle child grapples with the question of who she is, and in particular of her role in the family. She may have a poor self-concept. (3) Withdrawal and/or behavior problems. Because the middle child often feels cheated of parental attention, he may become shy or withdrawn in an attempt to cope with his lack of uniqueness in the family. Or he may develop behavior problems to get noticed.

Now that you're familiar with the basics of MCS, there is one final, most important feature to recognize about this syndrome: It doesn't exist. Oh, it exists in the sense that it has been popularized and held up as an explanation for some children's behavior, but as a clinical disorder, there's no such thing. *Middle-child syndrome* is a prime example of how to create pathology using only a name. The procedure is simple. Find a few behaviors or characteristics that cause a middle child problems. Observe that some other middle children have similar problems. Dub these a syndrome, and you have a new disorder. One catch: The new disorder is nothing but a description of some characteristics that any child, not necessarily a middle one, could display. Granted, some middle kids do have identity problems, or a sense of neglect, or a poor self-image, but why not call these troubles what they are—not a syndrome, but a child's unique perception of his role and status in the family.

The idea that birth order affects personality is a popular one, and in fact there is some research to suggest that birth order is weakly related to such qualities as achievement, independence, and self-confidence. But birth order itself doesn't breed these qualities. They evolve in part from how your parenting practices change over the years. You are the guiding force behind "birth-order effects."

Sometimes I wonder if *middle-child syndrome* is the start of a trend—the forerunner of a line of birth-rank disorders. Maybe someday we'll also have to worry about *only-child disorder, change-of-life-baby syndrome,* and *firstborn trauma.* If I seem to be stretching my point a bit, it's because I've already noticed early signs of this trend. For example, I have heard parents apprehensive about having only one child. They foresee all kinds of ill effects on a youngster growing up without siblings. Will he retreat into fantasies to occupy his time? How will he learn to share? Who will he play with? This doesn't sound like the life of an only child; it sounds like the life of one growing up in a vacuum! These parents are plagued by the same errant reasoning that underlies MCS. They envision trouble resulting solely from their youngster's place in the family. And they worry that the trouble will be too persistent to offset with their parenting. In a few instances, I've actually known parents to decide to have a second child primarily because of such worries.

Whether your Billy is your one and only, your first, your last, or your in-between, you are the prime shaper of his development. You needn't fear any automatic side effects of his position in your family structure. In the first place, the effects of birth rank are nowhere near as impactful as parents have been led to believe. In the second place, even if Billy does periodically misperceive his role in the family, your parenting can do much to correct his misperceptions. And finally, all of us are born with certain "givens," inescapable attributes present at birth. Whether we're male or female, firstborn, last-born, or middle fraternal twin, developing our potential largely means minimizing the disadvantages and maximizing the advantages of our birth status.

I hope we will never see the likes of only-child disorder, change-of-life-baby syndrome, or firstborn trauma. It's too bad we had to see middle-child syndrome. It's just as meaningless a disorder.

Some Abnormality Is Normal

I hope you're feeling reassured about your youngster's overall adjustment and about the fact that he's not likely, now or ever, to be a victim of one or more of the better-known childhood disorders. But what about those times when he acts in ways that look abnormal? What do those times mean? In the next sections we will uncover some behaviors that seem abnormal but are really more common than you might think.

No doubt you have your ideas about what particular misbehaviors are most serious. At the first sight of these, you would probably react strongly. Your youngster is doing something you always equated with maladjustment. To be sure, almost any misbehavior *can be* serious, if it's part of a pattern or recurs with increasing frequency. But quite often parents read too much into isolated appearances of strange or atypical behavior. They overinterpret because they overlook two maxims of parenthood: (1) kids can try just about anything once; and (2) some amount of abnormality is normal.

Kids will do anything once ...
and sometimes more, especially if it's fun!

You've probably heard somebody proclaim: "I'll try anything once." Maybe you've even uttered this battle cry a few times yourself. Well, we adults aren't the only ones who can live by this motto; kids can, too. In fact, they do. Kids will try some of the craziest things once, or twice, or perhaps many times, just because they're kids or just because they want to see how grown-ups will react. I could compile a long list of some very abnormal-looking behaviors that I've seen displayed by some very normal kids. And I'm sure a few of these behaviors would send the most nonreactive parent scrambling to look up the name of the nearest child psychologist. But in these cases, a call to the shrink wouldn't be necessary. These kids were only doing what almost all kids do from time to time while growing up—acting bizarrely. Here's a portion of the list.

B.J. was a highly rambunctious but otherwise pretty typical three-year-old who one night decided to shed all his clothes and see how high he could climb on the neighbor's TV antenna tower. Unusual? I know few three-year-olds who would scale a TV antenna even fully clothed. What was B.J.'s motive? Neither his parents nor I ever uncovered it. Did he ever try it again? Not that I know of. Apparently, he got cold, found he had a fear of heights, or, most likely, didn't like his parents' reaction.[16]

Holly was a quiet, generally reserved six-year-old who had been neglected in her younger years. In recent months, Holly's home life had improved, and she was slowly peeking out of her shell. During one visit with Holly, I noticed several circular, reddish welts on her arms. The welts resembled those that adolescent boys and girls exchange while petting, or, to use teenager vernacular, they looked like "hickeys." Holly said she had seen similar marks on an older girl and had asked her how she got them. After getting a detailed account, Holly experimented on herself, quite successfully. Did the marks represent some unidentified sexual hang-up? Were they a manifestation of unsatisfactory "oral stage" development? Were they the first hints of a move toward masochism? I don't think so. As I explained to Holly how unsightly and childish the habit was, she listened quietly. I never saw the marks again.

My four-year-old nephew Anthony is a regular visitor to my mother's home, and from what I know of him I have no reservations about diagnosing him "normal." But he is a precocious sort who likes to stir up his environment. One day he was playing peacefully in the basement (an immediate danger signal!), but I assumed he was just amusing himself with a spider web, a sweating water pipe, or some equally fascinating but benign object. The calm was soon broken, however, by a phone call from a telephone operator. She had received a call from someone who sounded like a little boy and who told her, "I'm going to light a fire and burn this house up." She had traced the call to our number. My nephew's threat caught both my mother and myself completely off guard. And though, with questioning, it became obvious that Anthony had no intention of following through with his plan (he didn't even know where the matches were!), neither of us could get a satisfactory explanation out of him for his actions. The feeble arson attempt flared up several months ago, and since then nothing similar has happened. I still feel confident in diagnosing Anthony as normal, although a bit more resourceful in his attention-seeking than most.[17]

Whether a particular incident involves unusual sexual curiosity, severe acting-out from an otherwise well-behaved child, elaborate fantasies, or story-telling, the point is this: Periodically, throughout the course of childhood, even the most well-adjusted kids do strange things, the cause and nature of which is limited only by their environment and imagination. Further, these behaviors generally don't point to some more pervasive underlying problem. Most often, they are just a child's unique way of reacting to or interpreting his experiences.

At this point, you may be thinking that every inexplicable behavior can't simply be a passing oddity with little significance. Definitely not. But don't be too ready to draw conclusions from behaviors that appear only a few times. You can better size up the seriousness of any incident by asking yourself the following questions: (1) What is the frequency of the behavior? Has it happened only once, or maybe a few times, and then disappeared as mysteriously as it came? If so, there's no reason to hunt for trouble that may never come to pass. On the other hand, if the behavior is presenting itself repeatedly, then it's serving some purpose for your youngster. Therefore, you will have to decide what steps you'll take to manage the problem until it fades. (2) Is your youngster otherwise acting pretty much herself? If so, the behavior is probably an isolated phenomenon, unrelated to other aspects of her functioning. Deal directly with the behavior itself and watch that you don't exaggerate its meaning. Magnifying problems in one area can give a greatly distorted picture of a child's overall adjustment.

One final thought about transient episodes of strange behavior: At times, such behavior is nasty, or inconsiderate, or destructive. In other words, it hurts another person or infringes upon another's rights. In these instances, even though your first impulse might be to try to analyze where the behavior came from and what it means, don't neglect the main ingredient of a good response—holding your youngster accountable for what he did. Too often, parents completely abandon their standard disciplinary principles just because a certain misbehavior is unexpected or baffling. They're too stunned to think clearly. After the heart-to-heart talk is over, the tears are dried, and life returns to routine, your youngster is still responsible for the results of his temporary insanity. Your making sure that he fulfills his responsibility will reduce the chances of similar behavior appearing in the future.

Two Normal Abnormalities

Whatever crazy-looking behaviors your youngster confronts you with will, by and large, be unique to you, her, and your situation. Don't expect to see the same oddities from your brother's kids, your neighbor's kids, or even from your other children. Every child has her own peculiar brand of idiosyncrasies and aberrations. There are two particular aberrations, however, that are not as aberrant as most parents believe, yet they disturb parents of all ages, in part because they're so misunderstood. What are the terrible two? Stealing and lying. First, the more dreaded of the duo—stealing.

Thou shalt not steal ... well, maybe just once.

If your son Rob wants to upset you, to make you feel an incompetent parent, he should try stealing something. Even a single, isolated act of sticky fingers would probably conjure up for you all sorts of frightening questions. Where did I go wrong? Why would he do such a thing? What does the future hold? One parent found—under a piece of pie, of all hiding places—two dollars taken from her purse by her generally trustworthy nine-year-old daughter. Her reaction was typical: "I felt like a bag of cement landed on my head."

Stealing stuns parents, even if it happens only once, because parents leap so quickly to conclusions about what the stealing means. But contrary to popular worry, an incident or two of thievery does not a thief make. Nor does it necessarily indicate erratic personality or character development. In fact, I think it's more the rule than the exception that at least once in a childhood a youngster will without permission take something that belongs to somebody else.

What possesses kids to steal, even once? The reasons are nearly as numerous as the kids themselves. Some kids are swayed by peers; others want the thrill of a risk; some don't resist the temptation to net a gain without a price; still others want the booty to "buy a friend." No matter what the motive, though, the fact is that a few bouts of petty larceny dot almost every child's life. Of course, any stealing needs your attention. It could point to other trouble spots. But if the stealing is not part of a pattern, you're better in the long run to resist drawing premature conclusions from it. You might convince yourself, and your youngster for that matter, of things that aren't true.

All right, you're willing to wait for more evidence before deciding you have a budding cat burglar on your hands. You're still faced with an unexpected and slightly unsettling behavior.

How can you be sure it won't happen again? Realistically, you can't. But I can offer some common-sense advice that again and again I've found most helpful in keeping an isolated stealing incident an isolated stealing incident.

First of all, work to maintain your composure. If you tell yourself that this isn't as alarming as you thought, you will better retain perspective. Driving yourself into a state of emotional upheaval will only hinder clear thinking. And if by chance part of Rob's motivation for stealing was to get a rise out of you, you won't be playing into his hand. Second, don't worry so much about what words to say or what masked meaning the stealing might have. You'll make extra and unnecessary work for yourself. Give the explanation you think best suits your youngster's abilities and personality, and give it once. Any more will probably be for your ears only. And if your youngster isn't willing to provide a reason for his action, don't try to wring one out of him. Let him know that an explanation is in his best interests, but that you're not about to pry one loose. In the end, you'll have a better chance of hearing the full story.

Finally, and this is most important, hold your youngster totally responsible for returning, replacing, and remunerating (the three "R's"). If Carrie took her friend's favorite *Swahili Made Simple* record, she should, if at all possible, take it back personally, apologize, *and* do whatever else is necessary to make up for every iota of inconvenience caused. Maybe Carrie's friend was without her record for six days; then Carrie owes her something to compensate for the lost study time—money, another record (different from the one taken; maybe Part II, *Swahili for Work and Play)*, or something comparable. The requirement of redressing inconvenince is the one most overlooked, and that's unfortunate, because it adds so much to any lesson about stealing.

What about punishment? In addition to the three "R's," some parents also place further unpleasant consequences upon stealing. For instance, they might take away outside privileges for a week or invoke an early bedtime. This is your personal decision. However, I might point out that in the adult world, a judge rarely lets someone off the hook just because he promises to return the stolen car, along with a sincere note of apology and a pledge never to do it again. Almost always there are other outcomes, such as a fine, probation, or jail. With kids, a lesson is usually more durable when it involves some milder parallel to what would happen if they did something similar as adults.

Playing To Tell the Truth
or *"I'm innocent even if proven guilty."*

Kids can bend, fold, and mutilate the truth in many ways. They can point a falsely accusing finger at a friend, and *will* point a falsely accusing finger at a sibling, to hide their own culpability. They can weave grandiose tales about their talents and achievements. They can give you their highly idiosyncratic versions of what really happened at school. We adults often manipulate the truth to suit our purposes, so we shouldn't be surprised when kids do the same. But there is one type of falsehood that puzzles and distresses parents more than any other. That is the "I'm innocent even if you prove me guilty" lie.

"I saw him break the plants but the more I questioned him, the more he denied knowing anything about it. He almost had me convinced I was seeing things." "Is it possible she really doesn't remember what she does?" These statements came from parents whose youngsters had maintained to the end that they were blameless of wrongdoing, even though there was solid evidence to the contrary. So tenaciously did these kids cling to their account of the truth that their parents actually began to question their own well-founded perceptions.

Some of the highest levels of parental exasperation that I've seen have arisen from these kinds of situations. As one father put it, "I feel I could show him a videotape replay of his behavior and he'd still tell me he's innocent. Sometimes I actually wonder if he knows reality from fantasy."

The child who practices this brand of lying habitually is of more concern, no doubt, than the one who does it occasionally or the one who does it only when she has something really big to hide. But regardless of the type of lie, virtually every child who lies knows reality from fantasy. She suffers no mental block over what she did. Nor does she truly believe she is innocent. Her steadfast denial is usually an attempt, however naive and clumsy, to skirt the impending repercussions of her actions.

Thirteen-year-old Gary had stolen several small tools from his junior-high shop class. Several students had reported to the assistant principal that they saw the tools in Gary's locker. Confronted by his dad with the accusations, Gary broke down crying, claiming that he never took any tools and that somebody must have hid them in his locker. Because of Gary's intense distress, both the assistant principal and Dad were ready to believe his story and let the incident drop. A few days later, other classmates saw Gary shove a tool into his coat pocket before leaving class. As bits and pieces of incriminating evidence trickled in, it became clear that although he was guilty, Gary was not about to admit it, even though Dad tried everything in his power to get him to do so. He reasoned, cajoled, threatened, even promised no penalty if Gary would own up to his behavior. But the more agitated Dad became, the more resolute Gary became. The impasse came to my attention after Dad started to wonder if some psychological anomaly was making Gary hang on to his innocence so adamantly in the face of overwhelming proof of his guilt.

Speaking with Gary assured me that he was perfectly capable of realizing his guilt. No emotional aberration, or selective amnesia, or hidden hatred for his father influenced his conduct. What, then, was his motive? Quite simply, he felt there was a chance, although slim, of sufficient payoff for not signing a confession. In the first place, as long as Gary asserted his integrity, Dad could never be 100 percent sure that Gary had done exactly what he was accused of. And as long as Gary could sustain the slightest doubt in Dad's mind, he hoped he could somehow escape Dad's full wrath. Second, even if Dad decided to punish Gary, Gary would be able to play the "unjustly accused" role and counter-punish Dad with guilt. Third, and perhaps most notably, the whole incident had mushroomed into a power struggle, and Gary was winning. He knew how desperately Dad wanted him to acquiesce, so he was all the more determined not to. His satisfaction came from watching Dad squirm and fret.[18]

Gary's case reveals several themes running through most episodes of "To Tell the Truth": (1) A youngster is most likely to deny behavior that is uncharacteristic of him or behavior that he knows you would make him pay a heavy price for. Kids disavow their actions so often after a stealing incident that I'm beginning to think the two behaviors are a package deal. (2) The lying usually doesn't cover some psychological streak or warped motive. It is most often a blatant stab at avoiding unwanted consequences. The child is well aware she's done something she shouldn't have, and she's downright scared of her folks' reaction. So she'll try to outlast any inquisition until the last hope that she'll emerge unscathed is dead. (3) The more you lecture, shame, and plead, the more you'll feed your own distress, and you still may not get any concessions. You'll probably succeed only in further convincing your youngster that any admission on his part will lead to, at the most merciful, being shot at sunrise. And suppose you finally do force a confession, at how heavy a price will it be for both you and your child? As one mother told, she could generally break her daughter down after a few hours of cross-examination. I wondered where Mom got her stamina. Obviously, a war of nerves was being waged, and even though Mom "won" that war in the end, she took a beating along the way in terms of time and mental exhaustion.

Indeed, many parents get pulled into the same battles this mother did; that is, they believe they must force, trick, or bribe a confession from guilty lips or else all manner of psychological business will be left undone and their child will have "gotten away" with something. This is just not true. You don't need to make your child tell the truth; she knows what it is. You need to show her that she will be held accountable for not telling it. Let me show you what I mean.

Suppose your son Linus has broken a garage window. Your neighbor (the reliable one, not the busybody on the other side) saw him do it. But when you approach Linus, he denies even knowing the garage had a window. He claims a bird must have blundered into it, blames an imaginary friend, or stammers through some other more or less plausible explanation, depending upon the limits of his creativity and fear. Ask no more questions. You have solid evidence that Linus did what he denies—a necessity, since you can't accuse him without evidence—so you present him with a choice. "Linus, I know you broke the window, so I'm only going to ask you once if you did it. If you tell me the truth, you'll only have to pay for the window by working it off at $1.50 a week. If you tell me you didn't do it, you'll have to pay for the window by working it off at $1.00 a week and you'll be without your bike for a week. Now think carefully, because you'll only have one chance to answer: Did you break the window?" Accept whatever reply you receive evenly and enforce your stated consequences without again later dredging up the matter.

The "I'm only going to ask this once" tack has numerous benefits. It keeps you from playing prosecuting attorney with a reluctant witness, thus interrupting an almost inevitable escalation of tension and ill will. It informs Linus of the results of both admission and nonadmission, thus easing his dread that confession will mean slow torture and death. And it makes clear your game plan for future games of "To Tell the Truth." That is, not bearing responsibility will only result in more troubles. It will not succeed in getting Linus off the hook.

In my experience, this approach works about half the time when it is first used, so don't be discouraged if, after your commendably calm words and choice-giving, you still receive a denial. After all, Linus has to find out for himself if your words have meaning. But the next time a window is mysteriously shattered, Linus will recall what happened with the last window and will be more willing to recognize reality.

What if you're not totally sure, though, if Linus is guilty? Then you will be forced to do what you do many times daily as a parent: Make a judgment. You will have to decide if there is enough evidence to hold Linus accountable despite his protests. You may judge wrongly, and you can freely admit it to Linus. But for the moment you have to rely on your assessment of the facts. And the facts may point to his culpability. Most likely, Linus will strongly dissent and will hurl a variety of accusations about how unfair you are. He may play the martyr role to the hilt for the duration of his punishment. Be prepared for these tactics, and don't let them weaken your resolve. It is better, I believe, to act assertively based on your judgment, with the chance you might be wrong, than to delay making a decision until you are 100 percent sure of yourself. Seldom do parents have the luxury of perfect certainty.

One More Time ...

An insidious trend is taking place in child-rearing today. Our view of what are normal ways for kids to develop, think, and behave is shrinking. More and more children are being labeled abnormal in one form or another or are considered victims of some vague disorder. Parents are vigilant for the smallest sign that their youngster might not be fitting the mold of the ideal child (as if such a creature exists!); thus their parenting is often complicated by unjustified anxieties.

One fact about kids stands out above all others: Kids are capable of nearly anything. Even the most well-adjusted have their share of maladjusted moments. Almost every child, at some time while growing up, will behave in ways that will make him a candidate for a label he really doesn't deserve. As a parent, you had better expect the unexpected from your kids and be prepared for the unusual. With every child, some amount of abnormality is normal.

Homework

1. In less than fifty words, write your definition of a "normal" child (pick any age). Ask your spouse, neighbor, or friend to do the same. Compare responses. Are there differences? Who is right? Re-read your definition. Is it a description of an imaginary dream-child who seldom has problems or, when she does, hurdles them easily 100 percent of the time? If so, you might be unconsciously comparing your youngster to something that doesn't exist.

2. Pick one of the following labels: hyperactive, emotionally disturbed, behavior-disordered. Initiate a conversation with other adults about this "syndrome." Ask them their perceptions of what the label means. How divergent are their answers? With "hyperactive," for example, you may hear anything from "he can't sit still" to "he giggles constantly" to "he plays so hard he needs medication to slow down." The wide range of answers you hear will probably all be "correct" according to some expert, illustrating the multitude of sins covered by these catchall terms.

3. Recall something from your school days that was frightening to you: the class bully, speaking in front of the class, taking a test—we all had our anxieties. Remember how catastrophic it seemed at the time? With a little stretching of the truth you could have probably developed a "school phobia" long before it became fashionable. Would your phobia have helped you deal with the bully or become a less anxious public speaker? No matter how phobic you were, you confronted your fears. So must your kids; they will not be ruined emotionally.

4. Think back to an isolated act of craziness you committed as a kid. If you can't remember one (funny how we get amnesic about these kinds of things), I'm sure a sister, brother, parent, or aunt could recount a few. Did this out-of-the-ordinary behavior predict more long-lasting maladjustment? Did it mask some buried problems? You were entitled to moments of temporary insanity as a kid, and so are your kids.

5. Play a new variation on the old game "Truth." The rules are simple. Everyone in your family, adults included, gets an opportunity to tell the truth about a past lie with no fear of negative consequences. Then everyone has to tell why he or she lied. Set the stage by going first. This will encourage your kids' cooperation. I think you'll be surprised at how straightforward your kids' reasons for lying usually are.

5

How to Talk Yourself Out of Authority

Thus far, we have concentrated on self-confidence and peace of mind as two keys to good parental mental health. In the next three chapters, we will focus on a third factor: authority. It is vital to your parental well-being, yet, like self-confidence and peace of mind, it seems to be in decline among parents. Because the word "authority" has come to have some negative connotations in recent decades, I want briefly to define what I mean by it. I don't use the term to imply a stiff-necked, dictatorial, "I'm the boss; you'll do as I say" parenting style. Such a style usually only increases the distance and breeds ill will between parents and kids. Authority is misused when it becomes an arbitrary imposition of a parent's power and influence to mold a child into what the parent sees fit. Not only does this suffocate both child and parent, but, ironically, excessive parental control almost never ultimately achieves the parent's original intentions. By *authority*, I mean a willingness to discipline, to lovingly and firmly place expectations and limits upon your youngster when you judge it helpful to teach her responsibility and self-discipline. Exercising confident authority involves the realization that part of doing a good job as a parent entails exerting your will over your youngster's when needed, even though you may hurt inside, feel guilt, or fret about the "effects."

No area of child-rearing seems to engender so much uncertainty and uneasiness for parents as discipline. Nearly every parent wonders and worries: How much discipline is healthy? Am I being too permissive? Too demanding? Will he resent me for what I'm doing? Isn't there a better way to get the same results? In just the last few generations, rapid shifts in discipline views and practices have taken place, and parents have struggled to keep up. The willow switch or hairbrush that were grandpa's standard discipline tools have generally given way to less physical, more psychologically oriented strategies for managing feisty "younguns." However, even though discipline practices have, by and large, become more humane as they have evolved, many parents are still tentative when it comes time to use their authority. Discipline is viewed as a breakdown in parenting, a reflection of failure at having to "make" a child act with consideration or responsibility. Most parents feel more unsure of themselves during discipline than at almost any other moments in their parenthood.

Why these doubts? Why are so many parents reluctant to assert themselves as parents? The answers lie in the same factors that head the assault on your self-confidence: the experts and other parents, your own irrational fears and ideas, and your kids themselves. We've already seen how others can rob you of your authority by robbing you of your trust in yourself and in your ability to act decisively. We will not retread the same ground we covered earlier. Besides, for most parents, other people are not the leading saboteurs of their authority. It is far more likely that your willingness to take control is being weakened by two much more powerful and pervasive influences on your parenting: you and your kids. In this chapter and the next, you will be the subject. We will look at how you might unwittingly be undercutting your own authority with misbeliefs and self-defeating discipline practices. In Chapter 7, your kids will be the subject. We will see how they, like most kids, seem gifted from birth at making you question your discipline and at finding chinks in your armor of parental resolve.

To talk yourself out of authority, you can draw from three main groups of notions: (1) what parents tell themselves about discipline; (2) what parents tell themselves about their kids; and (3) what parents tell themselves about themselves. Throughout this chapter, you may find yourself thinking, "Okay, I see why I'm surrendering my authority, but what can I do to get it back?" Answers to this question will follow in Chapters 6 and 7. For now, let's see why you might not be allowing yourself to be parent in your own home.

WHAT PARENTS TELL THEMSELVES ABOUT DISCIPLINE

Parents struggle with assorted worries and notions of what discipline is all about. Many of the worries are unwarranted and many of the notions are mistaken. And with discipline, as with any facet of parenting, it is misbeliefs that produce the most problems. The next several sections will expose prevailing misbeliefs about discipline that can fool you into relinquishing much of your authority. Certain of these misbeliefs are particularly treacherous because they can be self-fulfilling. If you don't act decisively with your kids for fear of triggering some unplanned side effect, you may actually begin to bring about the effects you are trying to avoid.

Peace at Any Price
or "It's easier just to let him go."

"When he begins to whine and nag, sometimes it's easier for me just to give in to keep him quiet." "I get so tired trying to get her to pick up after herself; it's quicker for me to clean up myself." "I know I should follow through on what I say, but he makes it such a chore. He batters my resolve until I let the whole incident drop." Familiar words of parents striving to do what may be the most demanding thing for parents to do: discipline consistently. No doubt about it, at times it does tranquilize your nerves to relent and give a badgering youngster what she wants. At least you've bought some quiet—temporarily. It certainly requires time and patience to stand over your five-year-old son Art while he scrubs each of his self-expressions in crayon off the bathroom wall. You could do a better job yourself in one-fifth the time. Of course, if you clean up Art's mess this time, what are you teaching him about next time? Instead of waiting through Beauregard's twenty-seven excuses for why he can't haul out the trash, it's less tiresome to spend three minutes and do it yourself, just to avoid all the prodding, irritation, and other garbage that the whole issue evokes.

Yes, in the short run, sometimes it is easier not to discipline, to yield to Rutherford's irresponsibility or defiance. But in the long run, your life will become more difficult. Submitting to problem behavior may initially be the way of least effort, but you'll soon find it takes more effort to live with the propagated misbehavior that almost always results from a lack of discipline. What's more, by not acting now, any energy you save in the present will be extracted from you many times over in the future.

It is toughest by far to discipline consistently, and thereby more calmly, if you have a temperamentally active or rebellious child, or if you've allowed a misbehavior to go relatively unchecked for some time. Assume your little Chastity presents you with both conditions. Not only is she overall a little spitfire, but in the last several months she has also developed an affinity for colorful language, the kind heard around harbors or, worse yet, in nursery school bathrooms. You've tried reasoning with her, turning a deaf ear, verbally chastizing her, even telling her what the words mean (you had to look some of them up!)—all to no avail. You finally decide to put a price on such language. Henceforward, Chastity will earn one half hour of sitting closemouthed in her room—without use of her toys, color television, and refrigerator, of course—for every profanity she utters. Naturally, the specter of a mere half hour of solitary confinement won't suddenly cure Chastity of her unchaste language. After all, when was the last time Chastity realized a lesson in just one try? So she talks herself into the penalty repeatedly in the first few weeks, no matter where she is, who's around, or what time of day it is, all of which makes it very inconvenient for you to enforce the designated consequence. For instance, if Chastity verbally blisters her morning school-bus mates, you have to remember to impose the half-hour price tag right after school. If she insults your choice of cereals in the store, she owes you an hour and a half when she gets home. If she can't even stifle herself in church, well, maybe it's best to hide in the back for awhile, but Chastity still has a debt to settle at home.

Through all this, your stamina is starting to wane. Maybe you should just hope Chastity eventually swears off her habit. Beware of the urge to follow the path of least resistance. It is the early phases of any new discipline tack that are most demanding, that evoke the greatest temptation to give up. Persevere through these energy-draining beginnings—and by "beginnings" I mean anywhere up to several weeks, or even months in some cases—and your need to intervene will slowly taper off. You will expend less and less effort as your child's conduct improves. Fail to survive the initial rough spots, and not only will you have to continue living with offensive behavior, but any future discipline will most likely confront a more durable, parent-resistant habit.

Indeed, it is hard to discipline. There is only one thing harder—living with an undisciplined child.

Parents Aren't Always Popular
or "Does discipline develop dislike?"

Not only is disciplining hard, sometimes it's downright unpleasant. In part, that is because discipline often involves a clash of desires—yours versus your youngster's. No matter how fair, how gentle your style, occasions regularly will arise when what you want to teach Wyatt is diametrically counter to what he wants to learn. In his eyes, you are the only obstacle blocking him from doing what he wants, like firing his cap gun two inches from Fido's ear to watch Fido sing and dance to cap music, or the only meddler making him do what he doesn't want, like turning in his cap gun for a week because he misused it. At these moments, Wyatt most likely won't appreciate your interference. He will neither understand nor accept your decisions.

For many parents the temporary hostility that kids sometimes present during or after discipline is unsettling. They fear that if they discipline "too much" or in the wrong way, over time their kids will progress from disapproval of their discipline to disapproval of them as parents. The isolated episodes of "I don't like you" (or the more staggering "I hate you"), whether conveyed in words or looks, will become more regular and lead to a feeling of permanent ill will on a youngster's part.

It certainly is possible to discipline in ways that will put emotional distance between you and your youngster. You can name-call, shame, put down, scream, and threaten, all of which are not only ineffective but also create an overall air of household tension. Ironically, those parents who discipline predominantly with these tactics are not usually those who worry most about provoking their kids' disfavor. Typically, it is those parents who are striving to be just and tolerant in their discipline. Unfortunately, their worry over being disliked hampers evenhanded, resolute action, and thus it is often the very thing that elicits more misbehavior and nastiness from their kids. By not disciplining confidently in the first place, these parents get yanked into more parent-versus-child feuds, in which the possibility of harsh words, regretted actions, and mutual antagonism rises.

Denise was a single parent of four girls: an eleven-year-old, a nine-year-old, and four-year-old twins. In seeking counseling, Denise had two goals: She wanted better discipline strategies, and she wanted to make sure her girls didn't dislike her. She didn't realize that the two usually go hand in hand. Denise explained that whenever she attempted to enforce routine and structure with the girls—unreasonable things like mealtime and bedtime—they would resist and counter with "I don't like you" comebacks. If Denise tried to press the issue, she encountered more opposition and negative vibrations, which unnerved her and usually effected her retreat. She couldn't stand the thought that her girls might dislike her, however temporarily, and the girls, even the two little ones, were acutely aware of this and regularly turned it to their advantage. In fact, the girls weren't nurturing any permanent bad feelings toward their mom. They only "disliked" her when she disciplined them. It was Denise's apprehension that was making her perceive bad blood that wasn't really present. And, as so often happens when parents are reluctant to discipline for any reason, Denise and her girls spent more time battling, with discord on the increase. Denise's feeble attempts at setting limits were only inviting confrontation, which in turn led to more distress on her part and more unmanageability on the girls' part. In the end, nobody won. Mom was doing little actual disciplining; she only thought she was, because she viewed discipline as nagging and arguing, and there was a lot of that.

I have yet to work with a youngster who dislikes his parents for disciplining him firmly and whenever necessary in the context of a loving relationship. Children with such parents learn young that Mom and Dad aren't bad guys (or bad persons) for making rules; rules and limits are a natural part of life. Also, because these kids are given clear guidelines within which to conduct themselves, they don't constantly test and push the folks in every direction to see where the limits are. They know where the limits are; they don't need to abuse time and feelings fighting over the gray areas.

If your fear of being disliked pushes you into a wishy-washy brand of discipline, your own worries may slowly fulfill themselves. You may indeed find your kids increasingly unwilling to tolerate your authority, and ultimately to tolerate you. But it is not discipline that leads to being disliked. It is the perpetual strife that inevitably arises when a parent is tentative in his or her authority. Ill feelings come from battles over discipline, not the discipline itself.

Consistent Discipline Does Not Equal Constant Discipline
or *"If I were consistent, I'd be on him every minute."*

A mother came to my office because, like so many parents, she felt she was forever disciplining yet her son Philip was only getting worse. Mom was afraid that one day soon she would lose all control and really harm Philip in a surge of exasperation and rage. As she spoke, it was evident that her main methods of "disciplining" consisted of nagging, pleading, preaching, threatening, and generally getting upset over much of Philip's nastiness. Mom spent most of her relationship with Philip locked in one or another of these communication modes, none of which had any impact and all of which heightened her feelings of hopelessness. Since Mom's most urgent need was to regain some sense of control, both of herself and of Philip, she and I put together a simple system of rules and results. We chose the most persistent of Philip's misbehaviors and attached automatic consequences to each. Likewise, we decided upon privileges Philip could earn by acting with some degree of thoughtfulness and maturity. Nothing fancy, just an elementary system to start reducing the incessant clashes between Mom and Philip. But as Mom assessed our plan, she commented in doubt, "I'm not so sure this will work. With as much as Philip acts up, I'll be on his back constantly if I discipline him every time he misbehaves. He'll never earn any privileges."[19]

This mother's idea of discipline was a major source of her spiraling distress. She measured discipline by the quantity of arguments, yells, and warnings she aimed at Philip. In truth, this is not discipline at all. This is the illusion of discipline—an illusion that will thrust you into repeated and ugly face-offs with your youngster. (There is more about illusory discipline in Chapter 6.) Legitimate discipline—calmly placing limits on your youngster's behavior, backed by predictable consequences—will not put you "on his back" constantly. It will have the opposite effect: it will take you off his back. You won't be forever reminding, or cajoling, or threatening him to act with some semblance of propriety. Instead, because your youngster will know exactly what your responses will be—pro and con—to certain behaviors, you will be freed from the role of fulltime overseer and enforcer. Once you have laid down definite guidelines, you'll actually have to discipline less.

Many parents, however, don't take advantage of this fact. They think that setting explicit consequences for perpetual misbehaviors will drag them into a state of perpetual discipline. They figure they'd better tolerate the trouble at least part of the time, or they will spend all of the time disciplining. This error in logic is easy to fall into, especially if a youngster acts up with clockwork regularity. Suppose your six-year-old son expresses his "agressive instincts" upon the body of his younger brother almost every time they play within sight of each other. Nothing you've tried thus far has prevented their playtime from ending up in a one-sided boxing match. You've been entertaining the idea of separating Rocky from his brother and placing him in a dining-room chair for a half hour each time he turns bully, but you've not yet implemented your version of a neutral corner for fear that Rocky will live the greater part of his next few years there, thus depriving him of the positive aspects of sibling interaction. Of course, up to now any positive interaction has been regularly shattered by the tormented screams of little brother. If you decide to adopt your plan, at first you will probably have to be prepared to act frequently. You see, Rocky may not take you too seriously, so he'll be willing to go fifteen rounds on this issue. But if you're willing to go sixteen rounds, you will watch your use of the dining room chair tapering off. Rocky's no amateur at being a kid. He's also no dummy. The mandatory neutral corner will help him think, before he swings, about the repercussions of bopping his brother. Contrary to what you thought would happen, Rocky is not growing old in the chair, and you are not refereeing squabbles nearly as often as you used to.

To say it again (at the risk of being on your back), it is not consistent discipline that makes for constant discipline; it is inconsistent discipline. If your kids realize they have between four and twenty chances before you act, or if they're never quite sure how you're going to act, they will learn to either ignore you or challenge you. This is what leads to your feeling of being "constantly on their backs."

The Spirit Isn't Weak
or "I don't want to break his spirit."

David was a fast-moving, indefatigable five-year-old. He was inquisitive, endlessly tampering with anything in reach to see how it worked or how it came apart. He averaged twenty questions per hour, wanting the *why* of everything from the basic laws of physics to the rules he was supposed to operate by. If I were to use one word to capture David's essence, it would be *high-spirited*. But his irrepressible nature also brought him more than his share of trouble. He was forever pitting his will against that of adults, particularly his mother and nursery-school teacher, sometimes to win, sometimes just to see what would happen. Unfortunately, David's innate spunk, coupled with his penchant for rule-breaking, gained him the dubious honor of being the first child ever "expelled" from his nursery school. Fortunately, David's mom wasn't ready to expel him from home, not yet anyway. But she was unsure how to handle her little dynamo. On the one hand, she knew she had to teach him to curb his impulses; on the other, she was afraid of "breaking his spirit."

If you have a youngster anything like David, you're probably nodding your head vigorously and sighing sympathetically as you read this. You too know you have to find some means to moderate him or he'll become impossible to live with, if he hasn't already. But you don't want to bridle him so much that you squash his natural inquisitiveness, or exuberance, or extroversion. Since I don't know your child, I can't give you specific direction about how to do one without the other. I can share with you, however, what I told this mother to help her overcome her own anxiety about asserting her authority.

To be sure, Mom could have disciplined David in ways that would have reduced his zest for life. But, like most parents with similar fears, Mom was nowhere near dictatorial. In fact, she underdisciplined. Because of David's nature, Mom needed more than a standard amount of parental perseverance and willpower, and this unsettled her. She had trouble carrying out any type of evenhanded, definitive discipline, because whenever David reacted negatively to her authority, which was usually anytime he was awake, Mom became anxious that she was inhibiting his spirit. Instead, she went to the other extreme and chose to live with his progressively uninhibited behavior. My first step was to reassure Mom that high-spirited kids usually do require more supervision and limit-setting than their more even-tempered counterparts, and that this does not break their spirits. Quite the opposite, it enhances them. It gives energetic children the self-control necessary to use their energy to its utmost potential. A child with unbridled impulses quickly becomes nongoal-directed and, like a pinball, erratically careens against the world and its realities, eventually coming away with a battered, if not broken, spirit.

My second and most important step was to give Mom some general guidelines regarding when to curb David's appetite for action and when to encourage it to feed itself fully. The guidelines were basic ones. If David's exuberant behavior is not hurting anyone, himself included, nor trampling on anyone's rights, then there is no need to intervene. What or whom is David harming by squirming through forty-six contortionistic postures per TV show? If Grandpa doesn't mind that David asks him fourteen questions a minute, why should Mom? If David sings himself to sleep every night, where's the problem? On the other hand, if David is using the living-room couch for a trampoline, or calling Grandpa "stupid" because he can't answer all his questions about the universe, or singing right through Mom's wishes that he be in bed by 9:00 P.M., then his actions are irresponsible, or infringing upon others' rights, or defiant, and they need to be tempered and even stopped. Doing so will not suffocate David's natural exuberance; Mom will be teaching him to moderate it and use it more constructively.

High-spiritedness and self-control are not mutually exclusive characteristics. Indeed, they complement each other well. A child who possesses both will maximize her inborn talents.

The Ogre Syndrome
or "Discipline makes me feel mean."

Many's the time I've heard a parent—a nice, kind parent—say, "I feel mean when I have to discipline. He looks so hurt ... or angry ... or upset ... or disappointed." Granted, disciplining has a way of making you feel like an ogre, even if you're not acting like an ogre. For when you discipline, you're typically doing something that you wish you didn't have to do and, needless to say, that your youngster wishes you didn't have to do. But here we must make a crucial distinction between discipline viewed in and of itself as mean and mean discipline. Most definitely, you can act the ogre as you discipline, blasting your child with verbal assaults and personal put-downs. Let's face it, in these instances you are acting mean! The purpose of your discipline is not mean; your style is. But discipline intended to teach such things as values and self-restraint, when done with quiet firmness and resolve, is *not mean*. It may be work, sometimes unpleasant, but it is not mean. Even if you were wrong in the assumptions that gave rise to the discipline, you still weren't mean. You were mistaken. And you're allowed that privilege as a parent, often.

Equating firmness with meanness can have the same impact on your parenting as nearly every myth about discipline we'll expose. It can be self-fulfilling. If you think you're a nasty person just because you discipline, you will effectively render yourself ineffective. Your own tentativeness, which your kids will instantly sense, will invite progressively more unruly behavior. In time, no matter how easygoing your disposition, you will become fed up with being ignored or abused, and your anger will begin to show itself. Then your discipline finally will become mean, and you may not even care, because you will have exceeded your limit.

To avert this chain of events, you need to see discipline for what it actually is—not a show of your intolerance or vindictiveness, but a fundamental function of parenthood that even the nicest parents with the nicest kids have to carry out. If your child were ill, would you not make sure he received proper medical care, even though it might be painful for him? Would you feel rotten because you did what was best for him, even if he didn't want you to? Surely not. You might hurt along with him, but where your child's health is concerned, you don't worry about being mean. You do what you must, confident he'll understand later. The same reasoning applies to discipline. When you discipline, you are considering your child's personal and social well-being. You are acting upon your judgment of what is beneficial to him. Eventually, he will understand that your motivations have nothing whatsoever to do with being an ogre.

Enforcing rules or taking action instead of just talking does not make you a tyrant bent on making your youngster's life miserable. A child is responsible for the repercussions of her own behavior. In a sense, she is the one who is treating herself in a mean way, as she is knowingly inviting unpleasant results by choosing to misbehave. To consider discipline itself as mean is a fallacy—one that will slowly erode your attempts to discipline justly and without meanness. Put simply, it is not mean to discipline; it is mean not to discipline.

WHAT PARENTS TELL THEMSELVES
ABOUT THEIR KIDS

Your willingness to parent with authority is affected not only by how you view discipline but by how you view your children. You can perceive your kids in ways that make you believe that you have little right to discipline, or that even if you did your discipline would have little effect anyway. These paralyzing perceptions vary greatly from parent to child, even within the same family, but a few are notoriously widespread. They rob many parents of the consideration and respect they are due from their children.

Ignorance Isn't Bliss
or *"He doesn't really know any better."*

I cringe when a parent uses this rationale to stand idly by, watching a preschooler bruise the leg of a nearby adult, pour Kool Aid down her brother's pants, or indulge in any of a wide array of obnoxious behaviors. The belief here is that because she is young, a child is somehow exempt from needing to learn appropriate conduct or some measure of self-control. Most of the time this reasoning is applied to kids under the age of four or five. However, I have heard it used to absolve the actions of older children—for example, an angry eight-year-old who flings curses whose meaning he doesn't fully grasp, or a raving teen who mauls a piece of property she didn't realize was so valuable.

Lest I be misunderstood, I want to define the sort of behavior I believe is mistakenly shielded under the *he doesn't really know any better* umbrella. I'm not speaking of the relentless touching, exploring, and experimenting that the toddler and even the older preschooler pursues. This is a natural developmental learning process, and whenever possible it should be encouraged, not squelched. The sensitive as well as wise parent knows to place valuable breakables out of range of a toddler's fumbling grasp. Most often, however, this is not what parents are talking about when they claim that a child doesn't know better. Instead, they are referring to nasty, defiant, or hurtful conduct. And even though such conduct is also a child's way of experimenting with his surroundings, it needs to be curtailed, as it is in direct disregard of your authority and/or of someone's rights or welfare. I once observed a three-year-old girl in a fit of jealousy severely pinch the hand of her cradle-bound baby sister, leaving a large reddish welt and even drawing a bit of blood. To my surprise, the little girl's mother watched in shock and then looked at me as if to say, "What can I do? She's only three years old."

In a sense, it is true that young children do not fully comprehend the nature of their behavior or all the reasons why they should or shouldn't do something, certainly not on the same level as adults, or even on the level of children with a few more years' maturity. A three-year-old doesn't think to himself, "I shouldn't spit at people because that is a demeaning form of social interaction," unless he is *extremely* precocious. Nor does he fully grasp your similar explanation in language at his level. At age three, his understanding is probably limited to "I'd better not spit at people because mommy puts me in a chair or gets mad at me," or, if he's a bright three-year-old, "Spitting isn't right to do so I won't do it." Whether a child fathoms the complete *why* or *why not* of a misbehavior is irrelevant to whether or not you discipline her. A young child has to be taught to occasionally check her impulses long before she entirely knows why she should. Indeed, the very purpose of discipline is to help her do just that. As she matures, her understanding of *why* will become more complete and gradually shift from external reasons, like your reaction, to internal ones, like a value system and moral code.

An analogy can be drawn to teaching a pet. In all but the simplest sense of the word, a dog is not capable of comprehending why he shouldn't use your carpet for his bathroom. Are you going to wait until he "knows better" before you teach him? I hope not; you'll get progressively fewer visitors at home. Besides, Spot will never know better *unless* you teach him. A two-year-old is infinitely smarter than even Lassie and able to learn far more rapidly. If you postpone disciplining tiny Beatrice because you want to wait until she's better able to realize what she's doing, you are doing her no favor. She will eventually have to learn the same lesson, only at a price that is higher for both of you. A two-year-old just starting to name-call will be much more amenable to purifying her language, even if she doesn't know why she should, than a five-year-old who understands why she shouldn't call people nasty names but has been perfecting her skill for three years.

One final point: You may have recognized a link between the rationale *he doesn't know better* and the personality reality *the earlier the easier* (described in Chapter 3). This personality reality states that it's easiest and most beneficial for both parent and child when the parent establishes who is parent early. The *he doesn't know better* rationale is a chief reason why parents overlook this reality and thereby unknowingly ask for trouble later. So the next time you find yourself tolerating obnoxious behavior, or listening to someone tell you that you should tolerate it because your child doesn't really know better, stop and think; you really *do* know better. Not only would you be operating under a false assumption, but you would be missing an opportunity to teach your child something at a time when she is most open to learning it.

Apathy: Kids Work Hard at It
or *"Nothing we try matters to him."*

Back in Chapter 2, I cited the lament of defeated parents: "We've tried everything. Nothing works." Often this lament has an addendum that goes something like: "He doesn't care what we do. Discipline doesn't matter to him." Once they have conceded this, parents risk getting dragged down one of two parenting routes. In the first, they can stop trying altogether to discipline with any regularity, since they feel that nothing they try will make any difference anyway. The end product of this route is usually parents who are prone to either submission or angry lashing-out when they're no longer able to endure their youngster's unrestrained behavior. In the second, more traveled route, parents can begin the long search for the magic consequences that will make their youngster instantly care, that will have enough weight to motivate him to suddenly begin controlling himself. The main drawback to this style is that the search leads nowhere. It is a draining trek through a hodgepodge of strategies, many of which would work if the parents would persevere with them. But they don't, because they are convinced that nothing fazes their imperturbable child.

Sinking into either of these courses is particularly easy if your youngster routinely uses words or actions meant to display an attitude of total indifference to discipline: the apathetic shoulder shrug/mouth twist upon hearing that a bicycle will be off limits for three days because it was ridden after dark; the "send me to my room, I don't care" parting shot after a bout of ill-tempered language; or, perhaps most typical, the seemingly complete lack of emotion or reaction upon finding out that he has brought undesirable consequences (at least you thought so) upon himself. Kids are masters at beaming signals to persuade you you're wasting your time trying to hold them accountable for their actions. If you tune in to all the signals, you'll find yourself lacking faith in everything you try, and thus less able to carry anything through to a successful end.

A rare rendition of the *nothing matters to him* theme was played for a teacher I know. It firmly convinced her she was helpless to manage an exceptionally unruly youngster. Regardless what she tried, this little imp would giggle, grin, or smirk at her as if to say, "Keep trying; you haven't found anything that makes me unhappy yet." And try she did, for several months. By the time she asked my advice, she was exhausted. She had ridden herself ragged, believing that if she stumbled upon the right motivator—positive or negative—she would know it *immediately*. How? The boy's mirth would cease. But she never stayed with any one plan long enough to let it work. She finally decided something had to be psychologically awry with any youngster who laughed in the face of discipline.[20]

This little guy's bravado, as well as other, more everyday nonreaction reactions, can best be interpreted a couple of ways. Most often, kids do care about being disciplined. What child actually likes suffering the unpleasant results of her behavior, whether naturally caused, like roller skates made rusty and useless from nights in the rain, or parent-caused, like a week-long loss of the skates as punishment for having left them outside for the third time in three nights? Under pressure, kids often act exactly the opposite of how they feel. And discipline can be a pressure situation. Therefore, your child's indifference to discipline is a highly unreliable barometer of how your strategy is actually going to work. It is better to watch the results of your plan. If a youngster truly didn't mind the loss of TV, stereo, or computerized roller skates, she wouldn't spend time engaged in these activities to begin with!

Then, too, for some kids nonchalance, possibly laced with impudence, is a preferred way to agitate the folks. They do indeed care about what you're planning, they're just not about to admit it to you or give you the satisfaction of knowing you've made yourself heard. They want to salvage some measure of victory from a struggle they perceive themselves to have lost.

On occasion, however, a youngster genuinely may not be bothered by the trouble he has brought upon himself. Your discipline does not move him—initially. But if you can placidly accept Buster's momentary apathy and maintain your resolve, you'll watch him slowly gain an insight into himself: Discipline does matter. Many a youngster has blandly accepted the repercussions of his actions, feeling no particular discomfort in complying with them, only to find that over time those repercussions are a nuisance. They become real reasons to change his behavior. A colleague's son had developed the peculiar habit of never putting his toys away. Tiring of the daily competition over abandoned toys, my friend finally added a new rule to the game: Any toy not returned to its proper place after play was confiscated for one week. The first several times Mom enforced her toy moratorium, she met with the attitude: "Oh, well, this is no big deal; I have other toys." However, much to his chagrin, Joey soon began to miss some of his favorite toys. He also ran low on things to play with. Finally realizing that he liked his possessions more than he thought he did, Joey showed more care for them. An added attraction of this approach was that he and Mom had virtually ceased playing around with the toy issue. Mom later confessed to me, though, that she had come within a toy of suspending her rule because of Joey's early apathy.

If you are the receiver of "I don't care" messages, I have a few ideas to make you a less assailable target and to allay your concern that your authority has little meaning to the younger members of your household. The overriding principle is that you do not stop disciplining because your youngster presents an indifferent front. If you can weather Buster's maddening apathy, it should cease to recur. Shoulder shrugs and "I don't care's" will continue only as long as they are successful in making you reconsider your decisions. Accept apathy as Buster's routine response to discipline. But believe, in most cases, that he really does care; it really does matter.

Second, when you hear an "It doesn't matter," "So what," or anything similar, you can reply, evenly and nonsarcastically, "I'm glad you're taking this so well. It's nice to see you calmly accepting responsibility for your behavior." Buster may be jolted by your comeback, but you'll quietly get your point across: You're not about to upset yourself over the fact that he's not upset.

The Devil Made Him Do It
or *"What if he can't control himself?"*

Remember little Billy in the last chapter—the boy whose grand-mother believed that sugar was the key culprit in his unruliness? To continue the story, part of Billy's wildness included rip-roaring temper tantrums if Billy slammed up against a rule or condition he didn't like. Grandma, convinced the sugar-devil made him do it, couldn't understand why Billy's outbursts continued at peak strength even after his sugar-free diet began. But one thing she knew for sure: Billy couldn't control himself. His explosiveness came from some internal weakness of will, constitution, or personality. And therefore he couldn't really be expected to answer for his actions—not while possessed by a temper spell anyway. Naturally, with this attitude, Grandma usually stood permissively by while Billy vented his destructive rage or handed him whatever was necessary to make him cease and desist.[21]

However misguided, Grandma's attitude was not as atypical as it appears. In fact, the *devil made him do it* rationale is used to explain and excuse a broad range of hellish behavior. It is most likely to be invoked by parents of little Billies—those youngsters with a flare for dramatic emotional outbursts. And the more intense and frequent the outbursts, the more likely a parent is to wonder whether a youngster really is able to control his own destiny. The real deviltry in this reasoning lies in its effect on your authority. As you question your youngster's capacity for self-restraint, you may also question your right to discipline her or expect appropriate conduct. All outbursts, you might conclude, should be handled the same way: Keep your requirements to a minimum, wait for the fireworks to subside, and protect against flying objects.

To ease any doubts about your youngster's potential for self-control, ask yourself this question (of course, answer it too): Does he show the same rampant fury no matter where he is or who's present? In other words, do his emotional explosions occur only at home and seldom at school, or vice versa? Or only at Grandma's house, but never when you're watching? In Billy's case, even though he acted up with equal abandon at home and school, never once in his entire eleven years had he exploded in his dad's presence. Billy adored, almost worshipped his father. He also

113

knew Dad would not tolerate such antics, and from the reports of those who knew Billy, he never performed them for him. I guess you could say Billy had periodic fits of self-control. This strongly indicated to me, though regrettably not to the grandmother, that Billy had more throttling power than she was giving him credit for.

Similarly, if your little Angelica is selective about where and with whom she has fits, you're pretty safe in concluding that the issue is not whether she can discipline herself, but whether she chooses to. But even assuming that Angelica genuinely can't calm herself, either immediately before or during a temper frenzy (and there are very few youngsters I would put in this category), how would this excuse her from needing to develop self-discipline? If no bounds or costs are ever placed on Angelica's violent episodes, how will she ever learn to extinguish or at least moderate them? Once again, a self-perpetuating cycle could ensue: You believe Angelica can't bridle her own impulses; therefore, you make few attempts to hold her responsible for her actions. Slowly, she loses what little self-control she had to begin with.

Definitely, children vary widely in their innate capacity for self-restraint, just as they vary widely in their innate capacity for developing any kind of skill. Some kids are born more emotionally reactive than others. For them, it does indeed take more work to compose themselves in times of frustration. But what other choice do they have? Either they learn to rein in their emotions at least partially, or they ride a lifelong emotional roller coaster, with all the stresses that brings. Neither option is easy, but the former gets easier with time, while the latter piles problem onto problem. If your young Oxford had to struggle with math, would you expect him to fail it every year because it didn't come easily to him? I doubt you would. You'd do what you could to assist him and expect that he put forth enough effort to pass. Every child enters life with no skill whatsoever in math; she only learns it if she is taught. Likewise, every child enters life with no self-control whatsoever; she only learns it if she is taught.

The *devil made him do it* rationale is allied to the *he doesn't know better* belief. Both can immobilize you as a parent, making you wait to discipline your child until he has somehow independently achieved the maturity to discipline himself. But without your discipline and supervision coming first, your child may never learn to discipline himself. And the longer you delay taking action, the more likely it is that his emotional trigger mechanism will get even touchier.

Balancing the Scale
or "He's a special child."

One of the fixed conditions of our existence is that life is not fair. It does not treat people with the same degree of kindness, not even the most innocent and helpless among us. Some kids are forced to live and learn with a handicap—physical, emotional, or both. Others don't possess the intellectual resources given to most. Still others have temperaments that make growing up a long, erratic process. In some form or another, and to varying degrees, every child has a unique—and unfair, if you will—set of handicaps or deficits. And children have no choice but to shoulder their disadvantages, adjust to them, and overcome them if possible. You are your children's prime helper and also the one who hurts most for them.

Because you feel her pain when a child seems to be a victim of a capricious and often callous world, you want very much to find some way to make things up to her, to turn her world into a nicer place. You somehow find more time to talk, whenever or however it's needed. You make a little more space on your shoulder for this child to lean on or cry on. You reach deeper inside yourself trying to feel what she feels. At times it may appear that there is not enough you can do. But in your desire to compensate for the injustices done your child, it's quite easy to go too far, to do the one thing that can undo much of the good you've gained by everything else: You can deny yourself the right to put limits and expectations upon your youngster's behavior. Indeed, this may be the single most pervasive way in which parents strive to balance life's scale.

That you could be drawn into this course of parenting is understandable. Your child already looks to be enduring more than her share of hardship, so you don't want to add any more. You'd like to hold her disappointments to a minimum. By no means, however, does this include exempting her from following rules and acting responsibly. With a special child, a suspension of discipline may be well-intentioned, but it is misguided. It will not make amends for an unjust world; it will only create more injustice—for you, immediately; for your child, with time. She will form distorted expectations of life. Other people won't be willing to serve her habitually or cater to her every demand, as do Mom and Dad. She will learn from painful experience that her special condition, which some may not even consider to be special, carries no license to treat others shabbily or command special allowances for her behavior. Ultimately, in addition to not righting the scale, forfeiting your authority may bring about the very same result you wanted to avoid in the first place. Instead of making your youngster more emotionally durable, more equipped to handle stress, she will probably become even less so, as she grows accustomed to obstacles always being removed. Two separate cases with the same result will illustrate.

Carlton was born deaf. His parents were initially shocked, then hurt, then angry. Why should their son have to contend with such a handicap? Since, in their eyes, life had already been unduly harsh to Carlton, Mom and Dad made a silent pact. They would redress Carlton by giving him whatever they could, not only materially, but of their own privileges as parents. If Carlton destroyed a toy, he was bought another. If he desired anything at any time, he screamed and it was given. If he wanted to play, to walk, to go anywhere, he grabbed Mom's hand and yanked or wailed until she followed. Anything less than immediate submission led to escalating temper tantrums. Bedtime was out of the question. Bedtime was whenever Carlton fell asleep. While Carlton was getting more unbearable to live with, Mom and Dad were still denying the need to discipline Carlton or lay down any sort of boundaries because of his affliction. Essentially, they viewed Carlton's deafness as an excuse for his behavior. When I finally came in contact with the family, the parents were desperate, and Carlton, at age five, was not yet socialized. An added result of Mom and Dad's excessive permissiveness was that an area school for the deaf would not accept Carlton because his behavior was so wild. Indeed, Carlton's behavior had become more of a handicap than his deafness.

Sylvia was seventeen years old when I met her. She didn't want to meet me, or for that matter anybody else who was aiming to show her other ways to direct her life. When Sylvia was seven, her parents were divorced. Sylvia idolized her father and had trouble coping with the separation. To compound matters, within a year after the divorce Dad moved to another state, seldom contacting Sylvia thereafter. From that point forward, because Mom felt at fault (though in fact she wasn't) for Sylvia's growing up without two full-time parents, she gradually discontinued almost all discipline. She only asked of Sylvia what Sylvia wanted to do. Chores and duties around the house were completed at Sylvia's whim. Mom struggled to fulfill nearly all of Sylvia's mounting requests for material pleasures, but requests soon turned to demands, and demands soon turned to righteous indignation if not indulged. Over a period of years, temper outbursts went from verbal harassment to destruction of property to aggravated assault against Mom. I saw Sylvia after she began skipping school and threatening suicide if Mom treated her "mean," which is to say, tried at all to restrict her reckless rebelliousness.[22]

The inequities of life that can push parents to try to balance the scale are nearly endless. They include physical conditions, mental retardation, hyperactivity and other assorted "emotional problems" (see Chapter 4), and being an only, a foster, or an adoptive child, to identify but a few. In addition to these, however, there are many other less permanent hardships that can foster a variant of the *he's a special child* perception. Let's call it the *he's a special child—temporarily* perception.

Every childhood has its stresses and disappointments: the death of someone close, a family move, a lost friend, a change in schools. No youngster, however young, is exempted from periods of transition and adjustment. At these times, besides his erratic and "abnormal" behaviors, a child might also display some unexpected misconduct. Periodically, every parent observes: "He's really been backtalking me lately, but that's probably because he's adjusting to a new school," or "She won't listen to me at all. I guess I should expect that; she just got a new baby brother." True, you can expect a surge in misbehavior when a child is facing change or stress. And yes, helping her deal with whatever is bothering her should bring about a decline in her un-manageability. But tolerating nastiness or irresponsibility because a child has a "special reason" for it doesn't help her ride out these rough periods. It won't give her an outlet for her tensions or anger. It will only foster patterns that may perpetuate themselves long after the initial stress has come and gone. While Clara is busy hating her new school and everybody in it, her grades head downhill. As they do, Clara discovers she likes the freedom of no schoolwork, so her academic descent gains momentum even after she's come to love her new school. The original reasons that inspired Clara's underachievement have long since passed, and a whole new set of motives are now pushing Clara to act unlike Clara used to act. The behavior was allowed to feed upon itself, and eventually gained a life independent of any stressful events.

Many parents accept unacceptable behavior during a "crisis" in a child's life, assuming that such behavior will disappear once the crisis passes and their child returns to "normal." Sometimes this is what happens; more often it is not. The permissive message, "I'll give you temporary license to treat me, others, and yourself poorly until you've adjusted to your situation," courts trouble on two fronts. One, it informs a child that certain circumstances free him to act with impunity, to act in a manner that hurts people, himself included. And two, it provides a short-term breeding ground for problems that may become long-term.

Special circumstances in a child's life, be they permanent or temporary, may indeed be reasons for misbehavior; they are not excuses for it.

WHAT PARENTS TELL THEMSELVES
ABOUT THEMSELVES

Just as you can grant your child special status to exempt him from your authority, so too can you give yourself special status that weakens your authority. You can consider yourself somehow less than a "legitimate" parent because you do not fit the traditional parent mold. That is, you are not one of two full-time biological parents with a spouse in the house. This arrangement, while it may sound as American as apple pie, actually describes less than 25 percent of the parenting configurations in our country today. So if it doesn't describe yours, you're in the majority. Unfortunately, much of this majority—including step-parents, biological parents not living full-time with their children, single, adoptive, or foster parents, working mothers, and any combination thereof—has the demoralizing habit of stripping legitimacy from their own parenting roles by convincing themselves that they are not the standard. They draw the demeaning conclusion that since they are "nontraditional" parents, they are less than deserving of a full measure of parental authority and rights. The paradox here is that without this full measure they become much less effective with the children they are charged with rearing. Although every parenting role has its own individual strains and stresses, all are equal in this respect: If the parent chips away at his or her rights and responsibilities through doubting his or her status, the parent's confidence and parental mental health suffer considerably.

The following sections will uncover some potential assaults on a parent's authority associated with the more common nontraditional parenting roles. My goal is to make you aware of these threats and to help you protect yourself against them. My goal is not to explore in depth the complexities of these parenting roles, as that topic is too far afield from the aim of this book.

Single-Parent Guilt
or *"I'm solely to blame for (fill in the blank)."*

Throughout this book, a major theme is that parenthood is a stressful job, even when divided by two. But if you're taking on the job alone, you can total all the stresses we discuss and multiply them by two for each child you have. This is why it is doubly important that you learn to recognize parenting fallacies; you have no full-time partner to help you resist them. In addition to fallacies that ensnare all parents, there is one trap that is uniquely yours: single-parent guilt.

A few pages ago, the story of Sylvia showed how a parent can relinquish her authority through considering her child a "special" child—in Sylvia's case, a single-parent child. Sylvia's mother, however, went one step further. She saw herself as personally to blame for creating her special child. She was the reason for Sylvia's absent father, and as such she devalued herself as a parent. To atone for her inadequacy, she allowed herself to place only limited and weak requirements upon Sylvia. This was Mom's way of saying: "Sylvia, since I deprived you of your father, which I'm afraid will cause you irreparable pain and damage, I'll make it up to you by making your life as easy as possible."

Sylvia's mother's guilt over her single parenthood was more intense than most. Still, a good many single parents feel deserving of some degree of reproach. They see themselves as failures in marriage, the by-product of which is children without two full-time parents. With their sense of culpability often comes a forfeiting of their parental control in an attempt to put minimal demands upon their children. Even enforcing minor daily responsibilities—coming inside before dark, drying the dishes before midnight, taking a bath before mold sets in—can arouse guilt if a parent believes he or she has already asked too much of the child by asking her to live with only one parent.

Close scrutiny of this mentality of self-blame, however, will show that it is founded upon several unsound assumptions. The first is that two heads of household are always better than one. Sometimes a marriage can deteriorate so badly that the first time the kids actually experience some semblance of peace and stability is after their parents have separated. In these circumstances, one parent may indeed be better than two.

The second unsound assumption is that one parent is solely to blame for a marital breakup. Rarely is this so. Further, my experience with divorced parents is that the parent who worked harder to hold the family together usually feels the greater pain when it comes apart.

If you remain determined, however, to cast yourself as sole villain, you will set yourself up for a third fallacy in reasoning—that you can ease your child's adjustment to her new circumstances by being a lax parent, by asking less of her than you otherwise would if you were still married. Such reasoning only brings on added hardships. For one thing, as Sylvia's mother found, lax parenting doesn't help a youngster adjust better to a divorce. Without you in charge, your child will guide herself through her one-parent childhood, most probably doing a very childish job. Whether or not you failed at marriage is completely irrelevant to whether or not you should assertively parent and discipline your children. You are still in a far better position than your children to rule your home and raise them.

Another problem provoked by the *lax parenting helps a child cope* rationale is more long-range. You give your children the

120

mistaken idea that life will somehow expect less of them because of their lack of two in-house, biological parents. In truth, none of us gets special privileges in any area of functioning—school, work, marriage—on the basis of our parents' marital status. To teach children that they are allowed to be less responsible, obedient, or respectful because they have suffered from a divorce prepares them poorly for adulthood. And kids *do* make assumptions about what is and isn't OK in the world based upon their experience at home.

The fourth and final fallacy may be the most self-sabotaging of all. It is the belief that somehow you will feel less guilty by sacrificing your parental status to make your child happy. In all likelihood, in addition to *not* making your child happy, you will end up feeling even more guilty. Why? Because kids don't achieve happiness by being constantly catered to. They only learn to expect kid-glove treatment regardless of their behavior, and to be unappreciative, even hostile, when they aren't receiving it. Relegate yourself to this "I give and you take; you demand and I comply" relationship to assuage your guilt, and your fears may come to pass. Your children may start to act as troubled as you worried they would because of your divorce, thereby furnishing "proof" of your blameworthiness. The only catch is that the effects of the divorce are probably no longer the main thing perpetuating your kids' unpleasant behavior. Your own self-imposed parental retreat is.

In this country, over four million parents are raising children without the support of a full-time spouse. Single-parent guilt is a pervasive and extremely complex phenomenon. As I said, my intent is not to analyze its myriad dimensions. In these few pages I can only identify single-parent guilt as possibly the most corrosive destroyer of authority in one-parent households. If you allow it to engulf you, it will do nothing but steal your ability to put the past in the past and to parent in the present.

Weekend at Disney World
or *"I'm only a part-time parent."*

Rick had a typical custody arrangement. Every weekend he picked up his six-year-old son Jason on Saturday morning and returned him to his mother's care on Sunday evening. Over several months, for about thirty hours a week, Rick and Jason had enjoyed each other's company. But then the fun began to leave their relationship. Jason was becoming whiny, disrespectful, demanding, harder in general to be around. Rick came to counseling hoping to uncover what was causing the change. During our first interview, Rick described Jason's mother as a nitpicking, inflexible taskmaster who used Jason as a sounding board for her own emotional needs. How much of this picture was accurate I can't say, because I never met Jason's mother. However, the accuracy of Rick's description of his ex-wife was not the focal issue. More important were his perceptions, both of his ex-wife and of himself as a "weekend" parent, for these shaped his relationship with Jason. Since Rick saw Jason as behaviorally suffocated and emotionally misused during the week, he thought he could offset this by giving Jason free rein on the weekend. In effect, Rick was struggling to accomplish two impossible tasks: One, he was trying to undo the damage he perceived his ex-wife to be inflicting upon Jason. Two, he was racing to pack a week's worth of parenting into thirty hours—thirty fun-filled, interesting, conflict-free hours.

As unattainable as these goals may sound, weekend parents often reach for them, in part by not allowing themselves to discipline or deny their children any request for fear of "ruining" their short stay together. And there's where Jason's father bought his trouble. For the first few months, Rick did manage to avoid having to disappoint Jason by accommodating Jason's growing defiance and "gimme-ness." No parent, however, can make every weekend, indefinitely, a trip to Disney World, and Rick began to fatigue, emotionally and financially. Jason, who had grown accustomed to a bottomless well of treasures and adventures without rules, didn't like it when the well started to run dry. He reacted with surliness, with accusations of unfairness, and finally with grumbles that he'd rather stay with his mother on weekends.

If you have limited contact with your youngster, not just as a result of a custody arrangement but for any reason, you know well how Rick could have unintentionally contributed to his own distress. Because you're with your child for a relatively few hours a week, you don't want your time marred by conflicts or unfriendly moments. After all, you don't have the rest of the week to clear up any misunderstandings or build your relationship. What then is one indispensable way to keep disagreements to a minimum and maximize the pleasure of your time together? Be not

122

afraid to discipline when necessary. Easy to say, very hard to do. But if you don't at least begin to say it, how will you ever begin to do it? You must show your youngster as early as possible that even though you are not in the daily mainstream of his life, you still expect to be treated with the same respect you give him. You too have expectations; they may differ from your ex-spouse's, but they are in effect when your youngster is with you. And, depending upon what kind of relationship you had with your child prior to your marital separation, clarifying your expectations may take time, with both of you enduring some moments of hurt. But if you are warm in your authority, and equitable, the moments will pass. You will lay the ground rules within which a quality, if not quantity, relationship can develop. Had Rick initially confirmed himself to be still a parent, and one with limited resources, he probably would have averted his troubles. Jason would have been more willing to accept his father first as a father, second as an entertainer and source of good times.

Probably the stickiest predicament for any parent without custody occurs when the ex-spouse exercises little control as a parent. If this is your situation, and every weekend a little, or maybe not so little, wild man enters your home, you face two choices: one, put up with two days of exasperation and mistreatment until Spike returns to your ex-spouse, giving you several precious days to recuperate before his next visit; or two, put forth whatever energy is needed to demonstrate that your home has a set of operating rules unlike those to which Spike is accustomed. No doubt the second alternative is tougher—initially—and will evoke more resistance from Spike—initially. But once you've made definite your expectations and your willingness to enforce them, Spike won't spend all his time with you working against you. Each weekend won't be an endurance test to survive but a visit to enjoy. Expect, though, that with you tugging in one parenting direction and your ex-spouse tugging in the opposite, Spike may take a few weekends to catch onto the idea that he has to adjust his behavior from parent to parent. But he will adapt without confusion or emotional ill effects. He'll simply learn to treat both Mom and Dad as they teach him they want to be treated.

To sum up, if you are forced to spend less time with your child than you'd like, one foolproof way to make that time unenjoyable is to assume that your "part-time" status does not afford you full-time rights. Whether you spend one hour, one day, or one week per week with your youngster, during that period you have the rights and authority of a parent. To accept anything less may postpone conflicts for a while, as it did for Rick, but overall you will be increasing the likelihood that your relationship with your child will evolve into something unpleasant, something both you and she will want to avoid, instead of something to look forward to.

Stepparents, Not Stepped-On Parents
or *"I'm just married to his mother."*

Single parenthood puts unique stresses on a parent's authority. So too does shared-custody parenting. But there is one other parenting role that competes well with the above two in presenting barriers to self-assured parenting. And—predicting by statistics, anyway—if you are currently either a single parent or sharing custody, you stand a good chance of entering this other role sometime. Then again, for rising numbers of parents-to-be, this "nontraditional" role is their first exposure to parenthood. Naturally, I'm talking about being a stepparent.

As the divorce rate has soared in recent years, so too has the remarriage rate. This translates into more and more families that must adjust to a change in parents, an adjustment that, to say the least, is not always smooth. In stories, stepparents have been stereotyped as villains, wicked and ugly. Just ask any Cinderella. But in real life, stepparenthood may be the most challenging parenthood of all, even if you're a kind and good-looking hero. As a stepparent, you take on full parental duties and responsibilities, often without enjoying full parental privileges and authority. Emergence as a legitimate family member can be an inch-by-inch, uphill climb, sometimes, it seems, with obstacles thrown up by everybody: your kids ("You're not my real father; I don't have to listen to you"); your spouse ("They're not your kids; you don't understand"); your spouse's ex-spouse ("He's not your father; I am"); and even you (what you tell yourself doesn't help either, and we'll turn to it shortly).

Like every parenting role, stepparenting has its own special complications. I cannot begin to advise you about your particular transition into your new family. My intent is to share with you some observations on what many stepparents do to themselves to delay their acceptance as a full-fledged family member.

As I have said, settling into an existing family structure is a step-by-step process. Stepparents often worry that if they don't immediately affirm themselves as mother or father, they will be doomed to impotence in their new role. Sometimes (usually on television) stepparents can assume their niche quickly and effortlessly. But outside of television land, this is not generally how it happens. Eager to gain respect, many stepparents charge forth like gangbusters, laying down wholesale rules and discipline only to meet overwhelming resistance. These stepparents underestimate the complications involved in moving into an already formed system with its own rules, alliances, and loyalties—spoken and unspoken. They don't realize that systems, and the people in them, are threatened by, and therefore oppose, change—even positive change. After their initial, unsuccessful tries at winning a place in the family order, many stepparents prematurely conclude that their efforts are fruitless and resentfully accept the role of "puppet parents." They may tell themselves that trying to guide and discipline their new children is a waste of time and may begin to shun the responsibility in any number of ways, such as acquiescing to the kids' demands or deferring all decisions to their spouse. In short, by giving up after the first failures, stepparents can make their own apprehensions come true.

To be sure, your ultimate goal must be to assume full parental authority. Without both you and your spouse in charge, your family will function much less steadily. But you may have to be patient; your authority might evolve gradually. How gradually? Naturally, that differs from family to family, but it is not unusual for the transition to take more than a year. Of course, if from the outset you have the complete support of your spouse, if your spouse gives you equal status in the family hierarchy, your road to acceptance will be far shorter, with fewer bumps. But full spouse support or no, it is important to realize that in many cases a slow, deliberate phasing into the family is necessary. You will be rewarded with more complete and permanent authority—assuming, that is, that you believe you have a right to such authority in the first place. This leads to my second observation.

Some stepparents don't believe they will ever be entitled to a "normal" level of authority. They relegate themselves permanently to second-class parental status, forfeiting their prerogative to discipline because they are not a youngster's "real" parent. And it is not only stepparents who neutralize themselves with this notion, but other "unreal" parents as well. I have frequently listened to foster or adoptive parents somberly confess to enduring behavior they never would have condoned if they had been a child's biological parents and thus had a legitimate, "God-given" right to discipline. But whether your child's genes are half yours or not has nothing whatsoever to do with the limits of your authority. Once you assume responsibility for a child's welfare, you are eligible for parent status, totally. Deny yourself that status and you will also encourage your stepchildren to deny it to you. They will use your own downgrading of your importance to distort their image of you. Why should they accept you as a parent if you can't? Too, even if the family is willing for you to settle in, you can keep yourself isolated with your misguided self-perception. The family is ready to call you "parent," but you're not.

Attaining authority as a stepparent can take time, but it is a right that is inalienably yours. It does not depend upon a biological link to your youngster. Indeed, many biological parents do not have a fraction of the love and attachment for their children that some foster, adoptive, or stepparents have for theirs. Bloodlines alone do not a parent make.

A closing word about authority

Many studies have examined how parental discipline styles affect children's personal and social development. These studies have consistently confirmed what common sense would predict. Either extreme of the authority continuum—the cold, rigid, power-wielding authoritarian or the lax, weak-kneed permissivist—creates problems for both parent and child. In contrast, those parents in the moderate range of the continuum generally not only raise more self-confident, content kids, but they themselves are more self-confident, content parents. These parents can rightly be called authoritative, not authoritarian. They give their children autonomy and respect as individuals, but they also set explicit limits and don't permit their children to push them around. Neither the authoritarian nor the permissivist parent but only the authoritative parent is in true control.

One More Time ...

Authority is not a bad word. It is part of good parenting, and a necessary part. For your mental health and your child's, authority belongs unequivocally in your hands. Unfortunately, you can unequivocally remove authority from your hands with erroneous beliefs and groundless fears.

It would be nice if you never had to discipline your child. Discipline is hard work, sometimes unpleasant, and often misunderstood by all concerned. Realistically, though, you can't escape the need for it. You can, however, keep your moments of discipline to a minimum by being at ease with your authority and letting your youngster know that. On the other hand, if your every occasion of discipline becomes an internal contest of ambivalent feelings and perceptions, you will most likely talk yourself into all the problems you are trying to avoid. You will create more conflicts; you will lose effectiveness; and you may become very nasty. An axiom of parenthood is that authority is used less often when you are *not* uneasy using it.

Homework

1. Pick a behavior that's "just easier to let go." Next time you let it go, start a log. Keep track of the amount of time—not to mention effort—you spend in the following activities: (1) worrying about the behavior; (2) complaining to yourself or anyone else about it; (3) preaching or nagging about it; (4) chastising yourself for failing to handle it; and (5) going on a rampage about it when you've had enough. Add up the total time. Do you think it is more or less than the amount of time you would have spent dealing with the behavior or developing a plan to deal with it? Where is the greater cost in frayed nerves?

Also enter in your log the date and time of the occasion when you allowed the behavior to run its course. Note how long—or, shall we say, how short—it is before the problem erupts again.

2. Select another behavior for which you feel you're forever disciplining your child. Make an inventory of everything you do in order to "discipline." Does it look something like this: ask, order, remind, nag, bargain, plead, lecture, induce guilt, threaten, yell, lose control, give in? Analyze your list. How much of it constitutes actual discipline and how much is just self-harassment or child-harassment? Becoming aware of the difference is the first step toward spending less time disciplining. To take the next steps, stay tuned to Chapters 6, 7, and 8.

3. When you hear your next "I don't like you," either directly or in so many words, wait a day and ask your youngster: "What was it about me or what I was doing that you didn't like?" I think you'll receive one of two reactions: (1) he's embarrassed to talk about the matter because he didn't really mean what he said or because he's long since over his pout; or (2) what he most disliked were the unpleasant adjuncts to discipline (for example, yelling, shaming, nagging) and not your actual disciplinary decision itself.

4. This experiment is for parents who wonder if their youngster "really knows any better." When you find yourself succumbing to this rationale, ask your child: (1) "What did you do?" and (2) "What happens when you do that? What does mommy/daddy do?" Almost all kids can tell you what they did, or at least recognize that their actions were a "no-no." Likewise, almost all kids can tell you what usually happens after their no-no. If little happens, Brewster will be quick to point out, "Daddy do nothing," or some such insightful observation. If something does happen, he will be just as quick to tell you ("Mommy sit Brewster in chair"). Your little one doesn't understand all the philosophy underlying the rules, but even at his young age, he understands all he needs to understand in order to acquire the foundations of self-discipline; "If I do A, B will happen."

5. If you suffer from guilt for being a "meany" this is your assignment. The next time you don't address a misbehavior for fear of appearing "mean," become aware of your feelings toward your child, both during and after the misbehavior. If the problem recurs, and you remain immobilized, continue to notice your feelings. Are they positive? If you're human, probably not. Are you experiencing a mounting urge to explode? Probably so. At these times, don't be fooled into thinking that such feelings will pass. They will eventually surface, in the form of resentment, tears, emotional outbursts, verbal blasts. In other words, by shunning the problem to avoid looking mean, you are unwittingly moving toward being the person you least admire—a meany.

6. This is an exercise for single parents. Make a list of five things you think your children need that children of two-parent households may not need. Does your list include items like more time with you, giving your kids a better understanding of your pressures and concerns, guidance from clergy or a counselor to adjust to a single-parent family, more family group discussions? How about items like relaxation of rules, more material possessions, fewer responsibilities? My hunch is that your list resembles the first group and not the second. If so, you've told yourself what is really important for your kids' well-being and what is not.

6

Surrendering Authority: A Parent's Handbook

You can talk yourself out of authority without realizing it. But even if you don't talk your authority away, you can still give it away through your actions. In this chapter we will see how you might be unwittingly making discipline an ineffective and emotionally draining chore. We will cover some often used but often useless "discipline" practices. Quotation marks surround the word "discipline" here because these practices aren't really discipline. They are the illusion of discipline. They make you feel you are teaching valuable lessons when you actually may be doing little of the sort. You may only be making life difficult for both you and your youngster.

This chapter will also give alternatives to these self-defeating practices, alternatives to help you discipline more quietly, more surely, more fairly, and *less frequently*.

Nagging
or *"This is the last ten times I'm going to tell you."*

If I had to award a prize for the most futile parenting practice, I would surely present it to nagging. Indeed, nagging may be the single most pervasive masquerade of discipline. In its popular sense, to nag means to ask or tell a youngster repeatedly to do something—a chore, homework, a "thank you" to Aunt Ida for the horsehair pillowcase. In our context, however, nagging is defined more broadly. Nagging is any repetition of words made in the name of discipline, be it a request, command, warning, or injunction. You can nag a youngster to begin something ("Arnold, eat your brussels sprouts"), end something ("Arnold, stop jamming your brussels sprouts under the tablecloth"), or continue something ("Arnold, two more bites of sprouts and it'll be over"). Just how many repetitions constitute nagging is hard to say. Are two sufficient? How about five? The answer varies from parent to parent. But in addition to mere repetition, two other features characterize true nagging. The first is a gradual crescendo in voice volume with each reiteration. The second is a rise in parental agitation.

As you may fast be surmising, I consider nagging highly hazardous to your parental mental health. And the hazards are many.

Nagging is counterproductive. With nagging, the more you talk, the less you get listened to. Continually mouthing the same appeal or threat, whether changing your words a little or a lot, does little to gain a child's attention or cooperation. It only trains him to tune out more of what you say. Just as those who live near a superhighway grow deaf to the noise of the passing vehicles, children who live near nagging parents grow deaf to the noise of the passing words.

Nagging is even more fruitless when done from a distance. The farther your voice from your child's ears, the less likely it will be heeded. A simple formula shows this relationship: $I = n \times d$. The degree of being ignored (I) is equal to the number of requests made (n) multiplied by the distance at which the requests are made (d). Also boosting the degree of being ignored is the "unseen" factor. This refers to the fact that many nagging words have no face attached to them. They come from a parent who is out of sight—around corners, down stairs, through far-off windows. Words without a face are that much easier to ignore. Therefore, if you nag from across two backyards, from across the house, or even from across the room, your chances of being disregarded rise dramatically. Distance is the great nullifier of a parent's words.

Nagging is exhausting. It saps you of much parental energy, energy you could use in more enjoyable pursuits with your children. Consistently, I notice that those classroom teachers most drained at the school day's end are those who for six hours have sustained a steady stream of pleas, orders, and warnings, few of which are followed by any consequences, only by the teacher's paraphrases of the previous directives. Far more effort is demanded to intrude verbally and unrelentingly upon a youngster's behavior than to decide which behaviors warrant attention and then to take action.

Nagging is dangerous. More often than not, nagging not only entails repetition, it also provokes an unpleasant surge in emotional tension. Like the feedback caused by placing a microphone too near its speaker, nagging words typically increase in volume and pitch and culminate in a verbal explosion. Nagging greatly increases the risk that when you finally do act, you will act in exasperation and anger, saying and doing much that is not meant nor relevant to the issue at hand. This nagging-anger feedback loop is so treacherous that we will devote an entire upcoming section to it.

Nagging is deceptive. It is, as I said above, the masquerade of discipline. You literally talk yourself into believing you are inspiring self-discipline and responsibility, when in reality no such lessons are occurring. Nagging creates the impression that you are forever disciplining. But it is authority founded only upon words, and if the words fail, so too does the authority. Whereas discipline means putting action where your mouth is when necessary, nagging means putting only more words where your mouth is.

Nagging is a destroyer. It wears away your child's respect for your authority. In a sense, nagging is pleading with your youngster to listen to you. It demonstrates to her that your ability to set guidelines depends solely upon her choosing to listen to them or not.

Lastly, nagging is a habit. It is a practice that can insidiously become second nature, evolving into your dominant mode of discipline. Almost always, the amount of nagging done is underestimated. I recall visiting with a friend whose little girl came upstairs from the family room to ask if she could have some ice cream. The dialogue went something like this:

Gina: Mom, can I have more ice cream?

Mom: No, Gina, you had some after supper. It's almost time for bed.

Gina: Please, I'll just get a little bit.

Mom: Gina, you know you never eat just a little bit of ice cream. I'm visiting now. Go downstairs to watch TV.

Gina: John (a visiting neighbor boy) wants more ice cream, too.

Mom: He had some after dinner, too. Now, hurry, you're missing your show.

Gina: But I'm hungry.

Mom: It's only fifteen minutes to bedtime and both you and John had snacks. Now go downstairs this minute.

Gina: That was only crackers and peanut butter. We want something cold.

Mom: Gina, I'm getting angry. I'm not telling you again to go downstairs.

The dialogue wore on like this for a few more minutes, and Mom did in fact tell Gina again, and again, to go downstairs, until Gina finally stomped away, out of arguments for the moment. At that point I couldn't resist asking if I could offer an observation, something I'm cautious about doing outside the office since psychologists can bring out the paranoia in people without even saying anything. Since my friend wanted my input, I asked, "Stephanie, how many times do you think you told Gina in some way or another that she couldn't have more ice cream and to go back downstairs?" Sheepishly, Stephanie said probably more than she realized, maybe five or six times. The actual tally was twelve; I had counted. (We psychologists do things like that; no wonder we bring out the paranoia in people!) But the story doesn't end there. About a half hour later, Gina returned, requesting an extension of bedtime. Stephanie, still reeling from her twelve rounds of verbal sparring, assertively told Gina that she had already stayed up past her usual bedtime and that it was time to call it a day. Then she proceeded to tell her basically the same thing ten more times as Gina argued her cause. Needless to say, I kept my second tally in my head.[23]

It is painfully easy to slip into a pattern of doing little but rewording your original decision, maybe altering your reasoning a bit here and there, but nevertheless embarking upon the same tiresome trek nearly every time your wishes collide with your youngster's. Without doubt, nagging is one tenacious habit, hard to break. But it is breakable. You just need to begin with a few alternatives.

The "say it once" rule

Since nagging is saying the same thing more than once, to cease nagging you need to learn to say the same thing only once. Sounds absurdly obvious, doesn't it? Takes a lot of practice, though, to perfect. But as you get into the groove of not being a broken record, making your point once will become second nature, as nagging used to be.

Okay, so you resolve to make your point only one time. What's to ensure that once will be enough, that once will get you the desired results? If you only *say* things once, you probably won't elicit any better cooperation than you ever have. The key is to back your words with action. Present your youngster with a choice: He can heed your words or reap the consequences. In a nonthreatening manner, ask something of him and then tell him what you plan to do if he ignores or resists your request.

Two of the best ways to talk without nagging are through *if-then's* and *either-or's*. Since both are essentially equal in their purpose, from here on we will use *if-then* to mean either style.

An *if-then* is a logical proposition. It conveys a message and information about the consequences of either regarding or disregarding the message. Here are some examples:

1. Wiped out from constantly prodding your kids to take off muddy shoes at the door? Try this: "Clay, if you track dirt into the house, you're responsible for cleaning and vacuuming everywhere you tramped."
2. Getting the worst of interminable arguments? You might end them better by saying, "Polly, this discussion is over. Please don't say any more, or you will cool down in your room."
3. TV interfere with family suppers? "Nielsen, I'd like you to turn off the television now and come to supper. If I have to turn it off, I'll decide when it can come back on."
4. Your kids' everyday responsibilities seem to be more work for you than for them? You may wish to use one mother's approach when she sensed she might have to overtax her vocal cords: "Please hang up your coat. If I tell you again, a quarter is coming off your allowance."

134

5. Of course, *if-then's* can be used to promise privileges, too. For instance, "Gardiner, if you have the lawn mowed by six o'clock, we'll have time to go out for ice cream."

6. Or they can be used to offer more than one alternative: "Macy, if you don't nag me to go shopping, I'll have an answer for you at lunch. If you ask me again, though, I'm afraid the answer will be 'no'."

An absolute *must* for successful *if-then-ing* is that you follow through on your stated consequences. I can't stress this enough. Without action reinforcing your words, the *if-then* alternative is merely another variety of useless nagging, or worse yet, of threatening. ("Fanny, I'm warning you. Do you want me to do what I said I'd do?") Repeatedly threatening disciplinary action springs from the eternal hope that threats will serve as discipline, and real discipline won't be necessary. But kids are too smart for that. They'll quickly realize that your warnings are generally meaningless; they are *if*'s without *then*'s. Far better for you to say nothing in the face of misbehavior and at least not lose credibility than constantly to promise action you only carry out an average of 13 percent of the time. Before you threaten, keep in mind this basic principle about follow-through: The closer to 100 percent sure your youngster is that you mean what you say, the shorter-lived will be the problem you've been nagging about.

Now that you have a general idea of what *if-then's* are all about, here are several guidelines for using them more effectively. And as their effectiveness improves, you'll find yourself using them less often.

1. Whenever possible, preface your requests with a "please." This will remind you to stay composed. It will also show your youngster that you are seeking his cooperation, not trying to bully him into doing your will. Likewise, a genuine "thank you" after he has cooperated is a simple, immediate way to tell him you appreciate his choice. Both "please" and "thank you" require so little effort, but they do so much to foster your child's willingness to choose your request rather than your consequences.

2. *If-then's* are best said quietly and matter-of-factly. They are straightforward statements meant to reveal choices. They are not vengeful reprisals to be slapped upon your youngster as punishment. ("Go ahead, Casper, disappear next time I ask for

help and you'll spend the next month without an allowance.")
Ideally, communication of *if-then's* should be good-natured. And
many parents do this naturally. They give a child her options
without any edge of hostility in their voice. Their tone and
manner are gentle, supportive, but nevertheless definite.

3. The closer you are physically to your youngster when you
state your *if-then,* the more weight it will carry. As distance
renders nagging more pointless, proximity makes *if-then's* more
meaningful. Physical touching—a hand on the shoulder, a rum-
pling of hair, a parting pat on the back—further tells your
youngster you are not bent on hassling him personally. Him you
accept; some of his behavior you don't.

4. Once you have said your *if-then,* don't endlessly remind
your youngster of your consequences. He knows what they are,
you told him the first time. And he hasn't forgotten them. Again,
re-reminding is just another form of nagging.

5. Choose consequences that are *realistic* and *clear-cut.*
Open-ended *if-then's*— "Dawn, you'd better get out of bed, or
else"—invite a youngster to think, "or else what?" Without
specifically stating your intentions, you leave a child to guess at
them. Sometimes open-ended statements work, primarily
through a youngster's fear of the unknown. But eventually, every
child is bound to check for himself just exactly what you mean to
do. And when pushed, you may act rashly in the heat of the
moment, with little predictability from one situation to the next.
Open-ended *if-then's* will spur more confrontation than their
clear-cut counterparts.

Another reason to keep *if-then's* simple and precise is to
make them easier for your kids to grasp. Younger children
especially have trouble linking their behavior to some vague,
abstract consequence. The more ill-defined a *then,* the more
slowly children learn what you're trying to get across. Clear-cut
consequences help kids of all ages, even grown-up kids, to realize
if-then connections more quickly.

If-then's must also be enforceable. Obviously a "Cliff, quit
climbing on the furniture or I'll break both your legs" is tough to
support with action. It may be good for the shock effect, but your
kids know you won't really exact such a heavy toll, not the first

136

time, anyway. Once more, both you and they are left to surmise what you'll really do should you be tested. You're forcing yourself to decide upon legitimate consequences *after* the problem occurs rather than *before*, not nearly as potent a deterrent. Additionally, promising spectacular discipline can paint you into a corner, especially if for once your little one believes you. A client had a four-year-old who liked to use her crayons on furniture instead of in coloring books. After the second or third colorful incident, Dad exploded, "If you ever color on this table again, you're going to eat it." A few mornings later Dad awoke to find his little Michelle Angelo spreading butter all over the coffee table. Why? Having again scribbled where she shouldn't, Michelle said that if she was going to have to eat the table, she wanted butter on it 'cause she liked butter. Stick to consequences you can carry out. Your kids will have fewer doubts that you're speaking with conviction.

6. It takes practice to think of effective *if-then's*. Therefore, don't feel defeated if for a while your kids can act quicker than you can think. In time, you'll become adept at anticipating problem behavior and intercepting it with an *if-then*. Until you do, whenever you're unable to formulate a good *if-then* right when you need it, hold off intervening for a few minutes. Don't say anything until you have one. Certainly, this won't always be possible—for example, when Leif is yanking up your plants by the fistful or when Derrick is holding his little sister upside down until she agrees to his terms. But in most situations, you have no such urgency to act. Stopping to conceive your *if-then* before you talk will keep you from resorting to nagging for want of a better approach.

Since coming up with useful *if-then's* is a skill that is well-worth practicing, I can offer you the following step-by-step procedure to help start you on the track toward successful *if-thening*.

A. List three problem behaviors you have not been able to curb. Make sure they are *specific* behaviors (for example, throwing food, swearing, smacking siblings) and not general personality descriptions (eating like a barbarian, having a trash mouth, acting like a bully).
B. Make "if" statements about these behaviors. "If you throw food at the table…" "If you say that word again…"
C. List five activities and five things your child likes. If you're having trouble with this, ask yourself, "If it were completely up to my child, how would he spend his time?" Make the activities specific. For example, if he watches TV, what are his favorite shows?

137

D. Examine both lists with the idea of linking them together in *if-then* statements from which your child will realize that his privileges and pleasures depend upon responsible behavior. In addition to involving a favorite pursuit, optimum *if-then's* have to meet a few other criteria:

1. Does the *then* happen close in time to the *if*? If not, better to use another *then*. As much as Chester might relish watching reruns of *Gunsmoke*, telling him he won't be able to watch it next Friday as he's about to flog his sister on Sunday afternoon won't carry the same deterrent power as something you can enforce *now*.

2. Is your *then* something you can do without putting hardship on you or the rest of the family? Even if shopping is Penny's preferred activity, cancelling an evening's mall outing to punish vulgar language is not the best *then* if it punishes other eager shoppers— you included.

3. Ask yourself: How might Penny try to outsmart me on this? Anticipating any escalation of misbehavior in response to your new style will further prepare you to handle calmly any trouble that occurs over and above the initial problem.

E. Present your *if-then's* to your youngster—*now*. Don't wait for problem behavior to occur. You will not only verbally commit yourself to handling misbehavior differently next time if happens, you will also have the opportunity to explain your plan in a warm, logical manner, free from the potential pressure of a disciplining moment.

7. One last point: After all is said and done, be ready for resistance from your kids. If you've been an inveterate nagger, your kids no doubt have acclimated well to your style. They gauge their behavior by it. They're not about to accept any drastic changes readily. One mother told me that when she began using *if-then's*, her son disgustedly retorted, "You never used to do this before. You've been talking to the psychologist again."

As many as are the pitfalls of nagging, so are the benefits of stating your wishes only once. First and foremost, you completely short-circuit the escalating cycle of words and emotions that so often accompanies nagging. You avoid the unhappy and ugly endings of a tiresome nag trip. Second, you appropriately place the responsibility for acting squarely where it belongs—with your youngster. You cease to be the reverberating machine that bombards him with words, trying to wrench his cooperation. Third, while you may initially expend more energy carrying out your chosen consequences, once you and your kids catch on to your new style, the effort both of you will be spared will be immense.

Of course, you might be one of those ever-so-fortunate parents who say but one word and your kids listen. You don't need *if-then's*. Consequences are unnecessary when words are sufficient. *If-then's* are most valuable if you've been hearing yourself drift into a nagging addiction or if you are already badly addicted and want to withdraw. Then the message of this whole section is for you: *If* at first your words don't succeed, *then* try acting.

Driving the Folks Mad
or *"I have to get mad; then he listens."*

Once, at about age eight, I was deeply immersed in some backyard activity when my mother's voice rudely invaded my space, calling me to the house for some silly interruption like supper or a bath. Well, as the old saying goes, once is not enough, so I stayed glued to my pursuits. Again my mother beckoned. This time I gave her the courtesy of an "OK, Mom," figuring that would temporarily put her off and buy me more time outside. It did, but it was soon followed by other, more adamant callings, as I slowly edged closer to the house. Within minutes, my younger sister emerged from the back door, warning, "You better get in here; mommy said a bad word." That was my cue to move. I had finally received a sure sign that my mother had reached her limit.

Kids sense with uncanny precision how angry a parent has to be before he or she means business. And generally, kids don't move until a parent means business. *I get mad—then you listen* is a two-way, self-perpetuating loop. It traps you into having to lose your cool to be heard, and it urges your kids to stay oblivious until you do overheat. Granted, a vocal or emotional frenzy may periodically provoke some results in the sense that your kids will at least respond to you. But even so, the price paid for being caught in this loop is heavy, for everybody concerned.

First of all, the angrier you become, the more likely you are to say things you'll later wish you could unsay. You might verbally flail your child's character or dole out hefty doses of shame and condemnation, in front of his friends no less. Or perhaps you'll mouth threats that after simmering down you'll have no intention, or even wherewithal, to enforce. Can you *really* deny John bathroom privileges for a week because he left his underwear on the floor again? Then, too, you may fire forth absolute accusations like "You *never* listen to anything I say," or "You *always* want *everything* your way." Such all-or-nothing declarations are seldom true; they only arouse defensiveness and more resistance. Words said in anger all too often are words remembered with regret.

Second, as anger goes up, credibility goes down. Your point may be well taken, but it is obscured by so much verbal and emotional turbulence that it loses impact. Your kids, even should they want to listen, may not be sure what you're actually saying. To better understand this point, picture yourself as a clerk in the complaint department of a large store. Customer A returns a defective garden hose and in a tirade tells you how worthless the whole store is. He blusters that if he doesn't receive immediate and full remuneration, he plans to have his attorney pay a visit to the owner, the manager, and even you if he has to, and on and on. Right behind him, Customer B, shoddy garden hose in hand, approaches you politely and in a steady voice says that he has had similar problems with defective merchandise from the store in the past. He hopes the store will rectify the problem or he will cease to shop there and will tell his friends of his bad experiences. Now, who are you going to take more seriously? Even if Customer A actually planned to sue the store and everybody in it, you'd probably give him less credence because he was so agitated as he spoke. Your youngster perceives your reactions the same way. She will be much more willing to count on your words when you show her you are in full command of yourself as you say them.

A third cost of the *I get mad-then you listen* loop concerns some unexpected properties of anger. Your emotional upheaval, as unpleasant as it might seem to you, can be rewarding to your youngster. It tells him: "Look how upset you can make me with your behavior. I'm at your mercy; you act bad and I get mad." Your youngster may not enjoy facing your wrath, but he may still continue his irksome behavior if he sees it can adjust your emotional idle. Putting up with anger or even discipline may be quite acceptable in return for the power to temporarily drive the folks mad.

Anger rewards kids another way: The more upset you become, the less you are able to plan ahead and pursue some course of discipline evenly. Your kids will no doubt recognize the advantages of keeping you off-balance and thrashing about for a discipline response. When you're mad, you're easier to out-think. A fourth toll of this self-sustaining cycle relates to energy output. Emotional outbursts, especially when they are prolonged, can be quite tiring. Make a pattern of swelling toward an emotional peak every time you want results and you'll soon begin to ignore or tolerate much that you shouldn't, for the sake of saving your sanity. If the price of asserting your authority is an unpleasant emotional climb, then it will truly get progressively easier "just to let him go." But as we observed in Chapter 5, this rationale will steer you onto its own exhausting course. We will shortly consider other ways to achieve better results at a fraction of the energy cost.

The final futility is that over time even anger loses power. It elicits less and less attention. If your children have become "tone-deaf" to normal tones of voice, and you've steadily had to turn up your volume to be heard, what's to say they won't become tone-deaf to your anger? A parallel can be drawn to developing tolerance to a drug. Tolerance is the process of needing increasing amounts of a substance to achieve the same reaction. The body habituates, or grows accustomed, to doses that used to produce effects. So it is with anger. To get a reaction from your kids, you will have to suffer higher and higher doses, with the cycle propagating itself to excessive levels.

So you see, the *I get mad—then you listen* habit is destructive, draining, self-perpetuating, and ultimately unworkable. The key word here is *habit*. Certainly, you will experience many infuriating moments as you raise your kids. My guess is that the average parent traverses the emotional spectrum 136 times per child per year of child-rearing. In fact, getting upset has its benefits. For instance, it is one surefire way of communicating to your youngster exactly where you stand on certain behaviors. Problems develop when anger becomes a style, when getting upset is your main means of discipline. Then you are stuck within the nagging-anger loop. Fortunately, you do have ways out.

One way out we have already discussed. You can become proficient with *if-then's*. By short-circuiting nagging at the outset, *if-then's* automatically shut down the entire nagging-anger cycle. Your words will have meaning the first time without your needing to underline them with rage. And even when an *if-then* doesn't bring about the results you had hoped for, it will still keep you from escalating from speaking to yelling, because your second step is not more emotion, it is action.

Of course, not always will you use an *if-then* the very first time you speak. Often, you may hear yourself mouthing an appeal three or four times, then sensing beginning anger pangs. It's never too late to halt mushrooming anger with an *if-then*. Each time you do it, it will leave you a bit more sensitive to your emotional state next time. In other words, you will learn to stop yourself progressively earlier in the nagging-anger cycle.

Another means of snapping this no-end loop is through rules. In nearly every household, much nagging and tension is caused by a few main problem areas—carelessness with toys, backtalk, shirking chores or homework, agitating siblings. To keep from harping at Waldo every other minute for repeated misbehaviors, draw up a set of rules with consequences and rewards. Post your rules in a popular place, such as the refrigerator door or the TV screen. Suppose a chronic sore spot is Waldo's failure to be home at the required time. You might pass a new rule: For each minute late this time, five minutes home earlier next time. One week of perfect rule adherence leads to a half hour of extra outside time or TV time of Waldo's choice. For an elaboration of the rules system, refer to the case of Phillip in Chapter 5 (see "How the Story Ended," item 19). The main function of rules is to rid you and your youngster of the habit of constantly rehashing the same problems day after day, word after word, clash after clash.

The nagging-anger loop feeds upon itself. The more you use it, the more your kids will make you use it. Like every other self-defeating discipline cycle, the first step in breaking out is to recognize what you're doing. The second step is to work hard to replace old, diehard habits with fresh, workable approaches.

Addenda
or "Come here...now...right this minute...
I mean it...Do I have to start counting?"

Thus far, we've been stressing an inescapable reality of discipline: Words aren't always enough. But this is a lesson you most likely learned early in your parenthood as you watched an ample percentage of your words falling on deaf ears. What was worse, the percentage seemed to be steadily rising! Something, you decided, had to be done about this unacceptable trend. Somehow you needed to give your words more "oomph." So, if you're like most parents, you developed addenda. What are addenda? They are words attached to the end of a request, directive, or prohibition, designed to tell a child that she'd better listen this time because you aren't just idly talking. Or, to put it another way, addenda are more words added to your words. Being a one-of-a-kind parent, you probably coined some one-of-a-kind addenda, your own unique tack-on's for commanding attention. A few addenda, however, are particularly popular and are versatile enough to be shared by everybody. Let's see which ones they are...now!

ADDENDUM #1: *NOW*. This succinct command can be annexed instantly and conclusively to any statement in imminent danger of being ignored. Generally, it is spoken with more force than the words preceding it. "Please come here...*now*." "Take your glass into the kitchen, please...*now*." "Close the bathroom door...*now*." *Now* is intended to be a clarifier. It tells Noelle you'd like her to take her glass into the kitchen not after the late, late show, not the day after tomorrow, not on Christmas, but this very moment. Understandably, you want Noelle to grasp your time frame fully. The only problem is, she already does. She's not remaining immobile because she thinks she doesn't have to budge until her eighteenth birthday. She's remaining immobile because she hasn't yet received the standard six warnings or sensed you getting sufficiently riled. To Noelle, *now* is a clarifier of a different sort; it's a cue that you're on the verge of anger or that if she doesn't act, you will.

Like getting angry to be heard, punctuating your words with *now* is a tempting trap in that *now* does get some results— for a while. But in time it falls the way of all nagging words: It loses impact. Louder and more emphatic *now*'s are needed to evoke the same degree of motion from your kids.

An even greater disadvantage of *now* lies in its unintended impression: "When I say *now*, I expect you to respond. Otherwise, you can take your time until I get upset." Temporarily, *now* may emphasize anything it follows, but it simultaneously lessens the authority of like statements said without it.

Substitutes for *now* include right now, right this minute, right this second (instant, moment), immediately, at once, pronto. All can be used interchangeably, and all needlessly encumber your discipline.

ADDENDUM #2: *I MEAN IT.* Whereas *now* is added to emphasize time, *I mean it* is added to emphasize resolve. It tells a youngster you're not just talking to hear yourself talk. Whatever you said you fully intended to say. The main snag here, once again, lies in your unspoken message: "Whenever I *don't* reinforce my words with this telltale marker, I don't mean them quite so much. Therefore, they can be more safely ignored." Is this really what you mean to say, or, more exactly, not to say?

The cliché "Say what you mean and mean what you say" provides one sound guideline for disciplining. Words that are meant don't need to be repeated or followed by more words to be convincing. They are clear in themselves. On the other hand, words that aren't meant can't be infused with purpose no matter how much extra talk accompanies them. If your youngster repeatedly sees that you don't support your words with action if need be, even *I mean it* will quickly come to mean you really don't mean it.

Variants: I'm not kidding, I'm serious, I'm not joking, this is the last time I'm saying this, I'm not going to repeat myself, don't make me tell you again.

ADDENDUM #3: *COUNTING.* This also is a time-frame addendum. While the time frame for *now* is immediate, counting allows for a shade more flexibility, depending of course on how high you count and how fast. The two most popular counts are to three (favored with younger children) and ten (metric-system alternative, preferred with strong-willed children). Counting, in effect, says: "You have a certain period of time before I'll repeat myself, get upset, or act." Counting may be the most alluring of all addenda for it does seem to work so well at first. But its minuses outweigh its pluses.

One, counting generates the conditions for a contest of wills. Who can outlast whom? And even when parents prevail, nearly every child waits until the split second prior to the final bell before he complies. Thus he says: "OK, I'll cooperate, but not until I absolutely have to." As with any countdown, as the numbers roll, the tension rises.

Two, what happens when the magic three or ten is spoken and Conroy is still doing exactly as he was back at one? Kids being kids, you can count on this inevitably happening. Unless you have a backup plan upon reaching your final number, the whole system is valuable only for its effect as a bluff. Remember one of the guidelines for using *if-then's:* The more specific the better. Counting is a vague *if-then.* It translates: "If you don't respond by the time I'm done counting, something is going to happen." But what? I knew a grandmother who had a counting ritual for calling her grandchildren into the house. She would stand at the back door, beckon a few times, then begin a ten-count. In the early days of the count, by eight or nine the kids would start scurrying for the door. But one fateful day, grandmother found herself closing in upon ten and nothing was happening. As the kids let the final bell toll, Grandmother puzzled over what to do next. She called more loudly, threatened a bit, and finally stormed back into the house. She had fallen victim to a risk common to playing the numbers. She let the count itself become her discipline, thereby neglecting to develop any consequences should her numbers come to naught.

Three, counting outlives its usefulness as children pass age four or five. As I noted above, counting works better with younger children who are more apprehensive of the unknown—that is, what follows three or ten. But even with preschoolers, counting eventually evolves into a means of dragging out discipline.

What is my advice about addenda? Not unexpectedly, my first suggestion is to drop them from your discipline vocabulary. Certainly an occasional *I mean it* or *pronto* may be good for emphasis, but the danger lies in their becoming a blossoming habit. Therefore, it's probably best to go cold turkey with addenda, a process that may be painful, especially if your addenda are still working some percentage of the time. But if you have something to take their place, you'll find you won't even miss them when they're gone.

What's to substitute for these familiar standbys? Two alternatives you've already read about. Both *if-then's* and rules serve quite nicely to get you heard without piling word upon word. As noted earlier, rules are especially helpful when a problem behavior occurs seemingly on the hour. Much of the time that kids misbehave they're not really sure what your response will be, and they're willing to take their chances. By eliminating the guesswork over your reaction, rules help a child resist the temptation to act for the moment and worry about the consequences later. So if Noelle consistently abandons her glasses and plates in front of the TV, you might tell her that in the future, whenever you discover her clutter, you'll call her back from wherever she is—outside, at a friend's, on the phone—to clean it up. Such predictable approaches will lend more meaning to your initially calm requests than one hundred *I mean it's* or *now's*.

My argument against using addenda is not an argument for expecting your kids to jump the moment your last word clears your lips. Alas, parents should have such fortune. Almost all kids seem to have a built-in delay switch that kicks in whenever parents speak.* And although resorting to addenda may initially shorten a child's reaction time, in the long run it only adds excess verbal baggage detrimental to your efforts at decisive discipline.

Putting Discipline in Question
or *"Don't you think we'd better not ask too many questions?"*

"Don't you think you've had enough candy?" "Isn't it time to start your homework?" "Why don't you put your bike away?" These questions all have one thing in common: They're not really questions. The parents aren't actually seeking the children's candid answers, for if they were, they might hear something like: "No, I don't think I've had enough candy." "As far as I'm concerned, it's never time to start my homework." "I'm not putting my bike away because I'm counting on you to do it for me, dad." Each question is in fact a statement. Translated, they say: "I think you've had enough candy." "It's time to start your homework." "Please put your bike away."

By all means, if you can make clear your wishes and

---

*I did once read about a boy whose reaction time to his parents' words was less than a second. He is currently being studied at a leading university's center for rare phenomena.

146

expectations indirectly through questions, no need to change your style. Enjoy your status as one of those few truly blessed parents whose youngster obliges with "You're right, mom, I believe I have had enough candy," or "Oh my, thank you for reminding me. It is past time to begin my homework." But if you're in league with most parents, questions are at best a questionable way to get action. They may seem a "nicer" way to state your message, but much more often than not they don't suffice, and you're forced to take a more direct route and *quite* explicitly assert your wishes. As a rule, questions not only tend to go unanswered, they tend to go unheeded.

So what's one good way to keep your questions from becoming forerunners of nagging? Simple—don't ask them. Since you're not really seeking an answer anyway, you lose nothing by bypassing the question and moving straight to its translation. Doing so has two major advantages. First, you greatly clarify what you are saying. You're not seeking an opinion; you're giving one. If your desire for Candy to limit her sugar intake to four pounds per sitting is nonnegotiable, you want to convey that plainly. Questions do exactly the opposite; they communicate the impression that the sugar ceiling is open for discussion. After all, you asked for Candy's input, didn't you? Second, you will be less likely to be underestimated. Your youngster may interpret a question as a sign of weak commitment to a particular issue. This in turn can lead to apathy on his part. Your conviction doesn't seem solid, so why should he rush to respond?

One other line of discipline questioning bears mentioning. That is the "I'll put myself in your boat" query. Samples are: "Don't you think we've had enough candy?" "Isn't it time for us to start our homework?" In addition to the previously mentioned problems inherent in "question discipline," this style has yet another drawback. It can be heard as insincere, as an insult to your child's intelligence. However much you may want to share Candy's burden (at least in words), I don't think she'll see your good intentions. She knows *you* don't have to do what you're asking her to do. You don't have homework; you're not eating candy. Why, then, are you including yourself in her hardship? Better, once again, simply to state your position. Without question, you'll lower the likelihood of misunderstanding. Have we made ourselves clear on this point?

Bargaining
or *"Let's make a deal."*

Rewarding a youngster for his behavior is a cornerstone of good parenting. Praise, compliments, attention, privileges, allowances—these are but a handful of the innumerable ways to show a child you're pleased with how he handles himself. In psychology jargon, such practices are called *reinforcement,* and they constitute a most powerful means of encouraging behavior you'd like to see more of. But there is one reinforcement practice in particular that will backfire on you. That is the practice of *bargaining.*

Bargaining differs from smart reinforcement in a number of dimensions. First of all, bargaining does not reward desirable behavior; it rewards the ceasing of undesirable. The difference is not semantic; it is crucial. Essentially, the bargain struck is this: "You stop acting so unpleasantly, and I'll give you something." For instance, little Horton, performing a patented grocery store checkout-line tantrum, is promised a pack of gum if he cancels today's performance, at least until he reaches the car. With bargaining, the reward becomes available only after the misbehavior has begun. (I've always wondered if checkout lines are bordered by candy and gum displays to provide easy access to the stuff of negotiation.)

Second, the most powerful types of reinforcement are not material in nature. They consist of intangibles—a smile, a compliment, a show of pleasure. Besides being more socially beneficial and enduring, nonmaterial rewards also happen to be less expensive. On the other hand, bargaining *is* expensive. It almost always involves dispensing some material payoff. When was the last time you heard yourself or another parent promise, "Bunny, if you stop nagging me to buy honey-coated carrot crunchies, I'll pay you a compliment"? Bargaining convinces a child she deserves to be reimbursed for regaining control of herself. Savvy reinforcement in no way resembles bribery, but bargaining does.

A third difference concerns timing. Rewards can be given at any time and place, freely. But bargaining usually occurs under duress, while a child is acting obnoxious away from home and in the presence of others. These conditions exert intense pressure on you to get the situation under control *immediately*, thus making you highly vulnerable to bargaining. You reward because you want to; you bargain because you feel you have to.

The dominant argument against bargaining, however, is that it is self-sustaining. The more you bargain, the more you have to bargain. While bargaining may calm the present storm, it actually spawns more frequent and severe future storms. Any youngster who thinks a few steps ahead—and this is *every* youngster—will realize that a pack of gum is only a temper blast away. All he has to do is become unmanageable at the right place and time and he will begin the chain of events leading to a bargain. In short, you're training your child to blackmail you. Bargaining reinforces the very behavior you are trying to get rid of.

Instead of bargaining your way to momentary peace *after* a storm has started, a better alternative is clearly to tell Horton consequences of a storm *before* it begins. This will take some looking ahead, but I'm sure you suffer regular reminders of where your bargaining trouble spots are. And even when Horton's behavior catches you by surprise, spurring strong temptation to bargain, you can still replace any dickering with an exact statement of your position. Promptly tell Horton what will happen if he continues his behavior. And that's not negotiable!

Should you also want to use material rewards to show your appreciation for Horton's mature store conduct, certainly do so. I'm not suggesting you shouldn't. However, these tangibles would be more productive if you awarded them on a *variable-ratio* schedule. Translated into shirt-sleeve English, this high-sounding term means you reward every so often. Most potent of reward schedules, the *variable-ratio* is the one on which slot machines are based. A player never knows when he'll hit the jackpot. It may be one try in six, it may be one in twenty. Nevertheless, he keeps trying, anxious that his stick-to-itiveness will pay off. Similarly, if every so often you give Horton a treat in appreciation of his behavior, you'll accomplish two things. You'll be encouraging him to try harder, and you'll be teaching him that he won't be "paid" each and every time he acts with social grace.

As a final offer, if you stop bargaining with your kids, send me proof of purchase of this book along with a self-addressed stamped envelope and I'll send you a pack of gum of your choice!

Delegating Authority
or "Wait until your father gets home."

The cornerstone of successful counseling with children and adolescents is the forming of an open, trusting relationship. In whatever way possible, I try to show the kids I value them as persons. But every so often my therapeutic relationship gets used untherapeutically. That is, a well-meaning parent will try to curtail his youngster's misconduct by promising to "tell Dr. Ray" all about it during the next visit. This is done in the hope that the child, who supposedly desires to stay in my good graces, will thereby be motivated to straighten his course. Aside from not having the braking effect the parent desires, such promises cast me in the unwanted role of the "heavy." They also do little to enhance the parent's own authority.

Similar dynamics underlie the old discipline line, "Wait till your father gets home." Of course, as traditional parenting roles overlap, more kids are probably being confronted with "Wait till I tell your mother." Such lines warn of stern measures yet to be meted out by a parent who wasn't even present when the crime transpired. They set the other parent up to do the dirty work without firsthand knowledge of what actually happened. He or she literally walks in and has to discipline.

Certainly, you will want to discuss many incidents with your spouse before taking action. Maybe little Felina ate the cat's food again, and you'd like two heads to converge in solving this distasteful dilemma. Much of the time, however, misconduct is the stuff of day-to-day parenting and can be handled on the spot by the parent present. It doesn't require waiting for the absentee parent to serve as the enforcer.

Regularly deferring action to your spouse gives your youngster the impression that you lack confidence in your own judgment and authority. And ultimately, this will tempt him to challenge you more, especially in the absence of your enforcer. When you leave your discipline to another, you may escape appearing the meanie for a little while, but you will soon find yourself battling the urge to be mean as you are pushed more and harder.

One other point to consider before you delegate your authority. Delegation encourages "credit-card behavior"—that is, "act now, pay later." Anyone who uses a credit card knows that purchasing something gets easier the farther away the payment. Would your long-distance calls last as long if you had to pay for each minute as you talked? Similarly, kids are much more willing to shop for trouble now if the price of their spree comes later today or maybe even tomorrow, when the bill collector comes home.

You work too hard at maintaining your authority to give it away. Authority is best shared equally with your spouse. But delegation is not equal sharing; it is unequal and unfair sharing. Deal with what behavior you can when it occurs. And *share* your discipline when you deem it necessary. Your credibility with your child will rise, and your use of your authority will decline.

Discipline Debates
or "Let's argue about this later, when the kids are around."

A client once summarized his failing relationship with his girlfriend by saying, "We're so incompatible we have nothing in common to argue about." If you and your spouse have children, this is one statement that can never be made about your relationship. You do have something in common to argue about—child-rearing. In fact, if you never disagree about how to raise your kids, you're not typical.

Some child-rearing experts advise that it's all right to air parenting differences in front of the kids. It shows them you're individuals and reveals your true feelings about certain issues. Other experts caution that such open conflicts are an absolute parenting no-no because they inevitably spawn detrimental two-or-three-against-one alliances. My position is somewhere between these two poles, leaning more toward the "save the debates for later" side.

Debating discipline within a youngster's earshot does not necessarily court trouble. The crucial qualification is that your debates be a rational, respectful, and mutual mulling-over of

151

alternatives, and not individual attacks on each other's methods. Give-and-take debating can indeed help your kids accept that you and your spouse have your own styles and opinions, along with distinctive parenting features such as boiling point, panic-button sensitivity, and voice volume. Debates are even less risky if you clearly show your children that although Mom and Dad don't always see eye to eye, each will back the other's discipline. For instance, say your house phone limit is fifteen minutes. Your wife, having listened to a busy signal for more than an hour while she was stranded in the rain with a comatose car, has just revoked Belle's phone privileges for five days. (And just where were you during this telethon?) Even though you might think her action all wet, as long as you present your view reasonably, and stand by your spouse's decision if she resolves to stand by it, you won't send Belle a signal to fight her disconnection notice.

On the other hand, the case *against* discipline debates is compelling if the debate torpedoes either parent's authority. Destructive debates most often occur when one parent tries to make the other retract a spoken decision or appear ill-natured and unfeeling for upholding it. They happen less directly but just as efficiently when one spouse later undoes the other's discipline by overturning or compensating for it. Getting back to Belle, still being held incommunicado, you can nullify your wife's decision by letting Belle use the phone when Mom's not home, by letting her abuse it after the five-day moratorium ends, or by excessively commiserating with her during the punishment period. Any of these maneuvers gives Belle a plain message: "Resist your mother's disciplne, and you gain an ally in me. I'll side with you if I disagree with her." And Belle's resistance can take many paths. She may target more complaints about your spouse toward you; she may do heavier verbal battle with her mother—after all, Belle's counting on you to feel the same way she does; she will probably appeal to you to overturn her mother's decisions (more about this in Chapter 7); she may heap affections on you to punish your spouse. Ironically, once Belle learns to play one parent against the other resourcefully, what's to say you'll always be the preferred parent? Make some discipline move Belle doesn't approve of, and you could abruptly find yourself on the outnumbered end of a discipline debate, with your spouse partaking vengefully because for once she isn't the picked-on parent.

Another argument against torpedo debates is that one parent is left to be the villain. Most likely, the discipline, however much you disagree with it, was well intended. Your disputing it openly conveys to your kids that your spouse did what he did primarily to abuse power. Even if his decision was premature, or a bit strict, or even unfair, his motivation was still probably your child's welfare. He may have made a mistake; he didn't deliberately try to be nasty. Talk over differences later, in private. Your spouse will be more open to other viewpoints when the whole family isn't ganging up on him.

So often a parent feels the urge to contest a spouse's discipline immediately because she thinks it is poorly timed, overreacting, inconsistent, and so on. In other words, the discipline is seen as "psychologically wrong." And the wrong must be instantly blocked or rectified lest it provoke "emotional damage." In my experience, I believe it safe to say that far more trouble is triggered by one parent undercutting the other than by a poorly thought-out or "incorrect" decision. Further, in any given situation the range of useful parenting moves is quite broad, and what is considered incorrect by one parent merely represents a difference in approach. A youngster will better accept and benefit from discipline if he believes Mom and Dad concur on it. On the other hand, no matter how fair or appropriate the discipline, if a child senses the folks are divided, the house may be conquered. (Recall the case of Brian and Marc in Chapter 3.)

Talking over discipline privately also provides a more productive forum for ironing out broad differences in parenting philosophy. What you may define as harsh or ill-conceived discipline your spouse may define as legitimate and appropriate. If so, undermining her in front of your kids or anybody else will probably only draw the battle lines further apart and make each of you cling more stubbornly to your positions. Far better to discuss philosophies when you're alone, with a "let's discuss our differences and settle on a strategy we both can live with" attitude. You'll stand a better chance of compromising and agreeing on plans to correct future misbehavior with a united front.

The best discipline can be rendered totally ineffective if sabotaged by either spouse. If your debates become "I'm right— you're wrong" confrontations, not only will both you and your spouse lose authority but your kids will adeptly find ways to keep you subverting each other.

One More Time...

Much that is thought to be discipline is not discipline at all. Nagging, questioning, bargaining, addenda—all are futile, self-perpetuating illusions of authority. Recognizing when and how you depend upon these forms of "discipline" is the first step to weaning yourself and your kids from them. Simple alternatives— *if-then's,* rules, anticipating misbehavior—constitute actual discipline. They are more straightforward, effective, and benevolent. Using them is like developing any skill. With practice comes ease, comfort, and confidence.

Homework

1. Ask someone who spends time with your family (for example, a spouse, grandparent, or neighbor) to choose a day (or days) in the next few weeks to count your nags. Have that person keep a running total of how many times you say something before you (1) get a response, (2) drop the issue, or (3) act. The critical requirement is that you should be aware neither of the day nor of the counting. Add the totals; take an average. I think you'll be surprised at the number of wasted words.

2. Ask the same person to listen for the number of nags that pass before you become angry. Your aim is to identify at what point in the nagging-anger loop you make the transition from talking to emotion. Again, take an average. This will provide valuable information about your own personal nagging-anger index.

7

Reacting to Discipline: A Child's Handbook

Talking yourself out of authority is one sure path to reduced parent status (Chapter 5). Self-sabotaging discipline is another (Chapter 6). But even if you stop being the main cause of your own undoing, you still have to contend with other formidable causes: your kids. After all, you're not the only one in the family with a personal interest in how you discipline. Your children too have at least one representative at every disciplinary meeting, a representative who wants input, verbal or otherwise, into what you're doing. Quite often, believe it or not, your kids will see your point, or at least reluctantly go along. Then again, just as often they won't concur with your proposals, and they will let you know that loud and strong. These are the times when disciplining is hardest, when you are most prone to give to your kids the authority that is yours. Truly, these are the times that try parents' souls.

Many have said often that children want discipline, the security of knowing there are those who care enough about them to help them master their struggle toward self-control and responsibility. I agree with this observation, but I think it needs one crucial qualification. Yes, kids do want discipline—over the long run, that is. But when the discipline is actually taking place, when children are being required to conform to rules or to answer for their actions, they don't always want discipline or appreciate it, and they will expend much energy opposing it. How kids challenge your authority and show their displeasure over discipline will be the focus of this chapter.

Escalation
or *"Don't discipline me, I'll get worse."*

Let's begin with kids' preferred and most disconcerting way to resist discipline: escalation. What is escalation? Essentially, escalation is an increase in nastiness, unmanageability, or misconduct in response to discipline. Or to put it another way, escalation is acting more undisciplined in the face of discipline.

Escalation comes in all forms and degrees. It is limited only by a child's creativity and knowledge of his parents' pressure points. A few samples should give you a taste of this phenomenon, although I'm sure if you have at least one child, you've seen it firsthand many times. Escalation is the four-year-old who, when placed in a corner chair for his transgression, (a) refuses to sit there, (b) sees which foot can kick the wall harder, (c) turns around fourteen times to give you fourteen reasons why he shouldn't be there, (d) screams at 110 decibels, (e) all of the above, (f) and then some. Escalation is the ten-year-old who, when bedtime arrives right in the middle of a movie you told her at the outset she wouldn't be able to finish watching, (a) throws an Oscar-winning fit, (b) unleashes a flurry of R-rated language, (c) drop-kicks the cat on her way to the bedroom, and (d) slams the bedroom door hard enough to wake all of her younger siblings and some of the kids next door, too.

The above are concocted, albeit representative, samples of escalation. But the following is a real-life example of one of the most intense bouts of escalation I've ever witnessed. Greg was a twelve-year-old boy in a special class for children with behavior problems. During a class group discussion, Greg took a small truck from his coat pocket and began running it along his desk, making assorted truck noises. The teacher asked Greg to please put the truck away. He refused (escalation #1). Whereupon she offered him a choice: Please put the truck away or lose it for the day. Again Greg balked, starting to argue that he could play with his truck and still listen (escalation #2). The teacher calmly walked toward Greg to take the truck, but he hastily jammed it back into his pocket. Wisely, the teacher pushed the issue no further and continued with the group discussion. Greg, though, wasn't about to quit; he wanted, shall we say, to keep on trucking. As soon as the teacher's attention was elsewhere, Greg threw the truck, nearly hitting a nearby classmate (escalation #3). Retrieving the toy, the teacher told Greg to go to the Time-Out chair in the corner for one hour, the classroom rule for throwing things. Once more, Greg upped the ante by refusing to move (escalation #4). At this point I offered Greg a choice: Walk to the Time-Out chair willingly and spend one hour there, or be moved bodily and spend one and a half hours there. He thought briefly and, seeing we meant business, slowly edged towards the chair. En route, though, he collapsed "fainting" to the floor (escalation #5). I should mention that Greg often used "fainting spells" as passive resistance to any rules he didn't like. The spells generally worked at home, but we gave them no power at school.

As long as Greg wasn't bothering anybody, we decided to allow him to spend his one hour in Time-Out on the floor, if he so wished. But after some minutes, Greg tired of lying down, arose, and with one full-armed swoop flung every article on the teacher's desk to the floor (escalation #6). I told Greg he would be responsible for cleaning all messes, but first he owed the teacher one and a half hours in Time-Out, and I would hold him there if need be. At that point, ideally, we should have removed Greg from the room. The class was an audience, and he was performing. But we kept Greg in class for a number of reasons. One, we had no other place in the school to put him where he'd stay. Two, we didn't want to send him home because that's exactly why he was practicing escalation. And three, we wanted to maintain Greg in the classroom, something no other teachers had been able to do successfully, as you can see why. If Greg couldn't adjust in this class, the next step was complete removal from a public-school setting.

After about half an hour of being restrained, Greg asked to spend his remaining time under his own control. I agreed, with the provision that I would resume holding him if he couldn't hold himself. For about ten minutes, Greg sat quietly; then he vomited—another behavior he used often to comment on rules (escalation #7). Getting no one's attention (the teacher, the other kids, and I had seen the vomiting before, and we all knew we had to ignore it), Greg began a barrage of verbal abuse (escalation #8). We maintained our oblivion, although it was getting harder. His anger feeding upon itself, Greg then knocked over a bookshelf, along with several desks (escalation #9). That, of course, couldn't be allowed to continue, so I resumed restraining Greg.

Deciding to remove Greg's audience, and also because the class was fighting nausea as Greg vomited a second time, the teacher took the kids and headed for another room. This did calm Greg somewhat. The volume of his verbal barrage tapered, and he finished his time in the corner. But he still had a score of cleaning jobs to do. Even while cleaning, Greg vomited twice more, flung over the remaining upright desks, crumpled most of his homework papers, and threatened to put his fist through a TV monitor and a window (escalations #10 through #18). All through Hurricane Greg, I essentially stood aside and watched, wanting to keep Greg's escalation from becoming a power struggle between him and me. When the storm had finally blown over, nearly three hours had passed. However, before he left for the day, Greg had straightened the room, apologized to his teacher, his classmates, and me, and carried several pages of homework home.[24]

I doubt you'll ever be the target of escalation as severe as that practiced by Greg. He was a youngster with problems other than behavioral. But his example does raise an important question about escalation: Why do kids do it? Primarily for two reasons. One, it's natural for kids to get upset when someone puts bounds on their impulses and desires. And sometimes this upset bursts forth as nastiness, destruction, aggression, or other misconduct. For the most part, such escalation is the reactive type. It is born of anger and frustration. This certainly doesn't excuse escalation, but it does make it more understandable and less shocking. To put it simply, one reason kids escalate is because they're unhappy with what's being imposed upon them.

The second force behind escalation usually evolves from the first. That is, although escalation initially springs from discontent, a youngster may soon discover that escalation has built-in benefits: It works. At this point her behavior becomes more calculated. Essentially, the idea is to act as bad as necessary to escape rules and limits, and to hope that Mom and Dad will opt for "peace at any price." The hazard of this "I escalate, you yield" style is that it will feed upon itself until it becomes a youngster's prime response to any form of discipline. Greg was a classic, if scary, example of the limits to which a youngster will go to get around limits. Beginning in his toddlerhood, Greg tried to escape his parents' efforts to socialize him. Initially his resistance was slight, but it occurred so regularly that his parents capitulated regularly, thus unwittingly asking for more escalation. Over a period of years, what began as crying and pouting gradually phased into temper outbursts, then destructiveness, then even physical assault, coupled with the fainting, vomiting, and other eccentricities Greg developed along the way. By the time I met him, Greg was well prepared to make life for his folks as miserable as need be to keep himself on top of any discipline. Greg's sticking power had grown stronger as his parents' had declined.

Again, you'll probably never confront the degree of rebellion that Greg's parents confronted daily. It takes time and hefty doses of parental cooperation for such an out-of-control state of affairs to evolve. But without a doubt, if your kids are kids they will periodically try to one-up your discipline. You will be better prepared for escalation by being aware of some of the factors that increase its likelihood.

The first is a child's temperament. As I have emphasized throughout this book, some kids are born more active or strong-minded or aggressive than others. And the more a child possesses such qualities, the more likely he is to set his will against yours when you have to discipline. There is nothing abnormal or wrong with such kids; they just have more of a mind to do things their way.

The second factor is situation. Kids are more willing to escalate when they read a situation as limiting your parental power: in a store, at Grandma's house, while you're on the phone. At these times, a youngster is banking that you can't practice usual discipline because of constraints, such as Grandma's sensibilities or your strong desire to avoid a scene. The more constraining the situation, the better the chances for escalation. In fact, the only time some kids escalate is when they think the time and place will support it.

The third factor enhancing the probability of escalation may be the strongest: the duration of a problem behavior. The longer you have let a troublesome behavior flourish, the more likely it is that you will have to overcome escalation when you finally confront the behavior decisively, imposing consequences designed to change it. All habits have behavioral momentum that resists outside forces such as parents or psychologists. Try to slow the momentum and you will encounter heavy resistance. In all but the rarest of circumstances, a long-standing problem won't go down without a fight. Take Elwood, for example. Elwood has made bedtime a crisis for the past three months, and his parents have been opening their bedroom to him on those nights when his agitation is particularly intense, or when their nerves are particularly frayed. Eventually, though, Mom and Dad weary of sharing their room and want predictable privacy. So they determine to make their bedroom unconditionally off limits to Elwood. Now he may wail with ferocity that makes the past three months look like the good old days—or good old nights. Before Elwood accepts his folks' new resolution, he will have to be convinced their nerves can outlast his vocal cords, an experiment that may take him quite a few nights to conduct.

Recall Parenting Myth II in Chapter 2: If you handle a situation well, your child's behavior will immediately improve, or *We've tried everything; nothing works.* Escalation is the prime recruiter of parents who fall prey to this myth. Typically, the first stages of any well-executed discipline meet with resistance, especially when you are tackling a long-lived problem. In fact, those approaches destined to be most effective usually evoke the greatest initial opposition from kids, as kids often seem to sense what is going to work long before their parents do. However, parents frequently interpret escalation to mean that a strategy is failing, so they discard it and move on to something else. But each ensuing approach is also doomed at the outset as long as a parent equates escalation with failure. Here's an illustration.

In your home, you have to work hard at getting your kids to do chores. You nag, the kids ignore, you get upset, the kids stall—you know the cycle. A new strategy is called for—no TV watching until chores are completed. The kids don't really believe you mean what you say, since as long as they can remember you've been locked into a *parent talks-kids ignore* style. They respond by stalling even more, doing poor jobs, arguing over who's to do what, and so on. Because your rule is being assaulted from all sides, you soon weary of administering it, conclude it's only making matters worse, and slowly let it fade from your house's book of etiquette. You are now back to square one on the chore issue—no, you're actually back to square zero. Not only are chores still a source of labor unrest, but now your kids know that if they strike long enough, they can return to the old order, which is you being upset and them squeezing chores into their schedule (or, as is more often the case, them squeezing chores *out* of their schedule). You didn't make it past the point of benefit with your rule—that is, the point at which the rule finally begins to take hold because the kids realize they are getting nowhere by fighting it.

De-Escalation

We've seen what escalation is, as well as some causes and some effects. Now, what can you do to counter escalation, or to de-escalate your discipline? It's unrealistic to expect to eradicate escalation from your child's stock of discipline dodges, not while he's still in childhood or adolescence anyway. But you can take some steps toward reducing the chances that an ordinary occasion of discipline will elevate into a protracted contest of wills.

De-escalation Rule #1: Don't use escalation as a gauge for determining the fitness of your discipline. So many parents become victims of the same reasoning: "If my discipline were reasonable, he'd never react so unreasonably," or "He gets so upset when I send him to bed at eight o'clock, I must be underestimating how much he wants to watch Music Video reruns at eight-thirty. Maybe I am being insensitive." Once these worries dictate your discipline, you'll in effect be allowing your kids to set their own rules and guidelines. And no child is capable of that. Additionally, if you waver or collapse from the shock waves of escalation, you invite your kids to escalate again the next time they're unhappy with one of your decisions. It is far better to evaluate your rules and techniques of discipline when you have time to reflect on them quietly, and not when you're in the middle of a situation that registers a seven on the Richter Scale.

De-escalation Rule #2: Don't assume escalation to be a symptom of emotional problems. Indeed, this can be a compelling assumption, especially the first few times you watch your three-year-old hold her breath so long she radiates nearly every shade of the rainbow and verges on passing out. Witnessing such demonstrations, you could conceivably wonder if your little one is (a) suffering from temporary insanity, (b) manifesting signs of a "split personality," (c) at least mildly emotionally disturbed, or (d) all of the above. Actually the most frequent answer is (e) none of the above. The degree of escalation *in and of itself* is no more a signal of emotional troubles than the number of freckles on your child's nose. If the only time you wonder whether your child is developing psychological hang-ups is when she escalates, stop questioning and apply Rules #3, #4, and #5.

De-escalation Rule #3: Be willing to discipline behavior that comprises the escalation. At times, this will push you to the ends of your resolve, especially if you already feel bad about having had to discipline in the first place. But to strip escalation of its power, you must be ready to hold your youngster accountable for any escalating nastiness, destruction, or irresponsibility. A child will be less inclined to escalate when he realizes that not only won't he circumvent your initial discipline, but he will also add problems to a situation he's already unhappy about.

For an illustration of de-escalation, let's use our little chair-balking four-year-old from the beginning of this section—call her Joy. If Joy refuses to sit in the chair, you might return her to the chair firmly, adding five minutes to her original time; swat her seat (Joy's lower anatomy, that is, not the chair) and return her to the chair; place her in the chair if necessary. If Joy kicks the wall, you can move the chair beyond leg-to-wall range and have her scrub the wall after her sitting is over, even if her kicks made no marks. If Joy turns around fourteen times, you might begin sit-time again with each turn-around. And if Joy screams at 110 decibels, you may, depending on your tolerance level, try to be oblivious; place her in her room behind a closed door (soundproof, if possible); or tell her that time doesn't begin until the screaming ends. Of course, you could respond in many ways other than these few. No matter what your approach, though, the ultimate goal is the same: Don't let escalation succeed.

De-escalation Rule #4: Anticipate. From hard experience, or maybe just plain parental intuition, you have a good idea of your youngster's escalation style. You know whether she's more likely to refuse to sit, kick the wall, or scream. One of the best ways to defuse a potentially explosive situation is to anticipate further misbehavior and use *if-then's* to head it off. Returning to little Joy, still carrying on in the corner, you might tell her, "Joy, if you scream, your chair time won't begin until you're quiet," or "Joy, don't kick the wall; you'll have to scrub it." A forewarning *if-then* will tell Joy you are prepared to meet her escalation straight on and that you will not be confused or intimidated by it.

Anticipation is also crucial to avert trouble at those times when, for logistical reasons or for everyone's sanity, you cannot follow through with your normal discipline. For example, if the last thirteen visits to Grandma's house have convinced you that Elmo won't accept any kind of discipline there without escalation, give him a choice before you leave home: "Elmo, if you fight my discipline at Grandma's, we will leave immediately and settle the matter at home." Or perhaps you aren't looking for some reason to leave Grandma's; maybe you like spending time with your mother-in-law. Then you might say, "Elmo, each time you ignore me at Grandma's, you will be losing one hour of privileges (such as TV or outside play) at home." Of course, you'd also better anticipate that the first few times you try these advance *if-then's,* Elmo will confirm for himself, the hard way, that you mean what you say.

Countless situations can temporarily curtail a parent's authority. Both you and your kids are probably well aware of the times and places that are your particular undoing. Fortunately, these situations don't last long, although they may seem to at the time! Eventually, you will be returning to conditions in which you have more latitude to respond to misconduct. Until you do, though, your youngster needs to be sure that you will carry out some kind of consequences, even if they are delayed a bit. To add even more weight to your anticipatory *if-then's,* you can tell Elmo that the results of his misbehavior will be milder if he accepts them at the moment instead of continuing to misbehave and taking his chances later. Example: The results of backtalk at Grandma's might be only fifteen minutes in one of Grandma's chairs, as opposed to a half hour in one of yours. You will be teaching Elmo that it is definitely to his advantage to exert some control over his escalation before it gets out of hand.

De-escalation Rule #5: Control yourself. In other words, don't let yourself escalate. This rule is nearly impossible to adhere to completely, but it is an ideal to strive for. Now that I'm safely away from the front line, I can confess that more than once I wanted to throttle Greg during his endless temper fit. But had I lost control of myself, I probably would have lost control of Greg. I would have become embroiled in a power struggle, with my behavior fueling, instead of extinguishing, Greg's.

A power struggle can arise if you threaten, argue, put down—in essence, challenge your child to misbehave further. Being a kid, he just might. During a power struggle, your agitation might equal your youngster's. Then, not only will you find it harder to think one step ahead of your escalating Edgar, but you will also lose credibility (recall the nagging-anger loop in Chapter 6). Why should Edgar put any faith in the words of someone whose speech is distorted by rage? Further, even if, through a tirade, you eventually impose your will, at what cost will it be? How much drained energy or regretted words or hurt feelings will have ensued?

Remaining cool-headed carries another big advantage. Almost all kids, some more than others, at times follow this disciplinary precept (reportedly popularized by Dennis the Menace): "You might be able to make me behave, but I can make you pay a price!" During discipline, a youngster sometimes sees herself in a "one-down" position in relation to her parents. So it makes sense that periodically she might want a little revenge, a turning of the tables for having her desires thwarted. Her escalation, then, is intended to "pay you back." And by losing control you accept her payment. Sometimes spending extra time in a chair or losing another half hour of playtime is worth it if a youngster thinks she can make you suffer for making her suffer. All the more important, therefore, that you keep your cool during escalation. Fortunately, the four rules described above should help you do just that. However, I can add a few more suggestions to prolong your stamina, just in case.

1. Develop a pep talk geared to reassure yourself that "this too shall pass," more quickly if you stay unruffled. Talk to yourself as you would talk to a friend who needs a calming hand. Mull over some of the ideas presented above; reinforce the benefits of remaining in control. At first your pep talk may have little success at soothing your swelling agitation, but like a persistent rain on parched ground, your words will gradually soak in, becoming convictions.

2. Mentally focus on anything that will prevent your dwelling on how obnoxious Edgar is acting. You might compile your shopping list in your head or fantasize about how you'd spend the grand-prize lottery money. The goal is to divert your attention from Edgar's efforts to bait you with backtalk or draw you into dead-end arguments.

3. Arrange to have your discipline consequence executed out of your eye- and earshot, if possible. Assume Edgar is occupying a corner of one room. You might seek shelter in a different room. If he is in some type of isolation (for example, his room, living-room couch, or bathtub), move as far from ground zero as possible. Edgar will be less likely to continue transmitting resistance if you're not there to receive it.

4. If you have younger children who can seemingly carry on without end, you might consider something as basic as earplugs (for you, not them!). You will not only temper your youngsters' voice volume to below the pain threshold, but you will also be able to endure reactions that would otherwise have provoked rage and exasperation.

I have given a fair amount of space to escalation. It deserves this space. Escalation is a common childhood phenomenon. It is a form of misbehavior, and all kids misbehave. But escalation, especially in its extreme forms, often goes beyond misbehavior. It becomes a youngster's way of saying, "I directly challenge your authority; I refuse to accept your right to discipline me." Escalation makes many parents feel powerless, held hostage by a child's willingness to act as unmanageably as necessary to escape rules. Indeed, nothing is better than escalation to mislead parents into thinking, "We've tried everything; nothing works."

Self-Assault
or "Don't discipline me, I'll hurt myself."

Escalation is a youngster's directing outward his dislike of discipline. It is behavior and emotion aimed at parents, siblings, or the environment in general (including unsuspecting doors and helpless toys). Not always, though, do kids direct their dissatisfaction outward. Sometimes they turn it inward toward themselves,

165

especially toward their own bodies. They might slap, pinch, even bite themselves in an expression of displeasure at meeting rules and limits. Like escalation, such self-punishment is typically born of frustration. Over time, however, self-punishment can become a self-reward through the effect a child gains on his parents.

Sammy was ten years old. In many respects he wasn't much different from most of the kids I see with behavior problems. He was defiant, ignored most of his parents' words, and wanted the household run as he wished. Sammy had one characteristic, though, that in its severity set him apart from most. When his parents tried to discipline him or refused to comply with his demands, Sammy would pull his hair, bite his hand, pinch his arm, and if these didn't unnerve his parents, he would threaten more serious self-directed violence.

Although the self-assaults never caused harm (Sammy didn't really like pain), the threats had been getting more frequent and more menacing. On one occasion, Sammy was denied the chance to play outside because he'd wandered far from the yard earlier that day. He pitched a rampaging temper fit that culminated in his grabbing a kitchen knife and pointing it toward himself. On another occasion, Sammy opened the door of a moving car and promised to jump out if the car didn't take him where he wanted to go. In both instances, for fear that Sammy would carry out his threats, deliberately or accidentally, Sammy's parents acquiesced to his terms. What began as a mode of expressing anger at discipline evolved into a high-risk game that Sammy played to hold Mom and Dad's authority at a level where Sammy wanted it.[25]

Sammy occupied the far end of the *if you don't do what I want, I'll hurt myself* continuum. The vast majority of children never begin to reach Sammy's extremes. His case, however, does bring out several questions about the self-assault-after-discipline phenomenon.

First of all, is this behavior abnormal? Is it a mark of psychological maladjustment or some predisposition toward masochism? Fortunately, very seldom is either the case. Even Sammy, with all his life-threatening ploys, was not psychologically abnormal. His behavior was unusual, but it is still best described as a means of controlling his parents. For most kids, self-assault after discipline is either a frustration response or a way to manipulate parents. Some children escalate when facing discipline; some assault themselves. Some even do both. And although self-assault is less common than escalation, it is still a fairly typical discipline reaction, especially among younger children. As kids get older and wiser, they realize that self-assault is not one of the more pleasurable ways to show displeasure.

To be sure, severe forms of self-assault, more accurately called self-abuse, are dangerous. But this extreme, where physical harm is possible unless the child is restrained, is highly unusual. Such behavior is exhibited by children with multiple intellectual, physical, and/or developmental handicaps. Also, self-abuse is not limited solely to times of discipline. Self-abusing children often seem to hurt themselves for no discernible reason.

It is vital to distinguish between self-abuse and self-assault. While self-abuse is rare and serious, self-assault is common and generally benign. Self-assault usually dies out as a child gets older, unless it strikes a reaction from Mom and Dad. This brings us to a second question about self-assault: Why do kids do it? Two of the reasons we've already noted: (1) they're frustrated, and (2) it works. But there is a third reason for self-assault. Sometimes kids just want to punish the folks for having disciplined them or denied them something. The nonverbal message is: "Look, I'm so hurt over what you did to me that I'm going to hurt myself more." Certainly, this can evoke your guilt, especially if you're tissue-dabbing the blood where Tina miscalculated and bit her knuckles too hard. But if you keep telling yourself that you will only hurt Tina in more long-lasting ways by allowing her to govern you with guilt, you will be better able to ride out her self-directed anger. Now, on to our last but most pressing question.

What can you do to take some of the sting out of self-assault, to make it less likely to recur? My first suggestion would be to learn to ignore it, or at least not to react emotionally to it. Your youngster will not assail himself with enough vigor to do serious harm. Even young children have a good sense of when to quit. Stripped of your reaction, self-assault will be a momentary display of emotion. Should you react, though—with worry, guilt, or even anger—you could provide a maintaining payoff. Like

Sammy, your youngster may impactfully realize he has hit upon a way to moderate your authority or to retaliate against you for disciplining him.

Of course, you may not always prefer to ignore self-assault. Sometimes you might wish to disclose more actively that you will not be flustered. My mother had a surprising response to my budding attempt at self-assault. Once, at about age four, I was operating on a toy that wouldn't open in the direction I wanted it to. Irate, I flung the uncooperative toy against the cement-block basement wall. My mother, washing clothes nearby, told me to collect the shattered pieces. Being me, I refused and counterordered my mother to pick them up herself if she wanted them picked up. (Wasn't I a lovely child?) To add impact to my command, I began hitting my head against the wall, warning my mother I wouldn't quit until she followed my orders. I had her, or so I thought. To my amazement, she started toward me, saying, "If you're going to hit your head, let me help you." She was actually reaching for my head! I immediately decided that head-butting was not all it was cracked up to be. Mom's meaning was clear: Self-assault was neither going to cow her nor get me out of cleaning up my mess.

Self-assault is like escalation. If your youngster finds he can control you with it, he may go to great pains to resist your discipline. If you're not afraid of his self-aimed upset, and you regard it calmly, it will most likely cease to be a disciplinary retort.

Appealing the Decision
or *"Mom said to ask you."*

We adults have our ideas about the advantages of two parents raising the same child. We've theorized on the subject at length in books, classrooms, and backyards. But were we to ask kids what they see as the advantages of being reared by both parents, we might be a bit surprised at their answers. And somewhere on their list of benefits might be a plus not even in our top forty: the chance to make an appeal, the opportunity to seek a second opinion, preferably one that contradicts the first.

Kids use two basic strategies to appeal a parental decision. The first is founded upon the "What Mom (or Dad) doesn't know won't hurt her (or him)" premise. Perry seeks a ruling from Dad, say, about whether or not he can go to Wendell's house and watch *The Video Game That Ate Chicago*. For whatever reason, Dad doesn't give permission. Whereupon Perry waits until he can isolate Mom, who is unaware of the ruling, and presents the same proposition. Of course, Perry will make no mention that he's already received an answer, hoping that (1) Mom won't ask, and (2) she'll unwittingly overturn Dad's decision. By the time both parents compare notes, Perry, having set up a Mom vs. Dad conflict on the movie issue, may already be at Wendell's, with Chicago half-eaten. Perry now has at least a fifty-fifty chance of seeing the movie, whereas prior to the appeal he had no chance.

The second strategy is an extension of the first. It is usually employed only after the first begins to falter because the folks get wise and start asking, "What did your mom/dad say?" Still contesting for a successful appeal, Perry may counter with: "Mom said to ask you," or "Dad said it's OK with him if it's OK with you." Once more, Perry is banking that the appeals parent won't check out the first parent's decision, and that he'll be well on his way to the movie before his move has been uncovered.

Children can resort to the appeals process only so long without risking discovery. Why then do some persist in their litigation even after they know their parents have caught on? Their motivation is straightforward: There's nothing to lose and a lot to gain. At the worst, Perry will get a confirmation of a decision he already doesn't like. At the best, though, he may get a verdict overturned, or at least get a hung jury. And a hung jury means the issue is still open to debate. Even if the debate goes against him, Perry still gains valuable information for the next time he wants to make a similar request: He knows who is better to ask first.

Kids have the mental agility of a trial lawyer in making appeals, but you are not without defenses, which we might term the *united we stand* defenses. Of course, if Perry doesn't use his appeals option much, you've no need to use any defenses. It makes no sense to question Perry's integrity without evidence; he is innocent until proven guilty. But if you do have evidence that Perry regularly tries to align you against your spouse, you can return a few verdicts that will change your adversarial system into a cooperative one.

Verdict #1: Any decision made initially by one parent will automatically be upheld by the second parent, whether that parent agrees with it or not. No doubt you and your spouse will disagree at times, but your immediate concern is to extinguish Perry's use of the appeals process, not to concur on all the parenting decisions you confront daily. The latter takes a lifetime of compromise, the former can be achieved in a few months. Iron out your disagreements later, out of Perry's presence, so that next time you will be more attuned to your spouse's mind.

Verdict #2: Whenever Perry seeks some privilege or permission from either parent, for a time he will be asked if he has already been given an answer. If he acknowledges that he has, and that the answer was negative, refer to Verdict #1. But suppose Perry tells you that Mom, who just left to go shopping, said he could go swimming today and weed the garden tomorrow if it's OK with you. Since you really don't know what Mom said, present Perry with his options. If you support your spouse's decision, and subsequently find out she said otherwise, Perry will have to pay the consequences for falsifying the records, which might consist of losing swimming privileges for the week and/or weeding the flower beds in addition to the garden. It's important to offer Perry his choices before he sails out to swim, thus giving him the chance to reconsider his story in light of the new conditions. Having to check Perry's word so carefully is unfortunate, but until he drops the appeals game, you will be heading off much confusion for you and much temptation to deceive for him.

The appeals process is an overlooked benefit of having two parents, at least from a child's point of view. A youngster isn't necessarily underhanded because she makes an appeal. She is just trying to find the most favorable of her alternatives. You have to counsel her that the appeals process is not how decisions are made in your home.

Guilty upon Request
or *"I know I shouldn't ask, but..."*

The appeals process is anchored in the old "divide and conquer" notion. Appealing works best when parents are separated by walls, buildings, miles, anything to keep them from communicating with each other, at least temporarily. But there is another, more versatile strategy that kids use, either in conjunction with or as an alternative to the appeals process. This is the *guilty upon request* tactic. It doesn't require that parents be divided to be conquered. They can even be standing side by side, consulting with each other. This tactic has power because it engenders guilt in parents by making them feel hardhearted or unreasonable if they don't comply with a request.

I first saw this tactic performed several years ago upon two quite softhearted and reasonable parents. Chuck and Darlene had three children, ages sixteen, thirteen, and ten. After a few family counseling sessions, I noticed that all three kids shared ideas on how to raise Mom and Dad. One of their collaborative endeavors was the *guilty upon request* tactic. Here's how it operated. One or more of the kids would want something—say, permission to practice hairstyling by giving Fido a permanent, or a ride to the pool where all the kids swim, somewhere in the next county. Now, in the kids' mind, a direct approach with either request had at best a fifty-fifty chance of sanction. These were not acceptable odds, so something was needed to tilt the draw a little more favorably. The kids knew that the proper approach would do wonders for extracting a "yes" from Mom and Dad, or at minimum a begrudging "OK." Therefore, they would gear up for a touchy request by assuming an appropriately deferential posture in all respects: nonverbal signals, verbal tone, and verbal content. They stood uneasily, shifting their weight from foot to foot; their eyes were roaming the floor, and their hands were hidden in their pockets. Their voices were subdued; at times they spoke in a borderline whisper (particularly effective in eliciting a request to speak up). They groped for words, implying uncertainty and reluctance even to ask ("I know what your answer is going to be, but..."; "Mom, I probably shouldn't even ask this, but..."). Taken together, the overall picture was unmistakable: "Mom and Dad, we come to you fully expecting that our request won't be granted because you deny us most things anyway." And nearly every time, this well-orchestrated approach had the desired effect. Chuck and Darlene struggled with self-images of being unfit and unfeeling parents. Consequently, they granted most petitions. Even on those rare occasions when they didn't, they felt bad enough so that they almost never turned down two requests in a row.

Chuck and Darlene's kids had the *guilty upon request* tactic down to a science. But many kids who practice this technique aren't even aware they're using it. They approach their folks in genuine doubt that their proposition will be accepted. Ironically, this is the very thing that makes their request so hard to weigh objectively. What basically kind-hearted parent can refuse a supplication so humbly proferred? Not too many. And I'm not saying you should. I'm saying that you need to consider any request on its own merits, unfettered by your own guilt. Certainly, there may be nothing wrong with swimming where all the kids swim. But if you know that particular days are notorious for alcohol or drug use at the pool, or if you've already made two twenty-mile round-trip jaunts to the pool this week, you need to respond to the swimming query in light of these factors, without striving to avoid appearing the wicked witch or warlock. Unless your judgment is free of extraneous considerations, you may find yourself acquiescing in something that's not in your child's best interests, or yours, for that matter.

But what if your kids really do think you're a nasty person whenever you don't satisfy a request? Rest assured, this is standard childhood practice; their perception will be temporary. You do far too much for your kids to be chronically judged as selfish or ungiving. At the absolute longest, their perception will linger until you fulfill their next request. Then you'll return to their good graces again. But, more important, you can't make decisions according to how your kids will perceive them or you. Your children's welfare and your rights as a parent come well before any passing shift in your children's opinion of you. Additionally, the surest road to permanent ogrehood is to comply indiscriminately with all requests. Rare is the parent who can stay abreast of a child's expectations and wants. Eventually, your time, finances, and energy will be exhausted. And your kids will be very upset at you, for they will never have learned to accept your human limitations.

Are there ways to respond to the *guilty upon request* tactic? I hope so. No parents should have to feel guilty merely because someone, even their own child, asks them to. One good response is simply to observe a child's behavior for him: "You look like you think there's no chance I'm going to say yes," or "I think you're trying to make me feel guilty if I say no." Follow this with the assertion that you won't let your decision be influenced by guilt, since that wouldn't be fair to either of you. Most kids, once they realize you're reading them accurately, will begin to make more straightforward requests. But even if they cling to their old style, at least they know exactly where you stand. Another suggestion: You needn't run through this explicit explanation every time. After a few replays, you can make your point better by saying, "Aha, the old guilty upon request tactic."

Of course, nothing takes the place of your own inimitable style. One father chose to answer his daughter's inquiries in the same spirit in which they were asked. With a gently mimicking tone, he would look down, shift his weight uneasily, grope for words, and counter with, "I know how you're going to react to my answer; I'm not sure I should even say it." Dad's talent for lighthearted mimicry both made his point and provided his daughter with a mirror in which to see herself.

Some kids calculate ways to make parents feel guilty at their request. Other kids get the same result through their genuine childish innocence. Either way, this is a subtle tactic that you need to recognize and resist. Otherwise, it will adversely color your parental decisions. It will also give you an opinion of yourself you probably don't deserve.

The Set-Up
or *"After all I've done for you, Mom."*

This sophisticated maneuver doesn't generally appear in a youngster's antidiscipline repertoire until age seven or so because it requires timing and negotiation skills available only to those who've reached the "age of reason." Behold a typical set-up. Slovenly Salina, age ten, is notorious for not picking up after herself, which produces ongoing conflicts between you and her. Salina receives an invitation from her girlfriend, nocturnal Nancy, to attend one of Nancy's infamous slumber parties in two weeks. Salina suspects she has two chances of obtaining your permission—slim and none. Salina may be slovenly, but she's not stupid. She immediately begins hanging up wet towels, throwing dirty clothes into the hamper instead of under the bed, and bringing used glasses from her bedroom into the kitchen before mold sets in, all without a single reminder from you. By now you're beginning to wonder, first, whether this one-person cleaning machine is a clone of your daughter and, second, what happened to the real Salina. However, you blissfully accept the sudden turnabout, hoping it means that Salina has finally decided to clean up her act. Then she pops the permission question on the eve of the slumber party. If the set-up has been well executed, you will find yourself in the same uncomfortable position as that posed by the *guilty upon request* tactic. Your pleasure over Salina's cleanup efforts is sufficient to interfere with your judgment regarding the slumber party. If you decide against the party, you may see one of Salina's finer theatrical performances, laced with lines like "You always tell me I'll get more privileges if I show responsibility. So I try and it doesn't get me anywhere." While you don't want to be a victim of this kind of emotional blackmail, you also don't want to discourage the notion that responsible behavior begets increased privileges. You're caught in a dilemma. But you can take steps to extricate yourself.

The first step is to advise Salina that membership in the family involves certain responsibilities. These responsibilities are expected to be performed from a sense of family commitment, and not to win something "extra" from them.

The second step involves confronting the sneakiness of the set-up ploy. You might say, "I'm disappointed that you behaved so well over the past few weeks mainly because you had the party in mind. I would have much preferred it if you had come to me directly when you got the invitation, let me know it was a special privilege you wanted, and then asked me what you could have done to earn it. Keep that in mind for next time."

The third step is to reinforce the idea that you judge all requests on their own merits, trying not to be swayed by irrelevant factors such as your own guilt or what your kids have done for you lately.

Chances are you will experience many set-ups as your kids move through childhood. They're a common dynamic, and a bright sign that your kids know how to act more responsibly when they want to. The steps described above should help you teach your kids that it is in their best interests to avoid set-ups, or at least to seek your cooperation in them from the very outset.

Tear-ible Misconceptions
or *"This hurts me more than it does you."*

This is a declaration meant to reassure a child during a moment of discipline. Although a bit of a cliché, it nevertheless holds true for most parents. But however sincerely these words are said, a youngster is not inclined to believe them, not while she's being disciplined anyway. Through her eyes, "this" hurts *her* more than it does *you*. She may understand why you disciplined, but that doesn't mean she likes it. No matter how gentle or fair, discipline is still not a child's idea of a good time.

Regardless of what your youngster believes, you probably do feel worse than she does when you have to discipline her, especially if you know how bad she feels. And few reactions can evoke a parent's compassion and guilt more than tears. Parents can usually weather a child's tears, aware that crying is a universal response to disappointment and that discipline often involves disappointment. It is not easy, however, to remain resolute and guiltless when you witness your child feeling so cheerless over something you've done. Further aggravating your self-chastisement in these situations may be a few widespread misconceptions about crying and its meaning.

The foremost misconception is that the intensity of a child's crying is directly related to her perception of how nasty and unjust you're being. While on occasion this may be true, in general no such relationship exists. As all children are individuals, so too all children have individual crying styles. Sunny may cry buckets over the smallest raindrop, whereas her brother Rainier can walk through a storm and not shed a tear. Many factors contribute to how often and how intensely a child cries—temperament, mood, situation, hours without sleep, who's present, who's listening. One of the lesser contributors is how much a child sees you as an ogre. In my experience, parents are too willing to rebuke themselves whenever a child sheds tears. Using tears to judge the equity and reasonableness of your discipline will badly misguide you. It will also make you feel as if you've done your child an injustice by trying to be a good parent. To reinforce a point brought out in the preceding two sections: Your decisions need to be measured on their own merit and not upon your youngster's reaction to them.

A second misbelief about crying is that the nature of a child's cry indicates the amount of internal psychological havoc taking place. Not only do children vary in the ease with which they cry, they likewise vary in their crying style, depending on time and place. In other words, the same child can cry many different cries. And one of the most common yet most alarming cries is the "Look what you're doing to me; I'm losing my mind" wail. (See the case of Carl in Chapter 2.) This cry usually occurs when a child is denied his wishes and literally explodes in displeasure. Suppose you have just told your son Clark that he has lost his morning cartoons for practicing his Superman leap off your coffee table. He reacts with a superstrength, half-screech, sometimes breathless, sometimes tearless wail. It looks terrifying. A youngster in the throes of one of these crying fits appears to be losing all mental balance before your eyes. But as we observed in Chapter 2, such a reaction, however intense, is a regular feature of a temper tantrum. And temper tantrums don't breed trauma, unless they are chronically successful. Then they perpetuate themselves and other forms of distress.

By the way, one telltale distinction of the "Look what you're doing to me" wail is its abrupt cessation upon removal of the offending condition. In Clark's case, this means that you could turn off his crying by turning on the TV.

Now, this is not to say that a child's distress at these times is not genuine. Usually it is. He is downright upset, and he's not about to spare you the full brunt of his feeling. But genuine distress or not, you can more securely contend with your youngster if you don't also have to contend with your own fear that you're watching maladjustment in the making. You're not!

A closing point: I'm not suggesting that you be totally insensitive to your child's tears whenever you make an unpopular decision. You could never do this, nor would you ever want to. Sometimes tears are words needing translation. However, because tears can so easily dissolve a parent's resolve, be careful not to let deceptive notions about crying misguide you into parenting in your child's long-range worst interests.

176

From the Mouths of Babes
or *"Don't discipline me, I'll say nasty things."*

Kids can expend much energy countering your authority or showing their distaste for discipline. We've by no means reached the bounds of their inventiveness or stamina; we've only covered their favorite methods. And like us adults, kids don't only use actions to convey displeasure. They use words as well.

Entertainer Art Linkletter has amused millions with "the darndest things kids say." I'm sure many parents have wished that they too had kept a daily log of all the kid-isms that have poured from the lips of their offspring. As children are capable of doing nearly anything, so too are they capable of saying nearly anything. In the next sections, we will listen to what kids say—particularly what they say when they don't like your style of parenting.

Parent Comparing
or *"But everybody else is allowed."*

In Chapter 1, I noted that kids have vested interests in swaying you towards "parenting by consensus," or looking to other parents to guide your own parenting. I won't reiterate all those interests here, but I do want to elaborate a few key points, since parent comparing is one of kids' better parent-confidence busters.

Put plainly, kids make comparisons to make you question yourself and change your mind—in their favor, of course. No comparison will ever be risked if it draws attention to a less obliging parent. Effectively, comparisons say: "Lucky's mom and dad are nicer, or better, or smarter parents than you are," and you're supposed to feel appropriately bad about that. What kids don't realize—and what you *must*—is that comparisons have little relevance for you. Decisions that other parents endorse with their children translate poorly into prescriptions for you to follow. You, your child, and your situation are unlike any others. Your parenting has to be grounded in your value system and circumstances and not those of Lucky's mom, or ten thousand Lucky's moms.

Naturally, I wouldn't expect your kids to agree, no matter how well you state your case. First of all, they're not going to view comparisons through the eyes of a parent; kids aren't good at thinking like parents. Second, since they want you to vacillate in their favor, they're not about to say, "You're right, Mom; my situation is different from Lucky's. I don't need to have a ten-speed."

The Grass Is Greener Anywhere Else
or *"I'm running away."*

Rare is the parent who navigates one full parenthood without hearing these words or some variant thereof. This is a pronouncement intended to convey unqualified discontent: "It's so bad here I would prefer living *anyplace* else." Generally, kids make this declaration rather sparingly, lest it lose effect. Fortunately, among all the inflamed words kids vent, these are among the least meant and least often carried out.

Before going further, I want to clarify what I mean by a runaway threat. I won't be addressing the burgeoning problem of teenaged runaways. This complex issue cannot be tackled in these few pages. Instead, I will be dealing with the more common, and much more benign, preadolescent vow to leave home.

Runaway threats are usually mouthed in a burst of fervor. They are meant to make you reconsider, relent, or just plain feel rotten. The words are primarily for impact, to let you know without a doubt that you're not making your youngster feel welcome and that if you remain on your present parenting course he will seriously consider finding alternative lodgings.

The *grass is greener anywhere else* illusion can assume many forms, depending upon who's doing the running. A friend told me of the first time her son John, age six, decided to move out. His decision reflected discontent that had been building over a period of ten minutes or more. It seems that John was irate because he couldn't play outside until he finished his milk. Pouting, he fired a number of verbal warning salvos at Mom, all meant to let her know he didn't like this condition one bit, but all nevertheless ignored. John decided to unleash his big gun: "I don't like it here; I'm leaving tonight." Still no response from Mom. "I mean it." Again no reaction. "And I'm taking Josh [his four-year-old brother] with me." I guess John figured if he couldn't jolt Mom with his departure, he'd raise the stakes and take a hostage. The plan fizzled. John finished his milk, played outside, and that night was too tired even to stumble to bed on his own. Besides, once he had played outside, home was sweet home again.

Another parent described her daughter's better-planned attempt to move out. Mom and Lisa, age nine, had spent one morning debating the degree of social freedom proper for a nine-year-old. Not surprisingly, Lisa wanted more freedom than Mom thought best, and she spent the rest of the day in a surly mood. That evening, Lisa emerged from her room with her suitcase packed and silently confronted her parents. This was Lisa's way of bypassing any preliminary discussion on the matter and moving straight to the brink of leaving. She wanted to give her parents a vivid image of her discontent, knowing that this one picture was worth a thousand "I don't like it here's."

Was Lisa any more serious than John? I don't think so. She just found a different way to say the same thing. Whether your child makes his wish to travel known in words or actions, you can be fairly sure of one thing: He doesn't really want to go anywhere. He's saying or doing something he hopes he doesn't have to pursue. What, then, might you do to show him that you, too, don't want him to go anywhere? (If, however, you do have days when you'd be glad to help Skip pack, you're normal.) With younger children, usually the best response is no response. Like John's mom, you needn't pay heed to words that are only that—words. Most children will carry the matter no further if they see you won't be bullied or upset by it.

Then again, you might prefer to let your youngster know verbally how you view runaway proclamations. My father had his standard rejoinder to my "When I become a teenager, I'm leaving." He'd reply, "Well, when the time comes, if that's what you want to do, fine, but don't let the door hit your backside on your way out." I heard what he was saying: "Don't manipulate me with threats."

With older children, exploring with them the ramifications of their proposed move sometimes helps. To illustrate, let's continue with Lisa's story. (Thought I was going to leave Lisa standing with her bags packed, didn't you?) Lisa's parents could have begun a conversation designed to reveal to Lisa the impulsiveness of her action. Here is a hypothetical interchange.

Parent: Lisa, it looks like you're planning to go somewhere.
Lisa: I'm running away.

Parent: Where are you going?

Lisa: I don't know, anyplace, maybe to Joanne's house.

Parent: She must know you're coming.

Lisa: Not yet.

Parent: I guess you'll have to find some way to get there, huh? Will you have food to eat and money for clothes and schoolbooks?

Lisa: I'll have to do work and chores.

Parent: Yes, and you'll need a lot of money to be able to pay all your bills.

Using this type of dialogue, Lisa's parents can nonjudgmentally point out to Lisa some of the potential hardships of her plan without backing her into a corner. They can close the talk by letting Lisa know that if she changes her mind, they'd certainly like her to stick around.

Most of the time, these responses will stabilize a runaway situation at what it is: a brief round of anger or manipulation, and not a genuine consideration. The main aim is not to panic. Most kids proclaim a wish to leave home many times before they achieve actual independence. Make clear to your child two things: one, threats won't buffalo you; two, he's welcome to stay where the grass may not seem the greenest, but at least there is some.

Telling It Like It Isn't
or *"You don't like me."*

The most frustrating thing about this accusation is that you know nothing could be further from the truth. It's ridiculous for your youngster to think that because you periodically have to rein in her behavior, you are doing so because you don't like her. Isn't there some way to make her see how absurd her proclamation is? Yes, there is, but probably not through any reasoning you might do at the moment she is saying it.

When a child charges you with not liking her, you can safely assume she has one of two motivations. If it is the first, she is fully aware that her charge is nonsense, but she is making it anyway because she's perturbed at you or wants to retaliate for having been disciplined. She knows from your words, your countenance, or your changing mind whether or not she's struck a nerve. If she has, she may continue her accusations, even though she knows they are totally unfounded.

The second catalyst behind such words is a genuine belief in their accuracy. To be doing what you're doing, you really must not like her. Such logic accompanies immaturity. It comes from an inability to take in the whole picture, to realize that your motives for discipline are in fact diametrically counter to any dislike on your part. Take heart, however. At these times, your youngster's feelings are fleeting. As young as she might be, she sees continuously how much you do show her you love her. She knows that most of what is positive in her life—solace, companionship, meals, entertainment—originates with you. Even the most trying youngster probably requires discipline less than 10 percent of your time together. That leaves more than 90 percent of your relationship to be positive in his eyes, to show him you "like" him. The impact of all this will overwhelm his brief feeling of being unloved at the instant of discipline.

Younger children (ages three to six) are most likely to feel unliked. As their reasoning becomes more sophisticated, they abandon this perception. But that doesn't mean they abandon this comeback. They may still sling "You don't like me's" if they see they can punish you with them.

Of course, your approach to discipline can do much to either foster or temper these remarks. If personal attacks or other demeaning assaults accompany your discipline, your youngster will probably attribute some ill will to you, even though you may feel little of the sort but are just fed up with him momentarily. No parent can always maintain perfect composure, but working to stay even-tempered, zeroing in on the lesson you want to get across instead of your child's personality deficits, should help keep false impressions from creeping into his head. At times they will creep in anyway, but you needn't help them along.

Related to the "You don't like me" comeback is the "You like (fill in the appropriate sibling) better" accusation. Sometimes a youngster sees an older sibling getting more privileges or personal freedom than he and concludes that favoritism is behind the differential treatment. You can certainly try to correct his perception, but don't be too surprised if you're not completely successful. Once again, his reasoning is constrained by his youth. As long as you are genuinely attempting to hold to what you deem age-appropriate guidelines for all your children, the "unfavored" one will eventually understand the method in your madness. He won't brew some deep-seated resentment toward his sibling or you. On the other hand, if you allot a child more freedom than you judge healthy in order to silence his charges of unfairness, you won't eradicate his belief. You will only temporarily placate it. You will also be convincing him that his accusations were right all along.

Another reason kids find favoritism where there is none has to do with the nature of kids, or, more specifically, with their respective natures. Cedric may, by temperament, be a more manageable child than Rufus. Therefore, you actually do discipline Rufus about three times as much as his brother. And try as you might to explain why to Rufus, he just doesn't understand. There comes a time to accept his nonacceptance and stop running your reasons against a stone wall. Every piece of discipline doesn't need to involve repeated explanations of why Cedric seldom has to redo his chores or why Cedric hardly ever spends time without TV privileges. Cedric is responsible for Cedric's behavior, and Rufus for Rufus's. If you discipline each son when necessary, Rufus will eventually figure out that his problems are coming from his own self-defeating actions and not from your sibling partiality. Until he does, though, don't allow yourself to favor Rufus by overlooking two-thirds of his misbehavior so as to spend equal time disciplining both boys. You will do neither any favors.

Every child passes through spells of misperceptions about her parents and their motives. And no amount of reasoning on your part will totally dispel her beliefs. Only time will tell her that they are unfounded and that you truly have her well-being at heart. Meanwhile, if you are the target of off-the-mark indictments, you can take some consolation from the fact that so is every other parent.

Selective Hearing Loss
or *"I didn't hear you."* (Translation: *"I wasn't listening."*)

A parent once told me she was contemplating a hearing check for her son Nicky. More and more, when she asked Nicky to do something—such as hang up his coat, hang up the phone, untie the bird—she would have to amplify her volume several notches before gaining his attention. Whereupon Nicky would answer, sometimes innocently, sometimes testily, that he hadn't heard her before. Mom asked me if I thought Nicky might have a hearing loss. Possibly, I said, but I couldn't make that diagnosis. I did ask, however, if Mom noticed any evidence of hearing problems in situations other than when Nicky was asked to do something—for example, when he was watching TV, playing with friends, or having a general conversation. She said she hadn't. On a return visit, Mom said Nicky's hearing had been assessed and found normal. This confirmed my suspected diagnosis: Selective Hearing Loss. The primary symptom of this condition is—deafness to anything a child doesn't wish to hear.

I asked Mom what she did whenever Nicky blocked out the sound of her voice. She confessed that she would usually repeat herself or else just forget the whole matter because it wasn't worth the exhaustion. You can see the dynamics. Nicky had found a way to escape his responsibilities, or at least to postpone them to a more convenient time.

Selective Hearing Loss (SHL) is an affliction prevalent among children. It can appear in the first several years of life and usually becomes chronic in the teen years. In fact, the adult form is said to be epidemic among marital partners. SHL is manifested by multiple "I didn't hear you's," which typically recur in the presence of some parental request or directive. This is not to say that a youngster's symptoms are never quite genuine. In the advanced stages of this disorder, many kids truly learn to tune out certain combinations of words, like "The garbage needs taking out," "It's time for bed," or "Did you take a bath?"

Is there a cure for SHL? Yes, a relatively elementary one: Make sure it is worth your youngster's while to hear you. How can you do this? In a conversational tone of voice (about 50 to 70 decibels, not the standard 75 to 100 parents unintentionally learn to use to wrench a youngster's attention), make your request once, stating the consequence for ignoring the request. In Nicky's case, for example, Mom could have made herself heard much more quietly by saying, "Nicky, supper is in ten minutes. Please be on time or your won't be able to go outside afterwards"; or "We have a new rule, Nicky: all homework must be completed before the TV is turned on"; or "Nicky, if I have to hang up your coat, you'll have to wash and dry my dishes."

But what about those times when Nicky actually didn't hear his mom? Should he be held responsible then? You bet he should! The problem is Nicky's chronic disregard for Mom's voice, not whether Mom's voice carries well enough to be heard. After a few lessons of feeling the results of his lax regard for his mom, Nicky would learn to be a little less deaf.

At this point, before I forget, I should alert you to a backup technique youngsters use in case the "I didn't hear you" isn't available. That is the ubiquitous "I forgot." Sometimes it is just not possible for a youngster to claim SHL. Perhaps he uttered an "OK, Dad," or gave an accepting nod, or maybe even looked up from the TV as you spoke. This is when the "I forgot" can be remembered. Garfield may not be able to claim hearing loss, but he can plead Juvenile Memory Deficit (JMD). Handily, the cure for JMD is identical to SHL. That is, a request is made memorable through consequences. Your words will gain renewed status as Garfield finds he will be held responsible for remembering them.

All kids will periodically ignore or forget what you say to them, and I'm not advocating that your every request come equipped with consequential weight. If, however, your youngster seems chronically plagued by either or both of these disorders, you can use the remedies indicated to alleviate his symptoms and free you from the "I'll keep telling you over and over so you'll listen and not forget" treatment. Not only does this treatment lack any curative powers, it abets your kids in doing the very things you don't want them to do—ignore and forget.

The States of Wrath
or *"I'm mad at you."*

During a workshop, a father commented that his son Tim seldom ignored him or "forgot" his responsibilities. Generally, Tim would respond the first time he was asked to do or not do something. From the envious expressions of other parents, Dad realized he had something of a statistical rarity on his hands. He semi-apologetically added that Tim was not always happy about being so obliging. In Dad's words, "He'll do what I say, but he'll be mad about it." Dad wondered how typical Tim was in this respect. In a word, quite.

Just because kids comply with a rule or requirement doesn't mean they agree with it or like it. Do you enjoy fulfilling all the demands made of you? How about getting up at 6:30 A.M.? Is it fun to sit at a red light at 3:00 in the morning when you're the only car on the road? Likewise, I don't know too many kids who relish turning down a stereo or cutting short a kickball game to get ready for a visit to Aunt Nellie's. And for children, an "I'm mad at you" is one of the first and most childish expressions of displeasure at rules and at the person who is enforcing them—you.

When a child proclaims "I'm mad at you," he may be saying any of several things: "I don't like your authority over me"; "I don't want to do this"; "I'm not actually mad at you, but you're the closest target"; or "in fact, I am mad at you." In other words, an "I'm mad at you" is not always an "I'm mad at *you*." Whatever a youngster is really saying, though, some anger over rules and responsibilities is quite human. Further, his wrath usually subsides as quickly as it arose.

Your own "mad," however, can make your youngster's "mad" briefer or longer. If you resent his feelings because you've done nothing to deserve them or because you're not being given credit for trying to be a good parent, you will be misinterpreting his words. They are not a personal attack on you. Rather, they are an expression of his feelings, and as long as they don't become disrespectful, you will respond to them best by acknowledging them but nevertheless standing firm on your discipline. If, on the other hand, you feel compelled to overrationalize your every move to an angry youngster, he will probably learn to be more angry whenever you do something he doesn't agree with. No matter how genuine, feelings of anger are no reason for you to overturn parenting practices and decisions you believe healthy for your youngster.

We've been listening to some standard kids' comments about discipline. There are many others: "You're unfair." "You're the meanest Dad anyone could have." "I'm going to treat my kids differently." "You never understand." "You never let me do anything." "I wish so-and-so was my mother." The list is endless.

Kids hold definite opinions of your discipline, and they aren't reluctant to give you those opinions, in whatever terminology. Most of the time their words stream from emotion. If you don't allow them to fluster you, they won't become a pattern. However, sometimes a youngster's words go beyond expressions of emotion and become expressions of disrespect. In these instances, you need to decide where to draw the line. It is one thing to disclose negative feelings; it is quite another to mistreat you verbally, both as a parent and as a person. No one has license to say whatever she pleases in the name of self-expression. Some restraint and tact is a vital part of communicating feelings, and you need to teach your kids you'll listen better to what they say if they say it with regard for you. Otherwise, they may move from giving their critique of your discipline to giving their critique of you.

One More Time...

Discipline is like exercise to adults. The long-term results are desirable. But the everyday effort, sometimes pain, needed to achieve them isn't always welcome. Every child will at times resist—in word and deed—discipline and rules. Therefore, every parent will at times meet anger, opposition and/or retaliation even as he or she tries to be a conscientious parent. If you don't allow such reactions to control your parenting, they will not become your child's dominant responses to discipline. Despite what he says and does in the short term, your youngster will eventually realize you are acting in his long-term best interests.

Homework

1. Begin an escalation diary. For the next few weeks, observe any bouts of escalation, identifying several variables: day, time, place, duration of the episode, escalation behavior, people present, and your reaction to the escalation. A chart listing each of these is an easy way to keep everything organized. As you collect your

"data," you will probably notice some trends. For instance, you might find that a particular siege of escalation lasts longer when you react with hollering. Or you might observe that Tallulah primarily escalates between 4:00 and 5:00 P.M., right after school, while the family's preparing for supper. Becoming aware of any such trends will help you anticipate and take concrete steps to head off troublesome times, places, and behaviors. For example, you could give Tallulah special toys to play with only before supper, or perhaps give her special tasks to make her feel more included in the family bustle. Or you might warn your relatives that Tallulah puts on a command performance more often in their presence and that they should be fully prepared for you to enter the act if necessary.

2. Share your observations with your youngster, assuming he's old enough to understand (roughly age two or older). When kids know that you have a working understanding of their habits, that in itself often alleviates a problem.

3. Whenever you're smitten with guilt caused by any of the following—a *set-up*, a *guilty upon request* maneuver, or a *tear-ible misconception*—ask yourself, "What am I guilty of? What have I done wrong?" If your answer is "I made a decision based upon what I believe is best for my child," then what is your crime? If your answer is "I didn't reward my child for setting me up, or for asking something in a humble, ingratiating way," then I ask you again, what is your crime? When you are able to evaluate automatically your unpopular parenting decisions using these questions, you will be less susceptible to guilt ploys.

4. If your youngster suffers from *Selective Hearing Loss* or *Juvenile Memory Deficit,* try this medicine (duration: two to four weeks; dosage: PRN—as needed). Whenever you request or direct your youngster to do something, make sure she looks you in the eye and repeats it to you. This will have two benefits: (1) It will keep you from repeating yourself endlessly. (2) Because kids don't generally like the taste of this medicine, to avoid swallowing it they will be willing to take drastic steps—like listening and remembering.

5. Note how often in any given month you entertain a "running away" fantasy—for instance, "How I'd like to have two

weeks away from this place" (your family or your job), or "Nobody appreciates me around here. I ought to let them fend for themselves for a while." If you have such fantasies, you're in league with every other human. All kids, ages three to ninety-three, have their own particular "running away" fantasies. These are a normal reaction to stress, a never-ending workload, or just plain boredom.

6. Recall your own childhood and the hours you spent scheming about how to ask your parents for something, using just the right words at just the right time. What was your goal? Was it to make your parents look bad? Or was it simply to tip the scale in your favor as much as possible? Most likely you weren't acting against your parents personally. Your goal was to get what you wanted, period. Looking back on your own childhood motivations will help you remember that the various manipulations and gyrations performed by your kids have always been a part of childhood.

Six Tested Ways to Drive Yourself Batty

Trying to parent without authority will frazzle your nerves. This is a theme shared by the past three chapters. Next, we will consider a slightly different group of parent-frazzling practices. Although not directly tied to discipline, these are nonetheless several of the stickiest, most fatiguing quagmires that parents sink into while pursuing ideal parenthood. And therein lies the deception. These practices *look like* what good parents should do. But in fact, they won't make you a better parent. They will only drive you batty, or, at the minimum, fray the edges of your emotional makeup.

Overreasoning
or *Too much logic is irrational.*

We humans are capable of sophisticated reasoning—a talent that sets us apart from all other animals, a quality that makes us human. Indeed, wouldn't the world be a nicer place if all humans were as reasonable as you and I? Alas, we both know you can't reason with all people all the time. And kids being people (well, most of the time), we both know you can't reason with them all the time either. The trouble is not in trying. The trouble is in knowing when to give up.

One quality of a "mature" person is openmindedness, a willingness to see more sides than one's own. Most parents readily recognize that not all adults are mature in this sense. Why, then, is this reality so hard to swallow when dealing with children, who by nature of their incomplete development *cannot* be as mature as grown-ups?

One mother reasoned that her reason for overreasoning came from an intense desire to make her family function as one perpetually harmonious community. Conflicts, she believed, should be rare, and resolved through liberal doses of "talking it out." She viewed discipline as a breakdown of the reasoning process, but more disconcertingly, as a sign that her family wasn't always the cohesive unit it was supposed to be. Mom further assumed that the consummate parent should be able to raise any child through reasoning alone, an assumption that made her a consummately frustrated parent.

Another inducement for interminable reasoning comes from kids themselves. Oh, they're crafty little wranglers. They flatter you with the impression they're genuinely interested in every inch of the rationale behind your decisions. How? Through seeking endless clarification. With each explanation you give, another *why* or *why not* you receive.

Dexter: Can I go to Steven's house?
  Mom: Not right now, they're eating supper.
Dexter: But why can't (#1) I go if I don't eat?
  Mom: Because you would be intruding during their family time.
Dexter: What if (#2) I go in another room while they eat?
  Mom: You're still at their house; I'm sure they want their privacy.
Dexter: Why can't (#3) I call them and ask if it's OK?
  Mom: Calling them would put them on the spot. You can call after supper.
Dexter: Does this mean (#4) I can never go over during their supper?
  Mom: That's going to depend on whether or not they invite you. Tonight they didn't; discussion over!
Dexter: Why (#5) are you so mean?

190

Multiple *why's* are deceptive. They foster your hope that with just one more step in logic, one last rebuttal, the issue will be resolved to everyone's satisfaction. In a moment, we shall see that this is often a vain hope.

The worst offenders at perpetuating the reason-at-all-costs philosophy, however, may be us experts. Whether we intend to or not, we regularly imply that there are certain "right" ways to talk to kids, foolproof paths to making kids hear the wisdom of your ways. The flawless way to present your point is there; you just have to find it. And if at first you don't succeed, try, try, try until your youngster finally beholds the light; "Oh, gosh, Dad, now I understand why I shouldn't eat so much junk food. Thank you for sparing me from the growth of additional, unnecessary fat cells."

Once parents are aware that I "shrink" children for a living, my mere presence seems to impel them into overreasoning. While Sylvester tortures the cat with flying ashtrays and tortures Mom with embarrassment, I cringe for both Mom and cat as Mom desperately gropes for the golden stopper:

"Sylvester, you know the kitty won't want to play with you if you tease her."

Clunk. Meow.

"What is Dr. Ray going to think? Do you want him to think you're a mean boy?"

Smash. Hiss. Defiant glare at me.

"If she scratches you, you'll have nobody to blame but yourself."

Crunch. Swipe.[26]

By now, Mom's logical approaches have about as much chance of success as the cat's pleas for rescue. Her overreliance on reason is temporarily blinding her to a basic axiom about kids: By nature, children are more focused on doing what will bring them instant pleasure than on doing what adults define as "reasonable." That's why reasoning, which can quickly become nagging, is so often an ineffective teaching tool. As we have seen, attaching consequences or rewards to reason-resistant behaviors is a much more productive strategy.

All of this is not an argument against reasoning with children. Quite the contrary, I believe reasoning is the first course to take. If you're heard, by all means follow through to a sensible conclusion. But for most kids in most situations, there comes a time to abandon logic. Unfortunately, a number of illogical assumptions can keep you reasoning long after it's sensible to quit.

The first is the one that plagued the mother referred to earlier in this chapter. She believed that mentally healthy kids in a mentally healthy family rarely need discipline. Parents who believe this are highly vulnerable to overreasoning, since turning to discipline leaves them with the uncomfortable feeling that something is "wrong" with their family's functioning. After all, shouldn't really adept parents be able to reason away all prospective parent-child conflicts? Quite simply, no! The truth is that almost all healthy, loving parents have to use discipline to limit their healthy, loving kids' behavior because reasoning alone can't do the job. Well-timed and benevolently executed discipline immeasurably adds to a family's overall emotional health; it does not detract from it.

The second illogical assumption is that you must, yes *must* make your youngster understand that you're not bucking for "tyrant of the decade" award, that indeed your main consideration is his welfare. Why won't he give you credit for being a good parent? He should feel fortunate to have parents who care as much as you do. Why does he persist in his closed-mindedness despite all your attempts to convince him you're acting for his good, not yours? Why? Because he's a kid. ("Kid" is defined here as a person under eighteen.) And by definition, kids don't reason like parents. They don't look nearly as far into the future, peer around as many corners, or anticipate as many pitfalls. They need years to learn these skills. In the meantime, you will regularly have to act in your child's best interests without his consent, cooperation, or trust in your motives. As long as kids are kids, parents will be misunderstood. Sometimes your only consolation will be the knowledge that some faraway day he will understand, maybe even be grateful. And isn't that much of what parenting is about?

Not only do parents feel pressed to make their kids understand them, they also seem driven to persevere at the most inopportune times. It is totally illogical, not to mention masochistic, to believe you can talk your way through to a child who is in the midst of an emotional convulsion, be it temper, tears, or general escalation. Would you argue politics with an adult who stopped being sober three hours before? If you would, your tolerance for futility far exceeds mine.

Ironically, the more emotionally agitated a child, the more a parent feels pressured to quiet him with reason, especially if others are present. Let's return to Sylvester, who has wearied of playing bombardier with the cat and is now going berserk because you are "abandoning" him to a babysitter for the evening. Valiantly you try to sedate him verbally before you leave, so the sitter won't prematurely retire as have your previous twenty-two. But the more you explain and reassure, the more Sylvester clings and wails (and the more the sitter realizes that keeping Sylvester company deserves more than $1.50 per hour). You are trying to douse a grease fire with lighter fluid. Almost always, it is pure folly to struggle to engage a child in rational discourse when he is so visibly upset over your actions. The only foolproof way to restore peace immediately is to grant your child his wish, which in Sylvester's case is that you scuttle your plans for the evening (a wish the babysitter probably shares). If you're unwilling to do so—and I hope you are, as scuttling your plans will invite Sylvester to repeat the performance on your next night out—then you'd best scuttle your plans to reason the evening away. For the time being, Sylvester will neither hear nor believe your reassurances. Give one explanation and then leave. Believe it or not, Sylvester will simmer down much quicker after you've gone and logic is no longer fueling his irrational fire. Any further discussion can come later, maybe tomorrow, when Sylvester is tranquil enough to hear your words and the sitter is safe at home.

Well, you say, Sylvester is only five years old. As he matures, you'll be better able to make him see your side. Overall, that is a safe assumption to make. He may grow in his ability to *see* your side, but not necessarily in his willingness to *accept* it. As kids get older, they get more independent in their view of the world. Your reasoning skills might rival those of Socrates and still not guarantee that your sixteen-year-old will embrace not being allowed both weekend nights for dating. With older children especially, one, maybe two explanations of your position are sufficient. If they don't accept that, they're not going to accept sixteen different paraphrases. Age does not necessarily make one more open-minded. If it did, as we humans grow older we'd all become more understanding and easier to live with. Do we?

Another fallacy behind overreasoning is that a child who bombards you with a dozen *why's* is truly interested in knowing *why*. Almost always, more than two or three *why's* are a sure giveaway that little Newton no longer cares about your rationale. The name of his game is "Keep 'em talking and they just might change their mind." And the game entails keeping the dialogue rolling, probing for a loophole or an opportunity to talk you into submission. You're the one who must decide to leave all those *why's* unanswered. You gave the reasons for your decision. Newton's *why's* trailing your every elaboration do not indicate that you aren't making yourself clear. They indicate that your reasons aren't good enough. To prove this to yourself, answer one question: When was the last time you answered one *why* after another and for your efforts were rewarded with, "OK, Mom. Now I understand your point. Thanks for explaining it to me."

Perhaps the most frequent reasoning question parents ask me is "Should I give my child the reasons behind what I want him to do?" I think generally that's wise. But the wisdom fades fast if every time you discipline or enforce a limit you have to replay past explanations. Give your rationale for a rule or consequence once, possibly twice if you'll feel better for having persisted. Any more is just for your benefit. A youngster's chronic "ignorance" of your motives seldom stems from his inability to understand; he simply doesn't want to comply. Repeating yourself ten times a day only tells him you feel compelled, even apologetic, enough to rationalize your every move.

The last reasoning misbelief is that every conceivable reasoning path should be traveled before discipline is called upon. This assumption effectively puts discipline in the "last resort" parenting category. How often I've heard parents lament, "We've tried talking to him every way we know how. We finally had to discipline him." If you discipline after your first tries at reasoning fail, you'll escape becoming entangled in a sticky, no-win web of logic. You also won't give misbehavior extra time to fester until you finally do resort to discipline. A child is noticeably more tolerant of a rationale when it is backed by action, when parents are confident enough to say, "These are my reasons. Like them or not, this is what I expect."

Overall, kids are much more reasonable creatures than they show their parents. They remain unreasonable only as long as they catch a faint glimmer of a possibility that they can reason you over to their way of looking at parenthood or family life. The more comfortable you are in your logic, the less you'll feel driven to repeat yourself and the more quickly your kids will grasp it. They still may not like it, but living with it is the first step to understanding it.

Quibbling
or *"Just trying to get the facts, ma'am."*

Overreasoning has a close relative: *quibbling*. What is *quibbling?* (Contrary to popular belief, it is not a medieval sport.) Quibbling is aimless wrangling over irrelevant details between a youngster jockeying to ward off some rule or consequence and a parent jockeying to justify and enforce same. More succinctly, quibbling is clouding the issue with "facts," as a child perceives them, that is. Here's a typical quibble bout. Rutherford has just tried to sneak into the house nearly two hours after school's dismissal. Acutely aware of Mom's stand on going anywhere after school without permission or a prior phone call, Rutherford nevertheless did neither. Now he senses Mom's worry-turned-to-wrath about to erupt. He has little resort but to quibble. A long shot, but better than no shot.

Mom: School was out two hours ago. Where have you been?

Rutherford: It didn't let out two hours ago for me. I stayed after to help the principal carry boxes.

Mom: School is over at 3:10. It's 5:05. You didn't help two hours' worth.

Rutherford: It hasn't been two hours' worth. Besides, after I helped, I walked home. That takes a while.

Mom: It's only a half-mile walk. It doesn't take more than ten or fifteen minutes.

Rutherford: Uh-uh. It's almost three-fourths of a mile.

Mom: Rutherford, I've driven it in the car. It's barely half a mile.

Rutherford: [Changing direction as he senses that particular quibble route closing] I asked you last night if I could go to Jeff's after school today. You looked right at me when I asked.

Mom: I looked at you but I didn't give you permission. I said "We'll see" [a standard parental euphemism for "no"].

Rutherford: You said "We'll see, *maybe.*" I heard you, so did Lisa. She was sitting on the couch. [A master quibbler cites as many eyewitnesses as possible.]

Mom: [Starting to become hopelessly sidetracked] Lisa was in bed when you asked. Don't use her as support.

Rutherford: No sir. She took a bath and then came back out to watch the movie, remember?

Such are merely the opening gambits of a quibble bout that will sustain itself for as long as Mom feels pressed to correct every piece of Rutherford's version of the truth. Rutherford won't be the first to abandon the fray; he has too much at stake. He senses something disagreeable is soon to befall him unless he muddles the issue long enough to slip through some loophole or irrelevant technicality. The main aim of quibbling is similar to that of asking multiple *why's:* to obscure the matter sufficiently to change a parent's mind or wear him or her down—or, failing these, to make the parent feel as uneasy and guilty as possible over making any decision because so many minuscule chances for error have been raised.

Generally, the older the child the better she quibbles and the greater her endurance. I routinely watch adolescents adroitly divert mothers and fathers from the central issue—say, a blatant curfew violation—with in-depth scrutiny of such pivotal factors as how many minutes fast is the kitchen clock as compared to the stove clock as compared to the car's clock as related to last year's curfew as related to ... In Rutherford's case, the main point was that he was quite late from school with neither permission nor a call. He was indeed helpful to the principal. But it doesn't really matter if he spent the whole two hours guiding sweet little old ladies across the street. He didn't let Mom know where he was, period.

Parents are dragged into quibbling for much the same reasons that they overreason. They hope that through enough clarification and discourse a youngster will understand and accept discipline. But quibbling can be likened to Hercules' battle with the multiheaded sea serpent Hydra. Each time Hercules removed a head, two grew in its place. For every piece of nitpicking you bother to dispute, two more will follow it. As with overreasoning, once the debate gets rolling, you almost never return to the main theme. The instant you recognize the unplanned turn the dialogue has taken, you can successfully end the dispute by saying, "We're quibbling over meaningless details. The issue is this: You were late from school without permission. And this is what we're going to do about it...."

Of course, you can't expect Rutherford to be pleased with your abrupt termination of the controversy without allowing him to completely present "his side," or "his sides." He will probably consider you unreasonable and closed-minded. But I guarantee that you will spare yourself and him cumulative bickering, anger, and resentment by taking charge of the exchange before it erupts uncontrollably. You'll also be more willing and able to choose a fair course of action because you won't be feeling overwhelmed and confused by an avalanche of useless information to consider.

It takes two to quibble. And since your youngster will quibble to the end, you have to decide when the end is at hand. Since most quibble volleys are self-sustaining, the earlier you terminate them the better.

Why's Aren't Always Wise
or *"Don't ask me why, I'm only the one who did it."*

Quibbling to the death or answering a thousand and one *why's* in the dim hope of making your young one reason like a parent is asking for aggravation. But you can get just as aggravated when you are the one asking the *why's*. In this instance, turnabout is not fair play. You wind up on the short end again.

Back in Chapter 2, we exposed a widespread parenting myth: You must know the reasons behind a behavior to change it, or *you must know why before you try*. This myth has special relevance for us here. Perhaps the most relied-upon method for tracing the *why* of childish acts is questioning the actors themselves—kids. Unfortunately, they are not always the most knowledgeable or reliable informants.

To date, no studies have tackled this subject, but my guess is that the average parent asking the average kid why he did something receives an unenlightening answer over 50 percent of the time. And when the first *why* fails to identify a motive, the odds against additional *why's* reaping gain soar.

Why are *why's* so unproductive? Don't worry; I won't give you an "I don't know." I'll try to answer. After all, it's my question.

First, sometimes a youngster really is unsure of why he acted as he did, especially if his action is uncharacteristic, like stealing, cheating, or carving his initials into the neighbor's aluminum siding. Insight into one's motivations and the ability to verbalize them are talents that develop with age and maturation. Asking a child to explore his sometimes complex, obtuse, or conflicting motives is a task he may not at the time be prepared or equipped to perform. His shoulder shrug or blank stare may be a truthful reply. The younger the child and the more incomprehensible his behavior seems to you, the more likely his professed ignorance is genuine.

Second, even if a child does know why, or can figure out why with just a little effort, he might not want to tell you. Reasons? Fear of looking foolish (I hit Gil because he sneezed), shame (I took it so I could show off at school), vengeance (I broke it because you wouldn't let Huxley come over)—the possibilities are many. Sometimes a child's motives for hiding his motives are too strong for you to overcome, for the moment anyway, no matter how many *why's* you ask or how skillfully you ask them.

Why's meet a dead end for a third reason. They're good for thwarting the folks. Teenagers are especially clever at playing dumb. Shoulder shrugs, barely audible grunts, "I don't know's" slurred so badly they come out "Iunno"—all are trusty tools to rankle a parent's composure. A youngster may know perfectly well why she did what she did, but she's not about to give you the satisfaction of knowing, too, not as long as not knowing is making you so upset. She has to salvage some measure of triumph from any impending discipline.

Even though asking why often meets failure, it is still a parent's first impulse. Why? Because parents naturally want to understand and, if possible, change the impetus behind a behavior, especially a negative one. Besides, much of the time your *why's* are indeed rewarded with a sensible comeback. However, asking why is like overreasoning. The benefits build from the first couple of attempts; the frustration builds starting at the third attempt and continuing through infinity. Therefore, if your initial inquiries are obtaining no answers, either in a particular situation or with a recurrent problem, you need to adjust your strategy. You can start by replacing your *why's* with a different kind of question.

With younger children, you'll get better results by asking "What did you do?" or "What happened?" instead of "Why did you do that?" For one thing, a *what* question is easier for a child to answer; it requires only a verbal description of the incident ("I hit the lamp with a pillow"). For another, a *what* question is easier for *you* to answer! You know exactly what happened; you saw the act or its results. Can you be so sure of yourself with *why* questions?

Next, follow with "What happens when you do that?" Most often, kids will identify some natural consequences ("The lamp falls over") or some parent-prompted consequence ("You spank me," or "You use my allowance to pay for it," or "You breathe fast, turn red, and say you can't wait till I have kids just like me"). Having your kids answer *what* questions will show that they are well attuned to their behavior and its results, even if they're not so attuned to its causes. The former two insights are forerunners of the latter.

With older children and adolescents, when no motives are forthcoming after one or two *why* probes, probably the wisest move is to abandon your quest. You can inform Norbert you are still wide open to talking about the incident, but in the meantime, he still has to answer for his behavior, even if he can't or won't answer for his motives.

Suspending your inquisition early has two other benefits. One, it keeps you from eventually arriving at wanting to choke forth an answer. And two, surprisingly, the older the child, the more likely he will volunteer some reasons if you quit pushing so hard for them. Call it the nature of the adolescent beast.

One more comment about asking why. A good person to direct the first questions to is yourself. Are you doing anything to evoke or maintain your youngster's behavior? Are you nagging it into prominence? Do you drive yourself mad about it? Is your discipline-consistency average about 36 percent? So often, exasperating daily misbehavior makes parents prematurely seek elaborate *why's*—hidden psychological forces, intricate interpersonal relations, emotional upheaval—when in reality the *why* lies in their own behavior, in how they are responding to their youngster. They may simply be letting her act with little fear of discipline. Indeed, one of the main motives behind kids' chronic misbehavior is that they just "get away with it." Change your reaction or your discipline, and perplexing behavior may cease to exist.

To keep the *why* trek from exhausting you, limit it to a series of steps: (1) Ask yourself about your behavior first. If you can't give yourself a satisfactory answer, then (2) ask your youngster about his behavior. But limit your queries to two or less. If you still get no insights, then (3) take action without a *why*. Why not try this and see how it works?

Ignoring Is Bliss
or *"Sit up straight when you backtalk."*

A parent, call her Amy, sat in my office with her seven-year-old, Todd, and recited a litany of Todd's disagreeable habits. It went something like this:

> If I ask him to do anything, he returns a smart remark or look—Todd, sit still and quit biting your nails. He doesn't want to help at all around the house. He must think he's too young to have—Take your collar out of your mouth. Of course, I don't know how much help I should expect. He seldom puts his own things away—Is your hat bothering you, Todd? Stop playing with it and put it down. Honestly, he misbehaves so much I don't think I can keep up with it all.

Amy was right. It is impossible for any mere mortal to parent as fast as a kid can operate. And trying to do so will wear you out before he cuts his first tooth. Parenting is not full-time surveillance; it is guidance. And guidance means knowing when not to guide, or, more exactly, when to ignore. Amy had not yet mastered the art of sorting those behaviors needing her attention from those needing to be shrugged off—an art basic to the long-term survival of any parent.

Certainly Todd's backtalk (or backlooks?) and aversion to housework required Amy's intervention. But his other "misconduct"—fidgeting, nail chewing, collar sucking, hat tricks—would best be relegated to the very bottom of Amy's "to do" discipline list, if they were on the list at all. As you can see by her reaction in my office, though, Amy was affording idiosyncracies equal status with actual misbehavior—a move that immeasurably compounded Todd's rate of "unruliness."

Most parents do realize that a host of childish habits and quirks are best overlooked. But they wonder: What do you ignore and what don't you? Any complete answer, of course, depends upon the parent and what his or her values and unique life circumstances are. For starters, though, I can give you the same suggestion I gave to David's mother (Chapter 5) for disciplining without breaking a child's spirit: Don't ignore behavior that is hurting someone, infringing upon another person's rights or welfare, or challenging your authority. Examples of this are defiance, abusive talk, aggressiveness, destruction, lying, irresponsibility—we've talked about managing these throughout this book. Do ignore behavior that is not harming anybody or taking advantage of anyone's rights or welfare. This list is much longer. A few items are chair squirming, hair twirling, finger drumming, dancing without music, talking to oneself and/or making weird noises, clinging to security blankets and/or toys, basic fidgeting, eating all the french fries before the green beans, and daydreaming (during TV watching, not during lawn mowing). These are habits that cause no real harm. They do have immense potential for irritating parents, and that's one reason they linger so long. But my hunch is you'll incur far greater irritation trying to eradicate these normal quirks than you will working to overlook them. Permit more effective influences—maturation or peer pressure, for example—to do the work of extinguishing these pseudomisbehaviors. If Harry persists in publicly picking his nose despite your picking at him to desist, other children will unmistakably give him their opinion of his hobby. It's surprising how many ever-loyal stuffed animal companions are left home once school begins, or how fingernails are finally allowed to grow after a single member of the opposite sex makes one biting remark about their condition.

Even backtalk, with all its unpleasant connotations, can be ignored at times. What is often considered disrespect is not actually disrespect. It is an expression of temporary discontent: "I'm the slave around here." "I'm leaving when I'm old enough." "You never let me do anything." Such remarks, if not blatantly hostile in tone, can probably be disregarded. They represent neither direct defiance nor verbal abuse. And given the amount of discipline commentary the average kid practices in a childhood, for your own sake you'd better determine which comments you're going to tune out.

You will definitely have to practice paying no heed to the many innocuous behaviors that can push you to the brink of insanity. But your effort will have three advantages: One, you will eliminate the possibility that your irate attention is the very thing feeding the behavior. Two, you will be left with sufficient energy to eliminate more serious problems. And three, you will spare yourself years of wearisome exasperation, as you could never keep up with the endless assortment of quirks that come and go with age.

Big Brother (or Mother) Isn't Watching
or "What Mom doesn't know won't hurt me."

A plaque hanging in my mother's kitchen reads: "God couldn't be everywhere, so He created mothers." A folksy piece of wisdom, but not altogether accurate. Even mothers can't be everywhere, nor fathers. Not even the two together. Just as no parent can parent as fast as a child can act, so too can no parent parent everywhere a child can act. Some do try, though, feeling obligated to do so if they are to be conscientious and ensure a well-adjusted childhood.

Three factors determine the direction a child's personality takes: his home life, his physical makeup and temperament, and his life away from home. You have prime control over the first. You can guide and discipline the second. The third you can affect only indirectly; here your influence is least. Especially as kids move into adolescence, they move out of your sphere of influence. School activities, dating, branching networks of friends, increased mobility—all bring greater social freedom and higher chances for mistakes and poor judgment. It is impossible for you to be physically present to counter every potentially foolish decision your youngster may make away from home. And to hold yourself directly responsible for his shortsightedness is to pursue a parenting course you can't hope to follow. You can no more ensure his making mature decisions than you can ensure that he won't find himself in some very undesirable circumstances.

Obviously, your parenting molds the base from which your youngster can draw her judgments. But the immediate path she

202

chooses in any given situation is not under your control; it's under hers. And to hold yourself as accountable for your child's mistakes as she is puts you at the mercy of factors far beyond your domain as a parent.

Any rule or parental dictum you establish carries with it one implicit and unavoidable rider: "If I catch you." The reality underlying all discipline is that you can neither enforce nor respond to behavior you don't know about.* Strive as you may to impress upon eight-year-old Jumbo not to use his 5 feet and 120 pounds to terrorize other children, if he's roaming the neighborhood tying helpless six-year-olds to trees and you're blissfully oblivious to his maurauding, what can you do? Jumbo need not consider your opinion to be binding on him. No matter how incensed you get over Winston's smoking, no matter how heavy a fine you levy to deter it, you can never ensure that Winston won't decide to puff out of your presence. And you will only thwart yourself and drive him further underground by straining to stamp out all potential smoking times and places.

An inescapable condition of parenthood (seems like there's a lot of them, doesn't it?) is that you can directly supervise your charges only part of the time, a part that gets smaller as they get older. You are painfully aware of this, I'm sure. So are they, although I'm likewise sure that this condition doesn't pain them nearly as much. Therefore, it is smart parenting to admit your limitations openly. As you elaborate your stand on such issues as skipping class, smoking, poor peer associations, and leaving the library for a beer blast, you will greatly aid your cause by telling Winston that you fully realize you can't hover over his every move and you don't intend to. He knows what the consequences will be should he test your rules and you discover his gamble.

Such an admission won't be encouraging Winston to act sneakily. On the contrary, it will be encouraging just the opposite behavior. By removing yourself from the impossible role of parental watchdog, you will be placing responsibility for decision-making squarely upon Winston. You will be giving him the chance to make wise decisions on his own, without feeling

*This reality is as much for your protection as it is for your child's. If you were fully aware of everything your youngster did, you might conclude that the only way to save her from total depravity would be to lock her in the bathroom until she's eighteen. Of course, you never acted foolishly when your parents were out of sight, did you?

compelled to make them because you are peering over his shoulder. Also, an honest admission of your "helplessness" in this sense will do much to alleviate Winston's temptation to sneak around your rules. You'll have taken some of the fun out of pulling the wool over the folks' eyes; you already admitted it can be done.

"But," you say, "I'm somewhat responsible for his decisions because my parenting made him the way he is." Your parenting plays *a part* in making him the way he is; it is a major part, but it is still only one part. The other two parts are temperament and the world he encounters outside the home. All three variables interact to produce the direction your youngster ultimately chooses in any given situation. And even if you believe you did the absolute worst job of parenting humanly possible, can you undo all your misjudgments by not holding Winston responsible for his? You may be firmly convinced the main blame for Winston's waywardness lies at your feet, but will you ever begin to turn him around if you don't make him personally answerable for any waywardness you find out about?

As your youngster gets older, your ability to oversee behavior lessens. You can never be personally responsible for another's behavior, even your own child's. He is. Your responsibility lies in holding him responsible, assuming of course, that you are somehow informed of his behavior.

All Is Fair in Love and War, but Not Parenthood
or *"Mom always treated you better."*

Carol set one goal above all others in her parenting: that she be 100 percent fair and unquestionably equal in her dealings with her three children. If she was to be a good parent, literally all things had to be equal. Fairness was not an ideal to strive for; it was demanded at all times, in all ways. Birthdays and Christmas were occasions for careful measurement of gifts, lest one child "get more" than another. Discipline was guided by the same principle: No child should be disciplined more than his or her "fair share," meaning not too much more than either of his or her siblings. To complicate matters, discipline was a last recourse, delayed until every other conceivable explanation or avenue was explored. In this way, no child would ever be disciplined accidentally or held too accountable for his or her actions. Naturally, Carol's obsession with fairness led to chronic guilt because she could never completely escape the specter of unfairness, as every day in parenthood brings abundant chances for miscalculation and inequity.

Although fairness is an attribute well worth your effort, multiple factors preclude your being completely fair, or even equal, in your parenting. The first is most obvious: your human fallibility and capacity for mistakes, overreaction, and misjudgment. Would you ever insist that you master any sport or pastime without long hours of practice, trial and error, and regular mistakes? Of course not. What's more, even at the master's level, any sport is a combination of miscues and expertise. And no sport, no matter how challenging and complex, could ever begin to touch the intricacy and demands of even one month of parenthood. You can work to lessen the incidence of parenting inequities and errors, but good parents still raise good kids with ample numbers of each.

The second hurdle on the way to fairness is your kids. They are not all equally easy to talk to, easy to reason with, or just plain fun to be around. And without question, each is unique to raise. You're not unfair because you have to work more—or less—at enjoying one more than another. You're encountering undeniable differences. You may love all your kids equally, but that is no guarantee they're all equally easy to like. (If it's any consolation, they probably don't like you equally either!) Nor are they equally easy to discipline. To Carol, equitable discipline meant meting out discipline in roughly comparable amounts. But this actually led only to inequitable discipline because it neglected a basic truth about children: Kids bring discipline upon themselves in very different amounts. And "fair" discipline may mean that one child gets disciplined twice as much as another because he or she acts twice as undisciplined. There is absolutely no system a parent can set up to ration discipline. Any such system would be patently unfair, as a child would sometimes get disciplined too little and sometimes too much just to keep anyone from feeling "picked on."

A third factor is situation. Often circumstances just won't permit you to be sure of being fair. You'll never be able to figure out what really happened, who started it, who finished it. The classic example of everyday parenting limbo is provided by the sibling brawl. In most sibling squabbles, you are called to the scene—by the losing party, of course—three or four rounds into the fight. Trying to retrace the trouble to its initial catalyst is typically an endless quest. Two or more versions of the truth are assaulting you at full volume in stereophonic sound. Chances are high that you'll never make sense of all the conflicting signals. But to be absolutely sure of being absolutely just, you'd have to determine exactly who did what to whom, when, and how much. How often are you awarded this kind of certainty, during sibling battles or at any other time? And if you wait to act until you feel totally without doubt about what happened, your wait may never end.

Circumstances don't allow for total equality in gifts and privileges either. And it's well they don't. As early as possible, kids need to meet the reality that the world is not totally fair. A parent who desperately tries to measure every gift, compliment, and privilege only gives a child a false impression of how things are. Never again will the child encounter others so regularly willing to weigh and balance every move or word directed toward him. It's an easy step from demanding complete fairness of the folks to demanding complete fairness of the world. It's an easy step, but it's one that leads to many hard-to-learn lessons.

Perhaps the ultimate irony of demanding total equality from your parenting is that you only create inequality. Kids deserve privileges, praise, and help on the basis of their behavior, age, and unique needs, and not upon an artificial standard of "fairness." Such rigid guideposts serve no purpose other than to misdirect and exhaust any parent vainly striving to adhere to them.

You will never be a totally fair parent. It is not possible, not as long as parents are human, kids are human, and life is uncertain. Accepting your own limitations and those thrust upon you by the environment is the first step to being a more fair and more relaxed parent.

Rules for a fair fight

Sibling squabbles may provide parents with their most recurrent opportunity to worry about being unfair and to feel guilty for having to act without full knowledge of the facts. Therefore, I'd like to offer some guidelines to help you preserve your mental well-being and your kids' physical well-being if you're finding yourself playing perpetual mediator during daily sibling squabbling.

In order to ensure justice and equality (not to mention domestic tranquility) it would be wise for you to decree, in the presence of all concerned parties, that all sibling scuffles (including but not limited to wrestling, kicking, shoving, pinching, jousting, karate and other martial arts variants, and stick-fighting matches) will henceforth be conducted according to the following rules of the house:

RULE #1. The officiating parent will make little attempt to ascertain what proportion of the blame lay with whom, especially when the combatants are close in age or size. More serious brawls, with accompanying arena damage, may require investigation, but these are rare.

RULE #2. All contestants will be apprised that "informing," otherwise known as tattling, will not elicit parental disciplinary action against the "tattlee." Discipline will be one-sided only when a parent had a ringside seat for the action or a firsthand sighting of the postfight results. Obviously, if Harry appears half-bald, proclaiming that his sister Barbara pinned him down while styling his hair, you have substantial evidence of the accuracy of his report. Otherwise, tattling is best given light-weight status. It is not a reliable means of weighing responsibility. It only prolongs the number of rounds in any given match.

RULE #3. If the noise level from the fight reaches the ears of nonspectators, meaning parents, both fighters will be disqualified and appropriate disciplinary action will ensue (refer to guidelines for mandatory eight-count in Rule #4). If the kids want to do battle, they can at least have the courtesy to keep it to a dull roar.

RULE #4. All squabbles will be assumed to take two to tangle. Therefore, discipline will be meted out to both contestants, above the outcries of "unfair" and "fix." If a match occurs during a pleasurable pursuit—such as TV viewing, sandbox sculpturing, bicycle demolition racing—temporary suspension of the activity will ensue for both parties. If no pleasurable activity other than the battle itself is occurring, each pugilist will receive a standing (or sitting) mandatory eight-count, meaning separation from the other for a predetermined period of time in a neutral area such as the corner, chair, couch, or attic.

RULE #5. The above rules may be temporarily suspended at the discretion of the parent when one combatant regularly uses superior size and strength to provoke mismatched contests.

One More Time ...

The road to better parenting is not paved with the practices described in this chapter. The road to frazzled parenting is. Overreasoning, quibbling, chasing *why's,* perpetual overseeing—these only look like what good parents should do. In fact, they will misdirect and frustrate your best efforts to be a composed parent. Vigilance in avoiding these parent paralyzers will spare you literally thousands of misspent parenting hours per child.

Homework

1. This exercise can follow your next futile attempt to overreason your youngster into accepting your idea of parenting. First give the fallout time to subside, be it an hour, a day, or a week. This will let you regain some of the favor you lost from your most recent fit of inexcusable closed-mindedness. When you think it safe, approach your youngster with something like: "Remember when we had our little disagreement about (whatever it was). Could I have said anything that would have helped you see my side? Was there anything you were waiting for me to say?" You'll probably get one of two reactions: (1) Your youngster won't be able to give you anything you could have said to help her accept your position; or (2) she will reply that she was waiting for you to change your mind or tire of the whole scene. Either answer says essentially the same thing: Nothing short of reversing your decision would have been satisfactory. No amount of reasoning, for the meantime anyway, is going to get you understood.

2. Recall something you wanted badly as a teenager. The only obstacle in the way was your parents. As you presented your case, did you even hear theirs? Were you at all interested in any of their reasons, or did you want only to change their minds? Sometimes kids actually don't hear your rationale because they are focused solely on what they want when they want it.

3. Make a list of your "terrible ten"—those behaviors you find most troublesome or for which you constantly "get on" your youngster about. Make them specific—that is, not "vengeful" but "pulls feather off the bird"; not "antsy" but "vibrates feet at 96 cycles per minute." Next, apply the acid test to each behavior: Does this actually infringe upon anyone's rights or welfare? Separate the *yes's* and the *no's*. Do some of your top ten fall into the *no* column? If so, you've identified "misbehaviors" that are most likely not worthy of discipline time and effort. In fact, any effort you put into not upsetting yourself over these irritants will be very well spent, as your overall discipline load will lighten considerably.

4. Select your eldest child for this exercise. For one day (don't include nighttime sleeping hours), keep track of the time he spends out of range of your direct supervision, meaning out of eye- and earshot. What is the percentage of "unguarded" time? Is it upward of 60 to 75 percent? If it is, you're in the average range. A brief reminder that parents can't be guardian angels.

5. This exercise is to better arm you against impending quibble bouts. Next time Justice does something he shouldn't have, first decide upon what you're going to do about his behavior, and then confront him. "Justice, you seem to have forgotten to shovel the snow again. Because you did..." At the first sound of an excuse or quibble—such as "Major called and wanted me to help him with his Boy Scout project"—offer no argument whatsoever, only something like: "I'm glad you helped, but you didn't shovel the snow. Now you'll have to..." Say nothing else. With any further bids to pull you off the track, reply in essentially the same way: "That may be true, but..." Do this no more than three times. If Justice is still wrangling, cut the discussion. The three-strikes-and-you're-out approach will get across two points: One, you won't argue technicalities. In fact, agreeing with them is usually the best way to stifle them. And two, you won't be driven off the main issue. Used a few times, this tack should solve the quibble problem for a while, maybe even a week.

⑨

The Oldest, and Hardest, Profession

Each chapter in this book has in some way or another aimed to make your life as a parent easier and more relaxed. For if you enjoy being a parent, your kids will more likely enjoy being kids. One final observation must now be made about parenting today. It is an observation meant to bolster your self-image, to help free you of undeserved guilt. Simply put, every unpleasant turn your youngster takes is *not* somehow your fault, nor is it automatically a result of your inadequacy as a mother or father. Hold this observation somewhere in the foreground of your parenting every day you are a parent—yes, even after your kids are on their own— for parents often blame themselves for even their children's adult mistakes.

Wanted: More Days of Innocence

The more I work with families, the more I am convinced of one thing: Being a parent *is* getting tougher. This statement is certainly not a revelation for our time. I would guess that nearly every generation in the last thousand or so had bemoaned some version of how impossible it is to raise a child "these days." My own personal survey of "parenthood stresses" is limited to no more than the past few generations, so I will stay within my experience in claiming that, overall, parenting is a more stressful occupation than it used to be.

Why do I maintain that parenthood is getting harder? To begin with, because kidhood is getting harder. Before going further, I'd best clarify what I mean by harder. I don't mean physically more grueling; in this respect, the load on kids has lightened significantly. Yesteryear's children coped with a more insensitive and demanding physical existence, and they had nowhere near the conveniences that today's kids enjoy and have come to expect. I also don't mean harder in the sense of shouldering heavier loads of responsibility. Forty years ago, many more children were prematurely thrust into adult roles because somebody had to quit school to become a breadwinner, or to help at home, or to assume the duties of mother or father because of a parent's early death. In contrast, the current trend seems to be toward added years of dependency on the folks. With more young people heading for college or searching longer for jobs that will allow them to support themselves, more prolonged financial and emotional support is being asked of parents. In fact, comparing the present picture with the past, I don't believe our kids grow up any faster than their predecessors, as is so often declared. Our kids see more of life's ugliness at younger ages, but in no way can this be considered synonymous with "maturing" or "growing up." And this brings me directly to what I mean by *harder.*

Being a kid is getting tougher because today's world offers far more opportunities for young ones to make foolish and potentially harmful decisions. As life-styles become more complex and sometimes chaotic, kids routinely meet situations that never used to occur in childhood. And they meet them at earlier ages, when they're less ready for them intellectually, socially, and emotionally. Tough choices coupled with immaturity can be a dangerous combination.

Until I was well into high school, the only drug I had any firsthand contact with was alcohol. I thought "grass" was something to cut on Saturday and "speed" meant to drive fast. This is not so much a comment on my own adolescent naiveté as it is a sign of the more sheltered daily life most kids were nestled in. After I discovered that these words had other meanings, I wouldn't have known where or how to obtain such drugs even if I had wanted to. Drug involvement, and this includes alcohol, was something that attracted only a tiny fraction of my classmates. It was almost totally removed from my day-to-day existence. Nowadays, though, day-to-day existence for most kids is quite a different matter. Drugs are filtering down from the high schools into the junior highs (no pun intended) and even into the elementaries. Twelve- and thirteen-year-olds describe for me "going downs" in school lavatories (drug buying, for those of you not twelve or thirteen). Even if I had witnessed such transactions at that age, I wouldn't have recognized them for what they were. Likewise, the drug scene is routinely portrayed, even glamorized, on television; rock stars, athletes, and other childhood heroes often admit to drug use. Drugs have become a very visible facet of society.

Today's youngsters also struggle with sexual issues at ages when their parents and grandparents were still holding hands. Commercial and cable television openly parade sexual themes and scenes; magazines and movies have become even more explicit. Sexual topics and terms are a part of everyday vocabulary. Sexual awareness is healthy. But sexual obsession gives kids a mind-set they are often too young to handle. Estimates are that well over half of all teens have had sexual intercourse before graduating from high school. And teenage pregnancies continue to rise. Trends like these, as well as the increase in drug use, point to a disturbing fact for concerned parents: The opportunities for impulsive or irresponsible behavior are plentiful. In contrast to a few decades back, if a child today wants to find trouble, he doesn't have to search quite so hard for it. And even if he isn't searching, trouble may still present itself to him.

Our kids witness and often have to live around more irrational, antisocial, and outright nutty behavior than any group of youngsters in recent generations. The soaring crime rate, for example, has affected the life-styles of nearly all segments of our society, including the youngest. Compare your childhood to your youngster's: Were the streets safe to walk only during daylight hours? How often did your parents remind you to lock the doors? Do you recall being cautioned about "strangers" as often as you caution your kids? In junior high I used to walk a quarter of a mile to my bus stop, often before dawn. Neither my mother nor I was too concerned for my safety. When my younger brother came along fifteen years later, though, my mother worried about him waiting alone at a bus stop around the corner. To paraphrase Rudyard Kipling, it is more difficult to keep your head when more of those about you are losing theirs.

When your child repeatedly encounters situations that test the limits of her judgment and maturity, the limits of your judgment and maturity are simultaneously tested. You are given stickier dilemmas to solve, and the questions come faster and more furiously from the mouths of younger babes. As societal norms diversify and relax, your kids are exposed to a wider array of choices and viewpoints. This is not necessarily harmful, but it does raise their risks of traveling down some dead-end paths. The task of helping them choose wisely from among their many options falls mainly upon you. And not only is your task becoming more challenging, but at the same time, I don't believe you're getting quite the support parents used to get.

Wanted: A Quieter Neighborhood

In past generations, if a parent did an incomplete job of raising offspring, society was more likely to do a little parenting of its own, for, on the whole, adult society expected its young to live up to uniform expectations. More pressure could be exerted on a wayward member to follow rules and return to the mainstream. Just as kids more readily learn what is expected when Mom and Dad agree with each other, members of a society more readily learn what is appropriate when other members agree among themselves.

The society that guides our kids, however, is not as predictable as it once was. It is shifting too rapidly in too many ways. Most impactful is the changing structure of the family. The number of divorces has tripled since 1960; one of every two marriages now ends in divorce. One effect of this is that more and more children are switching parents at some point in their childhood. Families are also more mobile. Between 1975 and 1980, for example, fully 45 percent of Americans changed residences. And as families branch out throughout the country, the aid of nearby relatives is lost. Pockets of support that traditionally have helped maintain families through uncertain times are slowly disappearing.

Our society is also experiencing a general loss of respect for all types of authority—churches, schools, laws—even under the most necessary and justifiable circumstances. Consider the abuse the image of the police has taken in recent years. They aren't so readily depicted as the good guys who stand between the lawful and the lawless. In fact, they are often viewed with disdain, skepticism, and fear. My sister and my nephew Anthony (remember, the call-in arsonist) were involved in a minor traffic accident some time ago. As a matter of routine, they sat in the police cruiser to complete the accident report. The officer was surprised that Anthony appeared so at ease with him. He remarked that many small children are deathly afraid of police cars and refuse to come close.

Another major societal shift has been in the status and respect afforded schools. Once more, compare your elementary school days with your children's. Did your school witness the level of defiant behavior found in schools today? How often were your classes disrupted or your student rights trampled upon by others who were unwilling to adhere to school policy and who often flaunted their disobedience? I am aware of a young man in a special class who physically assaulted his teacher early in the school year. At a school meeting to discipline the student, the committee was informed that suspending him would go against new state educational policies. After the perpetrator swaggered into the room the next day, his classmates too became noticeably more bold in testing the teacher.

When your child sees others behaving recklessly and incurring little, if any, punishment, the "Why not? Everybody else is getting away with it" attitude can take root. The task of countering such an attitude again falls upon you, and your lessons may demand much repetition, because your kids are learning competing lessons elsewhere. The pressure of peers is not necessarily a bad thing. It breeds trouble only when more peers are applying more pressure to do more reckless things.

Instilling in your kids a sound set of values takes more of your effort in a society that's changing too rapidly to give you needed support. And perhaps nothing is changing society so relentlessly as technology. While technology continually reshapes the way we live, it also reshapes the way kids think. Television bombards youngsters with unrealistic portrayals of everything from love and marriage to cops and robbers. Advertisements skillfully manipulate childish desires and convince Jean she won't have friends unless she wears designer sneakers and munches syrup-coated Candy Critters. Space-age news media daily drop the troubles of the world into your living room. And advances in transportation and communication have altered the speed and scope of our lives. In seconds, phones can bring your youngster into contact with any influence, good or bad. In minutes, cars can do the same. While the automobile has long been a force in teenagers' lives, the difference today is that nearly every teen has ready access to or owns a car. This is not to pronounce technology the root of all evil and to say that we need a simple life-style to raise good kids. Not at all. But I am saying that with exploding technology comes whole new sets of issues that parents and kids must grapple with and learn to use for growth and not for self-defeat.

Wanted: Happy Endings

We have touched upon only a few of the factors—besides kids, that is—that are changing the face of parenting and making it a more sizable job all the time. To talk about the rest, we'd need a few more books. Even though you are the single most potent influence in your child's life, the number and strength of competing influences is significant. What do all these changes mean for parents? Collectively, they mean that even the best of parents may watch their kids choose some undesirable paths, however temporary, on their way to adulthood. And these bad choices aren't always their parents' fault. Even if it were possible to be the "perfect" parent, a "10" in the parent ratings—and, of course, nobody would agree on what that is—you still couldn't be absolutely sure of being satisfied with the end product. There are just too many pushes and tugs other than parents themselves that can detour a child on his course to adjustment.

Contrary to what has been, for decades, the dominant view of child-rearing, I don't believe that parents are the only participants in making a child the way he is. For too long, parents have been made to feel solely responsible for how their child turns out. If he reaches adulthood in good shape, the parents feel grateful; perhaps they even get some credit. But if he doesn't, accusing fingers are immediately pointed toward the folks, who may already feel at fault, unjustifiably. I have stressed repeatedly that a child's temperament is a major determinant of his behavior. Now I want to stress that the world around him is another. And if that world is a bit more complicated or chaotic than it used to be, then a child's personality may reflect some of that confusion, regardless of how conscientious his parents are. Over hundreds of cases, I have learned that it is indeed possible to do a respectable job of parenting and still watch a youngster pass through some turbulent, sometimes downright scary, periods during childhood, particularly in adolescence. In no way is this meant to frighten you, because good parents still raise good kids; instead, it is meant to reassure you. Not all child or adolescent problems are caused by poor or mistake-riddled parenting. Quite bluntly, what Junior makes of his young life can't always be pinned on his parents.

A distraught Mom and Dad brought their fifteen-year-old son Danny to counseling. During the previous year or so, Danny had become progressively resistant to his parents' rule and advice. He seemed attracted to everything his parents had tried to steer him away from. Danny linked himself to a crowd that couldn't exactly be considered the Junior Jaycees. He'd been in some minor scrapes with the law, and his parents suspected him of dabbling with drugs. School interested him only slightly, and his grades were near failing. Danny's style could best be described as living for today, thinking little about tomorrow, and caring even less about where he would be next year.

Danny was the last of five children. His older brothers and sisters lived away from home, and none had created similar distress for their parents. Prior to his teen years, Danny gave few hints that he might be headed for some rough spots in his adolescence.

Danny's folks hoped that I could help him mature a bit, both in judgment and attitudes. Danny, however, didn't agree with our good intentions. He saw no reason to talk to anyone about his life-style, especially a head doctor. He considered himself the victim of much uncalled-for hassling from adults. If people would let him make decisions as he saw fit, he would be fine. Others were getting themselves all upset over what was his business.

As is regularly true with acting-out adolescents, Mom and Dad were the ones who were hurting most. They were torturing themselves with guilt as they scoured the past, looking for where they "went wrong." Maybe they should never have moved. Was allowing Danny to buy that moped a mistake? Was it because they didn't give him enough attention? Danny's folks felt that had they been better parents Danny wouldn't be drifting aimlessly away from their family. As I came to know Danny's folks, I was hard pressed to figure out what they might have done differently to make that much of a difference in Danny's attitudes. They were both caring, responsible people who had given their kids a solid home life. They had not seen or done anything to make them suspect that they were going to meet these problems with their youngest. Their four other children were progressing toward mature adulthood, and Danny's folks had assumed that the same basic course of events would transpire with him. So when it didn't, they looked to themselves for the explanation.[27]

I often have a struggle convincing parents in situations like this one that they aren't failures, incompetents, or bad people. I can show them the many factors affecting their youngster that are not under their control. I describe cases similar to their own. At times, I can point to their other children who are doing well. But all these arguments sometimes provide little consolation or redirection of the parents' thinking. They still remain haunted by the notion that somewhere they missed something, blundered at a critical crossroad, or just weren't sufficiently skilled to handle this particular child. In these cases, the parents hurt in two ways: They feel helpless and frustrated by their youngster's distance and unreasonableness. And they blame themselves alone for the unpleasant state of affairs.

Danny's Mom and Dad, and parents like them, could be considered casualties of the times. The distress they endured with their son wasn't caused primarily, or even secondarily, by deficiencies in their parenting. Danny's folks were anything but poor parents. The world held just too many fascinations and seductions for their young man, in his immaturity, to resist. Danny's parents

217

didn't realize how loud the "call of the world" can sometimes be for adolescents, and so they blamed themselves completely for his shortsightedness and self-defeating behavior.

Through working with many such children and their parents, I've noticed some parallels across the families. These observations may help you, or at least afford you something to hold on to, if you find yourself in similar straits. A fair number of drifting or rebellious adolescents have the benefit of stable home lives. This doesn't necessarily mean that they come from two-parent homes. It means that these youngsters were taught a healthy value system by whoever was their guardian. They were given a basis on which to make sound judgments and to learn from their mistakes. These are the youngsters with the best prognosis for favorable adjustment—*eventually*. Even though they may stumble through adolescence and young adulthood, asking for and receiving many hard-learned lessons, most often they do develop into reasonable and responsible adults, even if the evolution takes a while. And as they struggle, it may appear that whatever the folks tried to instill in them was lost or rejected with the onslaught of adolescence. Despite what their parents think, some things did sink in during those days when their young ones were easier to raise. The characteristics and values that seem to have been abandoned usually resurface and become part of the adult.

Many parents worry that their teen's immaturity and rebellion will be carried into adulthood as more serious maladjustment. The fact is that those troubled adolescents who become troubled adults seldom have had much opportunity to learn any kind of wholesome social principles to begin with. Even when they were young children their behavior was never very well directed or disciplined. For them, each bad move just linked itself to the one preceding it, with little to halt the lengthening chain of misjudgments. Such problem children turned problem adults are not typically the products of responsible, conscientious parents who have striven to raise their offspring in an atmosphere of consistent love and discipline.

Of course, I'm not implying that you should idly watch your youngster pass unchecked into unruly periods, permitting her to indulge her desire to do things her way, in the expectation that she'll straighten out in the end. During such periods, you need more than ever to continue with responsible parenting, making sure that your youngster faces the consequences of her poorly-thought-out actions, even if it appears that she's learning her lessons at a snail's pace. What I am saying is that even when the days seem darkest, when you think you've seen the very last shred of that lovable kid that used to be yours, the chances are heavily in your favor (and hers) that she'll be back. Never lose sight of this when you're at the absolute end of your rope. It may help you tie a knot and hang on.

One More Time ...

This world is not an easy place to raise children. But for now, anyway, it's the only world available. Therefore, since you must do your child-rearing here, always remember this reality: All that goes awry is not, *cannot* be, your fault. Too many influences other than your parenting have a potent effect on your youngster's personality. Good parents are still the best source of good kids, but those kids have to weave through a tricky obstacle course on their way to good adulthood.

10

Seven Principles of Composed Parenting

Parents deserve mental health as much as children do. For parents have to care about themselves in order to care well for their children—a double responsibility, or, depending upon the nature of the kids, maybe even a triple or quadruple one. The aim of this book has been to improve your parental well-being: your confidence, composure, self-image, assertiveness, authority. If you feel good about yourself and like your life as a parent, you will pass the benefits on to your kids.

In these last pages, you'll find the highlights of this book, the seven principles for composed parenting. These principles are not hard and fast rules; they are realities of parenthood, too often ignored by the "experts," and far too often lost to today's parents. Work to keep these at the very front of your parenting consciousness. Use them to believe in yourself.

Principle I
You Are the Expert with Your Child

Everybody knows how to be a parent, or, more exactly, knows how *you* should be a parent. And everybody is quite generous with their opinions, whether you ask for them or not. A standard parental hazard these days is playing target to an unending stream of advice, comment, and criticism about what you're doing wrong and how you should correct it. Indeed, an army of experts—professional, familial, parental, juvenile—is always close by and willing to direct your parenting. You can best sift through all advice using this principle: You are the expert with your child. The ultimate decision on what and whose opinion to follow lies with you. You can listen to no opinion if you wish. Or you can select what advice to put into practice on the basis of your values, your child's welfare and personality, and your unique circumstances. After all is said and done, you are forced to trust your own good-sense judgment. And it's well that you are, because you know your child better than anyone else does.

Principle II
A Relaxed Parent Is a Better Parent

Every parent would like to be easygoing. The advantages are countless. For one thing, you can think more clearly and anticipate better—talents crucial to raising children who like to outthink parents. Second, calm control adds much to the effectiveness of any approach, even the not-so-good ones. Third, you can more fully enjoy your kids, and they you, if each day is not filled with uptight second-guessing of your every move.

Relaxed parenting is an elusive goal. But with each of the following ideas that you accept, you will be one step closer to it. (1) Seldom is an approach right or wrong; it is better judged by how well it works. (2) More than 90 percent of parenting involves common sense. Instincts are a parent's best friend. (3) Mistakes are as integral to parenting as children are. Truly, the main thing to fear is a fear of mistakes. (4) Children are amazingly durable, resilient creatures. They cannot be easily damaged when handled by caring, though fallible, human hands. (5) Knowing why kids do what they do is a parenting bonus. You will regularly have to act without this luxury.

Principle III
Confidence Is a Key to Effectiveness

If I had to choose one quality crucial to controlled parenting, it would be confidence. Indeed, a mediocre approach or idea used confidently is more effective and beneficial than the most brilliant approach used tentatively. Confidence begins with the realization that in your home you're the expert and that your own good-sense judgment is your best ally. Confidence is so important to your parental well-being that at those times when you don't feel confident, *act* confident. The results will be similar. You'll encounter much less testing and resistance. Your kids will be more inclined to accept your decisions and to gain from them. And as you watch your methods consistently work better, you will genuinely feel more self-assured. As one parent insightfully observed: "It ain't the substance; it's the style." So often true.

Principle IV
Kids Are More Normal Than Adults Think

Both parents and kids have been the unintended victims of a pathology hunt. Too many are looking too hard for too much wrong with kids. The search may be well-meaning, but its zeal is taking it to extremes. The uniqueness of every child is magnified by the endless variety found among all children—in development, personality, intellect, behavior. Much that is labeled "abnormal" is well within the proper range of "normal"; it is just not typical. Further, into every child's life some abnormality must fall. That too is the norm. It is a wise parent who is prepared for the unusual, who expects the unexpected. One of the surest ways to take parenthood in smoother stride is always to recognize that kids are built to think, say, and do nearly anything.

Principle V
Authority Belongs to Parents

Parents and children are not equals. You have more experience, you're smarter, and you know better than your kids what is good for them. Children have rights—the right to unconditional love, respect, security, care—but they do not have authority. In your family, the authority rests solely and unquestioningly with you. Your home is not a democracy. It is better likened to a benevolent monarchy. If you feel your authority slipping away, look immediately for what might be taking it. Is some expert or "new" psychological theory talking you out of it? Are you letting your kids ignore or flout it? There are very few legitimate reasons why your authority should be taken from you. For your mental health and your child's, authority must be yours.

Principle VI
Discipline Is Action, Not Words

Most of what is called discipline cannot rightly be called discipline. It is rightly called "talk." Certainly there is nothing wrong with talk. It is a first approach. If it works, so much the better. But with children especially, talking quite often is insufficient and very often is useless. You can't nag, plead, coax, debate, question, or threaten a child to act appropriately with any regular success. No one is more acutely aware than kids that talk is cheap, and so easy to disregard. Raising children requires legitimate discipline—not words, but action. In fact, when you discipline, generally the fewer the words the better. Real discipline leads to less discipline. Illusory discipline—most often in the guise of words—leads to more illusory discipline—that is, to more words.

And if you worry what your kids will think of your action-oriented discipline, it will help always to remember that the true test of the fairness of your discipline is not what your kids think of you when they're kids, but what they will think of you when they're adults.

Principle VII
Responsibility Is Your Child's, Not Yours

Parents are unjustifiably made to feel responsible for nearly every problem their youngster has, every undesirable turn he takes. Somewhere along the line, they believe, their child-rearing skills must have been faulty or inadequate. Without doubt, your parenting is the major force in your youngster's development. But also without doubt, your parenting interacts with two other potent forces: your child's temperament (that is, his unique physiological makeup) and the world he encounters away from home. All these forces are inextricably bound together to produce the person your child is right now and who he will become.

Some kids are exceedingly difficult to raise. They seem bent on making life tough on themselves, no matter what their parents do. And all kids must grow up in an ever more complicated and tempting world. Therefore, it is totally erroneous for you to mark yourself as the sole cause of your child's behavior and choices. You can guide and discipline him, holding him responsible whenever possible, but only he is fully accountable for his actions. He must answer for his behavior, not you. You provide choices; he makes the decisions.

This book is dedicated to your mental health. The first page began with this sentence. May this last page find you convinced that your mental health is indeed your and your youngster's best friend. I trust that much in this book made sense to you and reinforced many ideas you already held but just needed to hear again. Let these ideas mark the beginning of a move toward more comfort in your parenting attitudes and style.

11

How the Story Ended

Chapter 1

[1]John's dislike for all things connected with bedtime had been building for about a year when his parent's sought my advice. They had tried numerous tactics, from reason to bribery to endless bedtime storytelling. About the only approach they hadn't used was spanking; they believed it had no place in their parenting. Each approach elicited the same reaction from John. He would escalate his resistance until his folks eventually gave in for fear of hurting him emotionally.

Since John's folks were reluctant to reinstitute blocking the bedroom doorway (they had used a large easy chair), even though this probably would have been the quickest means to end this stubborn problem, I made another suggestion: Totally ignore John when he is up past his bedtime. Act as though he doesn't exist. No snacks, no TV, no toys, no privileges of any kind. When he finally falls asleep, carry him to bed. If he wakes en route or shortly thereafter, resume being oblivious. After about two weeks of being a ghost, John realized there wasn't much reason to stay awake late anymore, and he remained in bed after being tucked in the first time. I don't think I ever totally convinced John's parents, though, that they weren't going to scar him psychologically by being assertive parents.

[2]Altering Keith's diet made little difference in his behavior; he still remained a management problem. And his parents chose not to resort to medication. In my opinion, disciplining Keith, who was basically an active young man, would require extra consistency and firmness. Temperamentally, he was strong-willed, and his folks' relentless search for explanations for his behavior only postponed their coming to grips with the real issue. They had to take charge with Keith and hold him more personally accountable for his conduct, regardless of whatever reasons they perceived as the cause of it.

[3]What did the mother do to halt the assault on her plants? Whenever Amanda reached for them, Mom firmly said "No" and placed Amanda in her playpen for about ten minutes, without her toys of course. The first few times, Mom explained to Amanda why she was being incarcerated. After that, Mom gave Amanda some appropriate warning and then put her in the playpen if Amanda ignored her. About three or four days of prison convinced Amanda to turn her attention elsewhere. Last I heard, it was toward her mother's china cabinet.

[4]I never did find out for certain whether the couple adopted this little boy. From the tone of some of their remarks during the workshop, however, I believe that although they were frightened by the prophecy, they still planned to follow through with their adoption.

[5]Like so many youngsters who have been resisting their parents' authority for some time, Diane became more unruly when her father finally began defining some rules and limits with enforced consequences. Eventually, Diane realized that this was not the daddy she used to shove around daily, and she gradually became more pleasant to be around. Did our therapy take several years? Not at all. The only way it could have taken years was if Dad and I had met once every six months.

[6]After our initial session, the mother and her son moved from the area, so I don't know what, if anything, developed from this little fellow's problems. I have kept watch in the papers, however, and have not yet seen his name!

[7]What happened to the vomiting? Well, even though it was an exotic and somewhat untidy behavior, at bottom it was still Tony's way of manipulating his mom. Therefore, Hazel stopped letting Tony use his talent to get his way, and she insisted that he help clean up all messes. Slowly, the problem came up less and less. After about six months, it settled for good.

Chapter 2

[8]The kissing did not smack of latent sexual problems. Actually, it was one example of those many worrisome "abnormal" behaviors that kids pass through in the normal course of growing up. Apparently, this little guy had picked up his habit from something he'd seen somewhere, most likely on television, and brought it to school. After his father's Hulk example, the kissing problem was licked. I wonder, though, if this tack would have worked had the behavior involved hitting, and not kissing, others.

[9]This formerly fleet-footed youngster is now a priest who counsels adolescents.

[10]This is a story with one of the more unhappy endings. In junior high school Carl was placed in a classroom for children with severe behavior problems. Mom was finally right. Carl had indeed become an easily frustrated, overreacting youngster. Because he was never required to overcome hurdles of any size, he had gradually lost his ability to conquer even the small ones.

[11]The school official didn't follow up this matter with me, so I don't know if this young man ever again urinated on the school's bushes. However, I'm assuming he didn't, since none of the shrubbery shows any signs of stunted growth.

Chapter 3

[12]Although Susan had learned a number of problem behaviors, the one most needing immediate attention was her erratic school attendance. Therefore, I consulted with Susan's teacher and principal about managing her resistance at school. Understandably, they were tired of having their mornings

periodically interrupted by sirenlike wailing and had experimented with several strategies to ease the problem. They had reasoned with Susan, but that only made her cry longer and louder. They had tried rewarding her for walking to class quietly, but that also failed because the school had nothing to offer powerful enough to override Susan's desire to stay home. And they had ignored Susan's fits in class, but as long as an audience was present, Susan could carry on indefinitely, putting a real strain on her classmates.

I offered another plan. Whenever Susan cried, she should be escorted to the nurse's room, where she could cry in isolation. When calm, she could come to the principal's office and ask to return to class. For the first week, Susan averaged about two hours per morning in the nurse's station. But gradually, after she realized that she could not cry herself home, Susan began to head for class with only a sniffle or two along the way.

Where was Mom while all this was happening? Usually, she had to be persuaded to leave the building because she never wanted to go while Susan was crying. Of course, Susan would remain crying as long as Mom remained nearby. Did Mom ever realize her role in Susan's tearfulness? I can't say, because Mom only attended one session of counseling.

[13]No extended counseling was necessary for either Jerry or his parents. Jerry's folks agreed that they had to learn more productive responses to his often exasperating habits. When I followed up Jerry's progress several months later, his mom summarized it by saying, "He has his good days and his bad"—which is about what one could expect as Jerry struggles to get along better with life despite his excitable nature. One hopes that the good days will slowly start to outnumber the bad.

Chapter 4

[14]By nature, Donny was a reactive boy. But his crying also served a purpose for him. It got a desired reaction from his mother. At least some of the time, when the tears began, Mom would dutifully strive to calm Donny, reason with him, even remove the frustrator if she could. All of this, although seeming the thing to do to stop the crying in the short term, was only

fostering it for the long term. Mom had to change her style. I suggested that she try underreacting to Donny's overreacting. Every time Donny became upset over small inconveniences, Mom could quietly respond with something like: "You're right Donny, the world's not fair," or "Life just doesn't always go the way you want it," or "I think you'll live," and then drop the issue, allowing Donny to learn that his crying would net him no further attention from Mom nor removal of the unpleasant obstacle.

Donny's behavior problems were another story, and how we handled them couldn't be summarized adequately in these few paragraphs. Suffice it to say that they didn't dry up as easily as his tears.

[15]Frank's case was truly one of things getting worse before they got better. Before it was all over, Frank's mother had taken even plain tap water off Frank's already limited menu. Believe it or not, Frank was not allowed to drink any undistilled water because of the minerals in it. A few weeks after this directive, however, Frank's mom unexpectedly discontinued all diets. It seems that a doctor had warned that malnutrition could become more of a danger than hyperactivity.

Some months have passed since Frank's return to American eating habits, and his behavior in school has changed noticeably in only two respects. He now works much harder to earn the privilege of going out for a treat, and he no longer drools on his neighbor's cupcakes at lunch.

[16]B.J.'s behavior could definitely be considered life-threatening. He could easily have injured himself temporarily or permanently. Therefore, his parents' response had to be fast, hard, and designed to reduce drastically his urge ever to try anything similar again. After explaining bluntly to B.J. how he could have hurt himself, B.J.'s parents then gave him a spanking intended to hurt him, coupled with an immediate bedtime and no TV for a week. A three-year-old cannot fully comprehend the danger of climbing a TV tower, but he can comprehend the danger of his parents' discipline. B.J. didn't understand completely why his parents reacted so sternly, but he probably realized he'd better never do the same thing again, which is exactly what his parents wanted him to realize.

[17]My mother, who took the call and who has the advantage of several decades of parenting hindsight, calmly thanked the

operator and just as calmly called Anthony upstairs. I was impressed with her composure, but I couldn't help wondering how she'd have reacted if I, her first child-rearing venture, had done something similar. Anthony must have been aware of the nature of his deed because, despite my mother's nonthreatening tone, he sheepishly climbed the stairs and looked ready for the world to cave in on him. Barely had my mother asked him what he did when he immediately began begging, "Don't tell my daddy. I'm sorry. I'll never do it again." So my mother offered him an alternative. If Anthony would apologize to the operator and promise never again to abuse the phone in a like manner, his parents would not hear about this incident. Of course, my mother had to elicit the operator's cooperation by making a first contact and then calling Anthony to the phone. In effect, Anthony was being given a chance for a suspended sentence. If he never repeated his offense, he would be dealt with lightly. Naturally, Anthony anxiously agreed to those terms.

[18]After giving both Dad and Gary my impressions of Gary's behavior, I advised Dad to follow the same approach I present at the end of Chapter 4. Lo and behold, Gary fessed up. I think a couple of factors led to Gary's admission the very first time he was confronted this way. First, he was listening intently as I detailed for Dad what I thought he was up to, and he probably figured the game was over, at least for today. Second, I often find that kids will make admissions in my office that they will not make to their parents alone. That may be partly due to their notion that they might as well tell the truth because the shrink can read their minds anyway.

Chapter 5

[19]In this household, as in many others, the perpetual discord was fueled primarily by only a handful of problem behaviors. However, as is also true in many households, the behaviors happened somewhere betwen five and fifty times a day. The three battle zones accounting for most of the strife between Mom and Philip were: (1) verbal abuse (on Philip's part, though Mom had to learn to rein in her anger, too); (2) chore-shirking; and (3) homework hassles. My initial strategy was to set up rules with

230

automatic consequences for each of these areas— "automatic" meaning immediately implemented without prior reminders, endless warnings, or debate. For any system to bring peace, both Mom and Philip had to know beforehand that certain behaviors would lead to certain results, thereby eliminating much of the threatening and counterthreatening that went on anytime Mom and Philip enjoyed the displeasure of each other's company.

VERBAL ABUSE. This was by far Philip's most serious offense—it occurred daily, sometimes hourly—and his favorite way of pulling his mother into verbal warfare. Therefore, each incident of "backtalk," as defined for Philip by Mom, earned Philip an immediate half-hour cooling-down period in his room. Backtalk en route to the room or in the room resulted in additional half-hours confinement. Any day that Philip minimally treated his mom as a fellow human (that is, no verbal abuse), he was given a half-hour extension of bedtime, because adult behavior begets adult privileges.

CHORE-SHIRKING. An allowance of two dollars per week was initiated. Completion of a range of chores was necessary for Philip to be paid in full. For each chore shirked—that is, not finished within the time limit established for the chore—Philip would lose a set percentage of the two dollars. Only when Philip completed all his chores for the week could he ask for extra chores to earn extra money. No other spending money was to be given. If Philip was going to be lazy, he was going to be poor.

HOMEWORK HASSLES. All homework had to be completed—correctly—at the kitchen table before Philip could watch television or head outside to play. How did Mom know if Philip had homework to do? He had to write all assignments on a spiral pad and have it initialed each day by his teacher or teachers. If the pad failed to make it home for any reason whatsoever—a dog ate it; we had a substitute; I left it in the bathroom—or came home unsigned or without the necessary books, no TV or outside activities were available that evening.

[20]I asked this teacher (call her Dolores) to think back to the first approach she tried with this youngster (call him Josh). She remembered exactly; she had written it in a log that she had

begun early in the school year and that by now looked like the Chicago telephone book. Dolores's first tack was standard classroom discipline: loss of recess and time spent in a chair off to the far side of the room for breaking class rules and not doing assigned work. These methods were abandoned two weeks into the school year because Josh appeared to enjoy himself equally in or out of the chair and with or without recess. From that point, Dolores began her still-in-progress search for leverage strong enough to quiet Josh's disruptive merriment. I had the strong feeling that more leverage wasn't necessary; most of Dolores's ideas seemed capable of improving class peace. Dolores needed to quit making herself so unhappy over the fact that Josh seemed so happy. From all appearances, Josh loved the idea that his smiling antics were driving his teacher to tears. So I advised Dolores to return to her September tactics—the very first things she tried— only this time working with all her will to ignore Josh and maintain an attitude of "These are your consequences, and I'm going to enforce them whether you're happy or not." I also suggested a time frame for her strategy: no less than two months. How was Josh doing two months later? Well, his behavior was about 50 percent improved—the fun had totally gone out of the chair—but Dolores was not fully happy with our methods. She wanted something that would take care of 80 to 90 percent of Josh's misbehavior. But no such strategies existed, not at school anyway, because at home Josh was regularly allowed to perfect new tricks, which he eagerly carried to school.

[21]Did Billy ever learn to control himself? At school, yes. With Grandma, no—unless Dad was close by. At school, Billy's teacher taught him that he'd better show restraint or be prepared to reap what he sowed. Any time Billy threw a fit, either in rage, in an attempt to get what he wanted, or just for general principles, standard procedure was that he would not be given what he was raving for, no matter how persistently he carried on. For example, if Billy went berserk because he couldn't go out for recess, he would not only miss the recess he wanted, but the next one as well. Also, Billy knew beforehand that every minute spent in a temper tantrum would result in three minutes in a "quiet chair" afterwards. Of course, the other side of the coin was that Billy could earn extra privileges for lengthening his calm between storms. Through the year the tantrums never completely died out

because whatever control Billy was learning in school, he was unlearning at home.

[22]Were Sylvia's suicide threats serious or mainly a device to stave off Mom's attempts at discipline? They were a little of both. Because she had been pampered for so long, Sylvia had never matured in her ability to handle disappointment or frustration, including her own long-festering bitterness toward her father. So she was genuinely depressed much of the time. On the other hand, it was Sylvia's style to drop such remarks on her mother as "Well, you're going to drive me to do something serious," or "I can't handle this; I'll find my own way to end it," whenever Mom attempted to put some constraints, however weak, on her behavior.

My advice to Sylvia's mother? Since Sylvia was attending therapy sessions, albeit reluctantly, she did have a forum in which to work on her depression and her legitimate ponderings of self-destruction. At home, though, Mom could not allow Sylvia to continue to exploit her with veiled suicide threats. If she did, not only would her own life be miserable, but the threats would become more frequent and more likely to be carried out, through spite, discontent, or both. I recommended that Mom place the responsibility for such remarks exactly where it belonged—upon Sylvia. If Sylvia made an ominous allusion to hurting herself, Mom could respond with something like, "Sylvia, I care what happens to you, and I don't want you to hurt yourself. But if you're intent on doing so, I can't always watch you to make sure you don't. And I won't let you do as you please just to keep you from threatening me." When Mom finally began to assert herself, Sylvia's warnings of self-harm did increase, but at the time of this writing she had not gone beyond threats, and in fact they were beginning to subside.

Chapter 6

[23]How might Stephanie have better convinced Gina to return downstairs the first time she was asked, or at the very least within the first five askings? She might have tried this: "Gina, I'd like you to head back downstairs. I don't want to ask you again, because if I do, you and John will have an early bedtime." It was

within an hour of bedtime at the time of Gina's ice cream inquisition. Assume, however, that bedtime wasn't for another three hours and that Stephanie would understandably be reluctant to terminate Gina's evening with her friend so prematurely. Plan #2: "Gina, we're done talking. Please go downstairs or you'll spend ten minutes sitting at the kitchen table."

In fact, later Stephanie asked me what she could have done to avoid her war of words with Gina. I gave her suggestions similar to the above two, and she replied she would have felt too "mean" doing either. The irony of that logic is that by the seventh or eighth repeat in both bouts, Stephanie was sounding pretty mean, and Gina wasn't too happy about the whole exchange either.

Chapter 7

[24]When Greg left school that afternoon, his mood was surprisingly jovial. He greeted his dad outside the building with a summary of events that was about 50 percent accurate (pretty good, considering), along with genuine delight in having rectified his actions. Alas, Greg's balmy spirits were not to last. The next day he aimed a similarly intense escalation at his teacher and nearby students. Had the school and the teacher had the means (a full-time aide, a quiet room), this aftershock might have been weathered, and Greg would have seen once more that his stairstep misbehavior would not succeed in delivering him from school. However, a school committee judged Greg's behavior too volatile and destructive to be handled in a public-school setting. Greg was placed in a home tutoring program. At the time of this writing, Greg was preparing to enter an alternative school in the area.

[25]Understandably, Sammy's parents wanted direction in managing Sammy's manifold gestures of self-harm. Since I suspected that sometime soon Sammy would again threaten to jump from the car and maybe even resort to the kitchen knife, I used these behaviors to illustrate my suggestions. First of all, as long as Sammy's parents remained intimidated by his manipulations, Sammy would continue them, most likely boosting their inten-

sity. Consequently, Sammy's folks would need to be prepared to withstand some tense moments while conveying explicitly to Sammy that they would no longer be terrorized by threats and that he was only risking hurting himself. As an example, the next time Sammy threatened to step from a moving car, instead of pulling off the road and trying to reason him into tranquility (which was like spraying oil on a raging fire), they should continue driving. And in fact, within the week Sammy reused his threat. Because the car wasn't headed in the direction he wanted, Sammy opened the door a few inches and leaned. Trembling on the inside, Mom nevertheless held her composure on the outside and, although she slowed down a bit, kept right on driving. Sammy shut the door.

Any replay of the kitchen-knife episode would also require steel nerves on Mom and Dad's part. If Sammy ever again grabbed the knife in fuming response to his parents' decisions, Mom and Dad were steadfastly to let him know their decision was final and walk away, leaving Sammy no audience to uphold the drama. Later, away from the high-tension encounter, they could apply some consequences to Sammy's highly unreasonable behavior.

Most of the therapy sessions included both Sammy and his parents. With my support, Sammy's parents stood up to Sammy and informed him that his days of controlling them were over. Mom especially needed reassurance that Sammy would most likely never hurt himself. She very much feared miscalculating Sammy's intent, but in the end I believe she realized that her regular submission was only raising the chances that Sammy would eventually act on his threats. After about ten sessions, therapy was terminated, with a follow-up at six months. Sammy was still resisting the idea that his way wasn't the only way anymore, but his miscellaneous gestures of self-assault had ended.

Chapter 8
[26]Tormenting animals is a behavior to be handled without hesitation. One does not attempt to talk a child out of his cruelty even as the cruelty continues. Mom's foremost concerns were to control Sylvester and protect the cat; discussion could come later.

And in this instance, no subsequent discussion would even be called for, as Sylvester was already well aware of the nasty nature of his game.

Some might advise Mom merely to get the cat out of harm's way—that is, outdoors—or to remove the ammunition—the ashtrays. My response to that advice is: Why should the cat have to adjust to Sylvester's mean streak? What would Sylvester learn about restraining himself for the cat's sake? No, in my opinion Sylvester was the one who needed to change, not the cat or the environment. Mom could have given Sylvester a choice at the first sign that words weren't stopping him: "Sylvester, the cat doesn't agree with your idea of fun. Cool it immediately, or you will leave the room and sit at the kitchen table until I think you can control yourself." Naturally, Mom didn't have to use the kitchen table; she could have chosen anything suitably boring for Sylvester in order to save what remained of the cat's nine lives. And if the cat has lived any amount of time with Sylvester, I don't think he has too many left.

Chapter 9

[27]Did Danny eventually straighten out? I'm happy to report that he did, although he took his own good time about it. What caused the positive changes? I don't think it was any particularly brilliant therapy on my part. Nor did Danny's folks find any better means of reasoning with him. Danny needed to suffer from many of his mistakes before he finally started to believe that his folks knew at least a little about living more wisely.

236

Index

E

Emotional problems. *See* Personality; Psychological problems; *and specific problems*.
"Emotionally disturbed" label, 66–69, 94
Equal treatment, limitations on, 181–82, 204–6
Escalation, 156–65, 186–87
dealing with, 161–65

F

Fairness, siblings and, 181–82, 204–6
Fears, 72–73
at night, 1
See also Phobias.
Freud, Sigmund, 42
Friends. *See* Relatives and friends.

G

"Godliness," professional, 7–10
Guilt feelings of parents, 223–24
of acting-out adolescents, 217–218
and discipline, 106–7, 128–29, 170–73, 175–76, 187
single parents, 119-21

H

Homework, 1, 29
Hyperactivity, 2, 10, 47, 48, 65, 66, 73–79, 94, 117
causes of, 74–75
definition of, 74
diet and, 74, 76–78
discipline and, 78–79
Hyperkinesis, 74

I

"I mean it" (Addendum), 144
If-then statements, 134–39, 141–42, 145, 162–63

Ignoring misbehavior, 105–6, 200–202, 209
Impulse disorder, 74
Infants, discipline and, 58

K

Kissing, inappropriate, 20

L

Labels of abnormality, 64–70, 73–84, 222
Learning disabilities, 1, 9, 65, 74
Left-handedness, 4
Linkletter, Art, 177
Lying, 90–93, 95

M

Media
child-rearing advice in, 3–6, 11, 19
influence on children of, 215
Middle-child syndrome (MCS), 65, 72, 82–84
Minimal brain dysfunction, 74
Mobility of families, 213

N

Nagging, 130–34, 154
if-then approach vs., 134–39, 141–42
Normality
definition of, 65–66, 94
See also Abnormality.
"Now" (Addendum), 143

O

Only children, 83–84
Overreasoning, 59, 61, 189–95, 208

P

"Parsimony, Law of," 34
Part-time parents, 118–19, 121–24

240